D0179712

a
FATHER
WHO KEEPS
his
PROMISES

a FATHER WHO KEEPS *his* PROMISES

GOD'S COVENANT LOVE IN SCRIPTURE

SCOTT HAHN, Ph.D.

PUBLISHED BY ST. ANTHONY MESSENGER PRESS
CINCINNATI, OHIO

Imprimatur: Most Reverend Gilbert Sheldon
                 Bishop of Steubenville
                 January 26, 1998
Nihil obstat: Monsignor Roger Foys
                 Censor Librorum

Scripture passages have been taken from the Revised Standard Version, Catholic edition. Copyright 1946, 1952, 1971 by the Division of Christian Education of the National Council of the Churches of Christ in the USA. Used by permission. Verses marked CEV have been taken from the Contemporary English Version of the Bible. Versus marked NAB have been taken from the New American Bible.

Excerpts from the English translation of the *Catechism of the Catholic Church* for the United States of America. Copyright 1994, United States Catholic Conference, Inc.– Libreria Editrice Vaticana. Used with permission.

Cover photo: © Dennis Frates, Oregon Scenics

LIBRARY OF CONGRESS CATALOGING-IN-PUBLICATION DATA

Hahn, Scott
A father who keeps his promises : God's covenant love in scripture / Scott Hahn
    p.   cm.
Includes bibliographical references.
ISBN 0-89283-829-9 (alk. paper)
1. Redemption.   2. God—Love.   3. Salvation.   I. Title.
BT775.H15   1998
234'.3–dc21   97-46002
          CIP

ISBN-13: 978-0-89283-829-5
ISBN-10: 0-89283-829-9

Published by Servant Books, an imprint of St. Anthony Messenger Press
28 W. Liberty St.
Cincinnati, OH 45202
www.ServantBooks.org

Printed in the United States of America
Printed on acid-free paper

09 10 11 12 13 20 19 18 17 16

To the Monday Afternoon Scripture Class:

Michael, Gabriel, Matt, Anthony,
Catherine, Sia, Katie and Genice.

And to my beloved wife, Kimberly, without whom this book
wouldn't have been possible or readable.

CONTENTS

PREFACE

I once asked my friend Peter Kreeft which of his twenty-plus books he regarded as his most important. He thought for a moment, and then replied: "I'd say it was the one I *didn't* write during the years that my kids were young and needed me around." Good answer. For me, this book nearly ended up in that category.

It started seven years ago, when Fr. David Testa invited me to teach a series on salvation history to his parishioners at St. Paul's in Hudson, New York. These talks were taped by St. Joseph Communications and subsequently transcribed. Ann Spangler of Servant Publications later suggested that I revise and publish the transcripts for people wanting to get to know the Bible better.

Not a chance.

I had just started writing what turned out to be a 775-page doctoral thesis. I was also working with my wife, Kimberly, on another book, *Rome Sweet Home*. A third book seemed to be out of the question.

But during my conversations with Servant, Ann Spangler and David Came suggested finding an editor to work with me on the transcript for publication. They found a good one in Pam Moran who did a fine job sifting through some pretty dense verbiage.

Meanwhile things got even busier: two more babies; full-time teaching at the Franciscan University of Steubenville; finishing and defending my doctoral thesis, and so on. Meanwhile, the manuscript just sat there, collecting more and more dust.

Along came additional help with some more patient editors, Bert Ghezzi, Heidi Hess and Paul Thigpen, who coached me along to the point where I could see the project to completion.

Finally, I can offer them my sincere thanks, and a finished manuscript.

However, what really made it possible to finish this project was being awarded a sabbatical for the Spring 1997 semester. I want to thank Franciscan University's president, Fr. Michael Scanlan, and the academic dean, Dr. Michael Healy, along with my colleagues in the Theology Department, for making the sabbatical possible.

The greatest motivation of all came to me one afternoon in the car when Kimberly was reading an earlier version to our two oldest boys while we were driving to Cleveland to see Michael Jordan and the Chicago Bulls slaughter the Cavs. I sat in the driver's seat listening to their comments, and it suddenly dawned on me that *they* were really getting into it. Both boys encouraged me to read parts of it to their high school classmates who met in our home every Monday afternoon for an hour and a half of Bible study. The same thing happened. All I can say is thanks, and this one's for you.

Of course, more than a few rough edges remain, and I alone am responsible for that. Here again, I draw consolation from one of my favorite writers, G.K. Chesterton, who said, "If something is really worth doing, it's worth doing badly."

After many years of teaching this material at various levels (high school, undergraduate and graduate), I'm more convinced than ever that it certainly *is* worth doing. In fact, I can't think of anything *more* worth doing than sharing the biblical story of God's covenant love in salvation history. That's what this book is all about. So it's not written as a textbook or academic monograph, but a simple retelling of the stories that make up *the* Story.

For the most part, I stick to the major characters and events, since the stories make up the Bible's main plot. My primary goal is to convey the "big picture," which has been lost to many readers of Scripture in our day. In the process, I also hope to show how much practical wisdom the Bible contains for the ordinary believer, especially "rank and file" Catholics. That is one of the reasons I emphasize the twin themes of the covenant and family, because they touch us right where we live. The other reason for focusing on these closely related themes is because the Bible itself does.

The approach taken here is anything but new. I follow the basic guidelines of the Church fathers and doctors, recent papal teachings, the Vatican II documents, the *Catechism of the Catholic Church* and the Biblical Commission's recent instruction on "The Interpretation of the Bible in the Church." This narrative approach to the biblical account focuses our attention on God's fatherly plan in making covenants with his family throughout salvation history. We employ the method known as "canonical criticism," which involves reading the Old Testament in the light of the New, and vice versa, following the wisdom of St. Augustine, cited in the *Catechism of the Catholic Church:* "The New Testament lies hidden in the Old and the Old Testament is unveiled in the New" (#129). Our approach is also ecumenical, drawing insight from Protestant biblical scholars, and ancient rabbinic and modern Jewish sources. All of this is especially evident in the endnotes, which I strongly encourage readers to consult.

One final word before beginning: This book is *not* designed to serve as a primary text for Scripture classes at any level. In fact, I am strongly opposed to anyone who would use it as such; there can only be one primary text for studying Scripture, and that is the Bible itself. On the other hand, this book might prove to be useful, in various contexts, as a supplemental guide for study.

Now without further ado, you are invited to read about the greatest Story of all, of a Father who keeps his promises.

Scott Hahn, Ph.D.
August 22, 1997
Feast of the Queen Mother

Kinship by Covenant:
The Master Plan for God's Family in Scripture

Everybody felt it: a moment of eerie silence, a low rumble and then the ground began to shake. Buildings swayed and buckled, then collapsed like houses of cards. Less than four minutes later, over thirty thousand were dead from a magnitude 8.2 earthquake that rocked and nearly flattened Armenia in 1989.

In the muddled chaos, a distressed father bolted through the winding streets leading to the school where his son had gone earlier that morning. The man couldn't stop thinking about the promise he'd given his son many times: "No matter what happens, Armand, I'll always be there."

He reached the site where the school had been, but saw only a pile of rubble. He just stood there at first, fighting back tears, and then took off, stumbling over debris, toward the east corner where he knew his son's classroom had been.

With nothing but his bare hands, he started to dig. He was desperately pulling up bricks and pieces of wall-plaster, while others stood by watching in forlorn disbelief. He heard someone growl, "Forget it, mister. They're all dead."

He looked up, flustered, and replied, "You can grumble, or you can help me lift these bricks." Only a few pitched in, and most of them gave up once their muscles began to ache. But the man couldn't stop thinking about his son.

He kept digging and digging—for hours ... twelve hours ... eighteen hours ... twenty-four hours ... thirty-six hours.... Finally, into the thirty-eighth hour, he heard a muffled groan from under a piece of wallboard.

He seized the board, pulled it back, and cried, "ARMAND!" From the darkness came a slight shaking voice, "Papa...!?"

Other weak voices began calling out, as the young survivors stirred beneath the still uncleared rubble. Gasps and shouts of bewildered relief came from the few onlookers and parents who remained. They found fourteen of the thirty-three students still alive.

When Armand finally emerged, he tried to help dig, until all his surviving classmates were out. Everybody standing there heard him as he turned to his friends and said, "See, I told you my father wouldn't forget us."

That's the kind of faith we need, because that's the kind of Father we have.

The Father's Grace: Free, But Not Cheap

Scripture testifies to how God has cared for his family throughout the ages, making a way for his children to live with him forever. The biblical record shows that our Heavenly Father has kept each and every one of the promises he swore concerning our redemption—at the cost of his only beloved Son. Because of God's grace, the gift of salvation is free, but it is not cheap.

The story of that unfailing love is the story of this book. We'll examine together what God has done in history to make us his family and to save us from the wretched misery of our own sin and selfishness. Along the way, we'll discover anew how passionately he seeks us, how firm is his intention to make us whole again and how deserving he is to receive our gratitude, trust and obedience.

For Fathers Who Aren't in Heaven

We constantly hear about fathers who become so engrossed in pursuing a career or some other goal that they end up seriously neglecting their children. The trite phrase "quality time" often describes their efforts to make the most of the little time they do give. Even the best of fathers are all too human, flawed creatures who sometimes break their promises or fail to be around when their children need them most.

I know that's true in my own efforts at fathering. Despite my best intentions to follow through on family commitments, inevitably some other pressing concern arises to wreck the plans we've made together and take me away from home. Even though I try very hard not to make explicit promises I might not be able to keep, still my kids are disappointed when the expectations that I encouraged are dashed by unexpected circumstances—some of my own making.

I want to help you catch a vision of a very different kind of father, the eternal Father who never fails to fulfill his word. No matter what obstacles arise, he never loses sight of his goal: to form and fashion a human family to share in the infinite love of the Trinity. As we consider what the Scripture tells us about how God has fathered his people over the ages, we should realize more fully just how great is God's personal love for each and every one of us, as members of his covenant family.

Scripture, the First Love Story

A few years after resigning my Presbyterian pastorate, as a newly converted Catholic, I found myself at midnight Mass on Christmas Eve back in my hometown, a suburb of Pittsburgh. The standing-room-only crowd buzzed with excitement, almost as if the Christ

Child might appear. Candles added a warm glow to an altar arrayed with poinsettias, while the sweet fragrance of incense wafted its way to the back of the church where I sat.

I was barely seated when the solemn tones of a cantor could be heard, chanting an ancient lyric that introduced the liturgy of the vigil Mass. Few seemed to be paying attention; however, I sat there enthralled by the celestial melody, which conveyed a message that I knew quite well, though I hadn't heard it sung before. Weeks later, I still remembered the profound impression it left but not the words. So I asked around until I found someone who got me a copy of the actual song. The printed page cannot do it justice, but the lyrics are enough to make a point:

> The twenty-fifth day of December in the five thousand ninety-ninth year in the creation of the world from the time when God created the heavens and the earth,
>
> the two thousand nine hundred fifty-seventh year after the flood,
>
> the two thousand fifteenth year from the birth of Abraham,
>
> the fifteen hundred tenth year from Moses and the going forth of the people of Israel to Egypt,
>
> the one thousand thirty-second year from David's being anointed king,
>
> in the sixty-fifth week according to the prophecy of Daniel,
>
> and one hundred ninety-fourth Olympiad,
>
> and the seven hundred fifty-second year from the foundation of the city of Rome,
>
> the forty-second year in the reign of Octavius Augustus,
>
> the whole world being at peace,
>
> in the sixth age of the world,
>
> Jesus Christ, the eternal God and the Son of the eternal Father,
>
> willing to consecrate the world by his merciful coming,

being conceived by the Holy Spirit, and nine months having
    passed since his conception,
was born in Bethlehem in Judea of the Virgin Mary, being
    made man,
the nativity of our Lord Jesus Christ according to the flesh.

Perhaps my delight over the chanting of this message puzzles
you. After all, who cares about "the two thousand nine hundred
fifty-seventh year after the flood," much less "the one hundred
ninety-fourth Olympiad"? Maybe I should tell you something
about that point in my life so that you can appreciate my sense of
excitement over the message of this ancient song.

After spending a decade intensively studying Scripture, I had
finally begun to see the "big picture" of salvation history, and how
all of the innumerable puzzle pieces fit together into a big, beautiful divine love story. All the many names, places and events in
Scripture often leave first-time readers feeling overwhelmed and
bewildered. Honestly, it took me years before I formed a "mental
map" to find my way around Scripture, especially the Old
Testament, without getting lost. But once I mapped out the peak
events of the mountain range of salvation history, I finally got the
big picture.

Then one night I found myself at the Christmas vigil Mass, surrounded by hundreds of ordinary Catholics, listening as a cantor
sang an ancient rendition of my newly formulated mental map of
salvation history. Slowly it dawned on me that I had just spent a
decade of study reinventing the wheel. All this time God had been
providing his children—in the Church's living Tradition and liturgy—with the means to map out the scriptural record of his
fatherly plan for his covenant family in history; if only we would
avail ourselves of these merciful provisions.

The exact dates attributed to the events by the ancient liturgist
were debatable, of course, but that wasn't the point. The basic

message was undeniable. Here was a panoramic view of salvation history hearkening back to the scriptural signposts that offered proof positive of God's enduring love for the human race. Looking back on that night, I realized that the congregation was being invited into a deeper awareness of how much went into preparing the world and all nations, the whole human family, for Christ's coming.

The Mystery of God's Love in the History of Salvation

This superbly condensed version of biblical history made it perfectly clear: Our Heavenly Father has been watching over us throughout all of history, saving us from destruction over and over again. He longs to convince us of his passionate love for each one of us, that relentless mercy which calls—and enables—us to share his own divine life, that fiery outpouring of love by which the Father eternally begets the Son in the Holy Spirit. Only an infinite, raging love such as appears among the Blessed Trinity can explain the mysteries of human sin and salvation.

Let's face it, we humans really don't want God to love us *that* much. It's simply too demanding. Obedience is one thing, but this sort of love clearly calls for more than keeping commandments. It calls for nothing less than total self-donation. That might not be a difficult job for the three infinite Persons of the Trinity, but for creatures like us, such love is a summons to martyrdom. This invitation requires much more suffering and self-denial than simply giving up chocolate for Lent. It demands nothing less than a constant dying to self.

You may be wondering, Why do we *have* to love like God in the first place? Scripture gives us an answer in two parts: First, the Old Testament shows that we were made to live *like* God by sharing love within the human family during our earthly stay; second, the

New Testament shows that we were remade to live *in* God by sharing the love of the Blessed Trinity for eternity in heaven. Both elements are essential for understanding what it means to be truly human, but only the second one is our true and ultimate end, what theologians call the Beatific Vision. We would completely fall short were we to attain anything less.

This means that from the outset, our stay on earth was only meant to be temporary. This explains why the New Testament views the Old Covenant as a period of probation—unnaturally prolonged because of sin—out of which man failed to pass, until Christ (see Heb 2:6-9). We can also see how the New Testament integrates the "this-worldly" orientation of the Old Testament into God's fatherly plan to teach his children—in different stages—to desire and obtain that which is divine and eternal.[1] As Jesus taught, the only way into heaven is to lovingly divest ourselves of the temporal goods of earth (see Mt 5-7). This is not because earthly things are bad, for in that case they'd be useless as sacrifices. On the contrary, it's precisely because earthly things are so good—second only to heavenly ones—that we're able to sacrifice the former to gain the latter. Also, if temporal loss can bring eternal gain, then seemingly extreme forms of temporal punishment, like those God meted out to Israel throughout its history, suddenly make a lot of sense: for "God is treating you as sons…. he disciplines us for our good, that we may share his holiness" (Heb 12:7-10).

Sin is thus exposed for what it really is, our refusal to live according to the perfect love of the Trinity. This divine love is reflected in the sacrificial requirements of the laws of the covenant. At the same time, we are enabled to grasp the inner logic of salvation, and to comprehend how it could only be accomplished through Jesus' sacrificial death on the cross. For that is where Christ took our humanity and transformed it into a perfect image and instrument of the Trinity's life-giving love, as a sacrificial gift of self.

The essence of sin is our refusal of divine sonship, because of its sacrificial demands; so Christ's death atoned for our sin by taking it out right at its source. "He ... partook of the same nature, that through death he might destroy him who has the power of death, that is, the devil, and deliver all those who through fear of death were subject to lifelong bondage" (Heb 2:14-15).[2]

The cross needs to be understood as a trinitarian event, but one that we weren't ready to receive, or even comprehend, until God took us through a long preparation. That's what the Old Testament is all about, and why we need the New Testament in order to see it.

If all of this sounds pretty heavy, or if it flew by too fast, don't worry. That's what the rest of *this* book is for. We'll take a closer look at important people and events in Scripture, and see how they fit into the various preparatory stages of God's family plan. Then after we're done, perhaps you might want to come back and reread this section. Chances are it will make even more sense.

History With an Attitude

As one of the most valuable family heirlooms we possess, Scripture records the highlights of a divine drama. These pages present not a dry, impersonal history lesson but a passionate love story, the astonishing tale of a God who came to seek and to save the lost at immeasurable cost to himself.

We often read Bible stories as if they were simply morality tales. The hero in the white hat defeats the villain in the black hat and rides off into the sunset to live happily ever after—with the beautiful woman, of course. Yet God inspired Scripture to teach us something much more profound than a simple moral. This book is a long love letter from the Father to his beloved children still on their earthly pilgrimage.

We're often tempted to view the Old Testament as a dull list of "begats." Instead, these pages come to life as we take a closer look at these very real people, people much like you and me. They overcame obstacles and tasted defeat, laughed and cried, loved and lost. And who watched over them through it all? God the Father, who brought his light into the human darkness, making a way for us to come home to live with him forever.

Our problem in the West is that we tend to reduce history to a secular chronology of politics, economics, technology and war. As a result we are preoccupied with elections, depressions, inventions and military battles. Not that these things are unimportant, it's just that the ancient Jews discerned deeper currents of divine purpose and action in history. And tracing such currents calls for faith in God's providential governance of nature and the events of history.

From a Hebrew perspective, the primary purpose of biblical history is to recount humanity's familial history in the light of God's covenant plan for his people. To achieve this essentially religious goal, God inspired the biblical writers in their use of literary figures, poetry, parable, prophecy and many other things you wouldn't expect to find in modern history books. But that does *not* make it any less historical, just distinct—*very* distinct.

The biblical view of history also stands in sharp contrast to the mythical view that was widely held throughout the ancient Near East. Time was understood in terms of a never-ending cycle ("the myth of the eternal return"). This was combined with a fatalistic view of the gods, who controlled every person's destiny. The net effect, in most ancient societies, was a deep pessimism about time, both past and future.

The modern Western approach to history is antithetical to the ancient Near Eastern perspective. If the modern view is linear, progressive, optimistic and secular, the ancient outlook tended to be cyclical, regressive, pessimistic and mythical. Meanwhile, the biblical outlook falls somewhere between both extremes.[3]

Consequently, modern readers sometimes miss an important aspect of the biblical message, one that reflects the ancient Hebrew outlook on time as salvation history. Even devout readers sometimes approach Scripture with a Christian heart but a secular mind. Such a combination is a mixed marriage, at best. Instead, a Christian heart calls for a biblical mind; but this requires careful effort.

For one thing, the prophetic nature of the biblical narrative of salvation history must be understood. The ancient Israelites believed that God created the world, just as he guides its history according to his saving plan. Moreover, they believed that God's Spirit moved the biblical writers (Moses and the prophets) to make them bearers of divine meaning. The saving deeds of God (creation, Exodus, conquest, kingdom, exile, restoration) are thus described in terms of the covenantal pattern of divine justice and mercy.

In other words, God "writes" the world like men write words, to convey truth and love. So nature and history are more than just created things—God fashions them as visible signs of other things, uncreated realities, which are eternal and invisible. But because of sin's blinding effects, the "book" of nature must be translated by the inspired Word of Scripture. This in turn calls for a truly sacramental imagination, which will enable people (once again) to interpret history and creation in terms of the sacred symbolism of Scripture.

When men write words in order to express love, they usually resort to poetry. And in a real way, the same is true with God. Mark Twain once said, "History doesn't repeat itself, but it does rhyme." So our ears must be attuned to this divine poetry.

This is the purpose and value of *typology,* which studies how Christ was foreshadowed in the Old Testament (Adam, Abraham, Isaac, Melchizedek, Passover lamb, temple), thereby revealing the profound unity of the Old and New Covenants. Thus, typology is what enables us to discern "in God's works of the Old Covenant prefigurations of what he accomplished in the fullness of time in the person of his incarnate Son" (#128).

In sum, salvation history is a sacred mystery—conveyed in the divine poetry of Scripture. As typology reveals the rhyme scheme, so God's covenant unveils the overarching purpose and meaning. For this reason, our book will focus primarily upon the typological and covenantal dimensions of the biblical narrative.

Kinship by Covenant

Once you begin looking for what was important to the biblical writers themselves, you'll find that the concept of *covenant* is a central thread woven throughout Scripture. The dramas that we'll examine describe how God the Father, through a series of covenants, has moved from dealing with one couple—Adam and Eve—to the whole world. Each step along the way has moved us further up the pathway to heaven, providing yet one more crucial component in God's plan to form a family of faith. Viewing the history of salvation through the lens of covenant helps us to see the fatherly wisdom and power of God, and will offer a clearer perspective on the human family.[4]

We'll find ourselves in good company as we examine salvation history through this lens. St. Irenaeus, one of the greatest theologians of the early Church, once said: "Understanding … consists in showing why there are a number of covenants with mankind and in teaching what is the character of those covenants."[5] By examining the divine covenants in salvation history, we will grow in our knowledge of God's fatherly ways and share more fully in the life of the Spirit, which Christ died to give us. This is why God has revealed himself—and still speaks to us—in Sacred Scripture, so that we might come to know, love and imitate him as the covenant Father who keeps all of his sworn promises.

Growth by Oath

What exactly is a covenant? It comes from the Latin word *convenire,* which means "to come together" or "to agree"; the English term "covenant" involves a formal, solemn and binding pact between two or more parties. Each party must live up to its end of the bargain. By this definition, a covenant is similar to a contract. In fact, modern secular law tends to treat covenants and contracts as virtually identical; whereas in biblical terms, covenants involve much more than contracts. While there are several differences, we can only touch upon two: first, solemn oaths versus private promises; and second, the gift-of-persons versus the exchange of property.

First, a contract is made with a *promise,* while a covenant is made by swearing an *oath.* In a promise, you make a pledge ("I give you my word"). A contract is made binding by your signature, your *name.* In oath-swearing a promise is transformed by invoking God's holy name for assistance or blessing ("so help me God"). The oath-swearer places himself under divine judgment and a conditional self-curse ("I'll be damned"). The oath is thus a much stronger and more sacred form of commitment.

Even our largely secular culture still recognizes some sort of contrast between promises and oaths. For example, in the courtroom, we take an oath and place our right hand on the Bible before taking the witness stand, because our society still considers justice in the courtroom to be an extremely serious matter. In the eyes of the law, lying under oath is not merely a sin but a serious crime: perjury (oath-breaking), which is punishable by a jail term.

Consequently, doctors, police officers, military personnel and public officials all take oaths whereby they swear to fulfill their duties to the community. They swear their very lives to God in the service of others. The oath (Latin, *sacramentum*) thus serves as the essential foundation of the covenant. Taking an oath binds a person by covenant in a way that transcends mere legality. A covenant is personal, absolute and utterly secure, because it is a holy commitment made before—and enforced by—a holy God. (Of course, this doesn't mean that covenant oaths are never violated—but when they are, God's judgment is triggered in the form of covenant curses.)

Another example of a covenant oath is the sacrament of marriage—again, a commitment made not just to the new spouse but to God—which binds two people so closely that they become "one flesh." God's intention is that husband and wife not be separated. Properly understood, the marital sacrament is an encumbrance that paradoxically yields freedom. The wife is free to grow old and wrinkled without fear of divorce, while the husband is likewise free to become bald and potbellied without fear of his wife's abandonment.

Covenants forge bonds of freedom in commitment on the basis of oath-swearing. This is how God deals with his people, to whom he gives personal promises and covenant oaths. A passage in Hebrews explains this within the context of God's covenant with Abraham:

> For when God made a *promise* to Abraham, since he had no one greater by whom to swear, he swore by himself, saying, "Surely I will bless you and multiply you." And thus Abraham, having patiently endured, obtained the promise. Men indeed swear by a greater than themselves, and in all their disputes an *oath* is final for confirmation.
>
> HEBREWS 6:13-16 (emphasis added)

God's ultimate purpose thus rests upon the weightiness of an oath, so when he "desired to show more convincingly to the heirs of the *promise* the unchangeable character of his purpose, he interposed with an *oath*, so that through two unchangeable things, …

we ... might have strong encouragement to seize the hope set before us ... a sure and steadfast anchor of the soul" (vv. 17-19).

If you remember this while reading about the key figures in Scripture, you'll discover one of the most significant differences between the Old and New Covenants: the Old Covenant is administered by God with human mediators who came under oath and then sinned—like Adam (see Rom 5:12-21) and Israel (see Heb 3-4)—thereby triggering the covenant curses. In contrast, the New Covenant is established by the God-man, Jesus, but only after he had fulfilled the terms—and borne the curses—of the Old Covenant. He thus became the mediator of the New Covenant (see Heb 8-9), which he ratified by oath-swearing.

In this connection, it hardly seems like a coincidence that the Latin word for "oath" is *sacramentum*. From ancient times, the early Christians understood the sacraments in terms of covenantal oath-swearing, as the means that Christ had instituted for keeping—and renewing—the New Covenant.[6]

Saving Bonds of Sacred Kinship

Another major difference between contracts and covenants may be discovered in their very distinctive forms of exchange. A contract is the exchange of property in the form of goods and services ("That is mine and this is yours"); whereas a covenant calls for the exchange of persons ("I am yours and you are mine"), creating a shared bond of interpersonal communion.

For ancient Israelites, a covenant differed from a contract about as much as marriage differed from prostitution. When a man and woman marry, they declare before God their undying love to one another until death, but a prostitute sells her body to the highest bidder and then moves on to the next customer. So contracts make people customers, employees, clients; whereas covenants turn them into spouses, parents, children, siblings. In short, covenants are made to forge bonds of sacred kinship.[7]

Scripture reveals how God has used covenants to forge family bonds with his people in every age. This is echoed in the common formula used throughout Scripture to describe God's covenant bond with us: "I will be their God, and they shall be my people.... I will be a father to you, and you shall be my sons and daughters" (2 Cor 6:16-18). Of course, the climax of the process is the New Covenant, when Christ opened up the inner family life of the Trinity for all of us to share.

So if you want to get to the heart of Scripture, think *covenant* not contract, *father* not judge, *family room* not courtroom; God's laws and judgments are meant to be interpreted as signs of his fatherly love, wisdom and authority. This does not imply a lower or less strict standard of justice, however, since a good father requires more from his son than the judge expects from a defendant, or the boss from his employee.

The terms of a covenant call for certain actions to merit rewards or benefits, while a breach of the commitment results in specific penalties and damages. This follows the pattern of family life, where children work to get an allowance, and when they grow up and prove their maturity, they can reasonably expect to be rewarded with an inheritance. However, if they persist in serious sin, they face the prospect of disinheritance. This is the biblical pattern of the covenant as well, for the Father blesses his children when they keep the covenant, just as he punishes them for breaking it. All of this is spelled out in the covenant, in terms of blessings and curses (see Dt 28). The blessings mean life, while the curses mean death; so God urges his people to choose life and behave in such a way as to enjoy his fatherly blessing.

Peering Into the Eyes of the Father:
A Forever Commitment

The Father wanted to convince his children, "the heirs of the promise," that he's absolutely faithful, unchangeable in character. He knew that the ancient Israelites were surrounded by peoples with fickle gods, benevolent one day and vindictive the next. Why should the Hebrews not expect more of the same? No wonder God went to such great lengths to convince his people that he was different. He swore an oath to "strengthen" their trust, accommodating himself to their weakness of faith in his initial word of promise. Like those ancient Hebrews, we need to hold on to hope as a "sure anchor of the soul," especially since we have a better covenant (see Heb 8:6), based on better sacraments, for "it was not without an oath" (Heb 7:20).

The basic message God wants to convey by a covenant, then, can be stated simply: "I love you. I am committed to you. I swear that I will never forsake you. You are mine and I am yours. I am your father, and you are my family." How astonishing that the Creator has such profound love for his creatures!

The more I learned about how God has fathered his children down through the centuries, the more this reality of covenant came alive. It ceased being an abstract theory and instead opened the doors of my mind to new dimensions of God's love. Much more than just an ancient term from biblical culture, it came to represent for me all the richness of family commitment. The Old Testament characters took on flesh as an awesome yet understandable web of kinfolk, the household of faith.

The Gravity of Covenant Law

As you study Scripture, you'll see how covenant laws are not arbitrary stipulations but fixed moral principles which govern the moral order. Moreover, they reflect the inner life of the Blessed Trinity. In short, "covenant" is what God does because "covenant" is who God is.

Covenant law is to the moral order of human relations what the laws of nature are to the physical order. We are familiar with certain fixed laws—like gravity—which govern material things like our bodies. Suppose one day I grow tired of the law of gravity and how it restricts my bodily freedom; so I climb to the top of a tower and jump—just to assert my freedom from the law of gravity. Would I break the law of gravity? No, I would only demonstrate it. The only thing broken, most likely, would be my bones.

The same thing holds true of covenants in the spiritual realm. We might protest and complain in the midst of painful conflict and walk away from a committed relationship. We even try sometimes to walk away from God in a sort of mute protest. But we don't thereby break or invalidate the natural moral law of the covenant, binding us to God and to one another. We only break ourselves and the lives of our loved ones. The moral order of human life may be invisible, but it is governed by covenant laws that are no less firmly fixed than the laws of physics.

Once we understand the permanence of the covenant, we begin to appreciate its grandeur. We can use it as a lens with which to view human history. We begin to see from a heavenly perspective how God has worked from generation to generation to keep the human family together. And when we peer through that same lens from earth toward heaven, we see the eye of our Father peering back at us, keeping watch over his people.

This mutual bond of obedient trust and committed love is the heart of the covenant. It's what the ancient Hebrews called *hesed*;

sometimes translated as "loyalty" or "favor," its essential meaning is that kind of "covenant love" that is shared by family members.[8]

Jesus told the parable of the Prodigal Son to give a poignant illustration—in concrete terms—of the beauty and depth of the New Covenant he had come to establish (see Lk 15:11-32). When we read the story, we might focus on the young man's sinful life; but that would be the same mistake that his envious elder brother made.

Instead, we need to remember that the point of the parable is not the son's failure but the father's constant love. No matter what the young man did to try to break or escape the family bond of covenant connecting him to his dad, he never succeeded. Even when he was far away in a foreign country feeding pigs, the covenant embraced him. It's what eventually brought him back home.

Parents who have had to agonize over their own "prodigals" know the kind of stubborn love we're talking about here. It's like an abiding law of nature: Our kids may test our love for them, but they can't break it. Jesus once told his listeners (see Mt 7:11) that if we—sinners that we are—are able to show a deep commitment to our children's welfare, then how much more confident should we be that the love of God for us will never be exhausted or overcome.

Our Spiritual Ancestors

Supported by a cast of thousands, the main characters in our covenant love story will be familiar to you: Adam, Noah, Abraham, Moses and David. What do these five men have in common? Each of them shared an intimate bond of friendship with God, a relationship initiated by God and founded on a personal covenant. In fact, this series of covenants leads up to and climaxes in the coming of Jesus Christ, the Messiah, who instituted the New Covenant and thus changed the course of history.

As you read through the Old Testament, you are literally studying your own family story, your own roots, your own spiritual ancestors. Adam, Noah, Abraham, Moses and David are all truly our older brothers in God's family. Pope Pius XI once said, "We are of the spiritual lineage of Abraham.... Spiritually we are all Semites because God's plan from the beginning has always encompassed the whole family of man."[9]

God's Family Tree at a Glance

For an overview of the divine love story that encompasses the lives of these figures, let's describe briefly the promises God made—and fulfilled—for each one of them:

- God called *Adam* to share in his blessing in the covenant of marriage with Eve (see Gn 1:26-2:3), and promised to deliver them from sin through the promised "seed" by crushing the head of the diabolical serpent tempter (see Gn 3:15).

- The Father pledged to *Noah* to keep him and his household safe through the flood, and then promised never to wipe out the human family that way again (see Gn 9:8-17).

- God promised *Abraham* the Promised Land where his natural descendants might be blessed as a nation, and then a kingdom, until eventually all the families of the earth would be blessed through him and his seed (see Gn 12:1-3; 22:16-18).

- The Lord used *Moses* to lead the twelve tribes of Israel out of bondage in Egypt, and to ratify a national covenant that made them a holy nation (see Ex 19:5-6), called to occupy the Promised Land of Canaan as their inheritance (see Ex 3:4-10).

- God covenanted with David to build a worldwide kingdom, by establishing an everlasting throne with the son of David, who was destined to rule—with divine wisdom—over all the nations, united as a royal family in their common worship of the heavenly Father within his house, the Jerusalem temple (see 2 Sm 7:8-19).

- Finally, the Father kept all of his previous promises by the gift of his Son, *Jesus*, who bore all the curses of the previously broken covenants—in order to ratify the New Covenant—in the self-offering of his flesh and blood that permanently binds all of us together, both Jews and Gentiles, in one universal divine family: the one holy, catholic and apostolic Church (see Mt 26:26-28).

If we look closely at our own lives, we'll find that all these fatherly promises apply to us: to deliver us from the mess our sins have made; to preserve our marriages and our families; to meet our needs; to make us strong; to unite us to others; and for God to be with us always. When we consider our corporate life as the people of God, we'll see how the Father has fulfilled each and every one of these promises to us as a whole—with loving wisdom and merciful ingenuity—by transforming his flawed and fallen children into the spotless bride of Christ.

A Broadening Focus

With each succeeding covenant, God broadened the focus of his dealings with the human family. At the dawn of creation, God made the first covenant with *Adam* in the form of a *marital* bond, under the sign of the *Sabbath*. "God created man in his own image ... male and female he created them" (Gn 1:27). And he blessed them and called them to be fruitful; this is why he made the marital covenant with the founding father and mother of the human family.

Our founding father, Adam, represents the entire human family. In his first encyclical, *Redemptor Hominis,* Pope John Paul II made the point that at the time of creation God established a covenant with all of humanity. He sees this as the foundational covenant from which all of the others in Scripture spring—culminating in the New Covenant sealed by Jesus, whereby God's original covenant plan is fulfilled and renewed. Citing Eucharistic Prayer IV, he describes Christ's accomplishment: "He and he alone satisfied that fatherhood of God and that love which man in a way rejected by breaking the first Covenant and the later covenants that God 'again and again offered to man.'"[10]

Ten generations later, God made a second covenant with *Noah* and his household, under the sign of the *rainbow*. As a result, God's family now assumed a *domestic* form. As you may recall, Noah was a married man with three grown sons who were also married. Together they formed an extended family. Can you imagine these four married couples trying to get along while living together within the confines of the ark for an entire year? Noah must have run a tight ship!

After another ten generations, God made a third covenant with *Abram,* with the sign of *circumcision* (see Gn 17); so God's family was enlarged to *tribal* proportions. When called to leave his birthplace, Abram was a patriarch who ruled over a clan, and in time he became the chieftain of a veritable tribe. In addition to his own relatives who accompanied him (such as Lot), this one man oversaw domestic servants by the hundreds, possibly even the thousands (see Gn 14:14). The covenant included this entire group. So the people of God grew from a married couple to a household to a tribe, which was made up of many households and many more marriages.

The fourth covenant was made by God with *Moses* at Mount Sinai, signified by the *Passover,* which transformed the twelve tribes into God's *national* family, Israel. This made it absolutely necessary to form a much more elaborate system of laws; God gave the Ten Commandments and other statutes to Moses so that Israel would have its own national constitution.

God established the fifth covenant with *David*, under the sign of the everlasting throne of the Son of David in order to elevate Israel to a *kingdom*, (see 2 Sm 7). This meant elevating the nation of Israel over the surrounding nations and city-states, incorporating them into the covenant, by giving them a subordinate role as colonies and vassals under God and his royal priestly Son of David. Since kings exact tribute from subject nations, this also meant that foreigners would be making annual visits to Jerusalem, where they would be able to hear God's law, and learn his fatherly wisdom from Solomon. As a result, the Gentiles learned to worship the one true God, while the Father prepared them to be eventually restored to his family, after the coming of the *real* Son of David, Jesus.

As you can see, each one of these covenants is fundamentally familial in nature. God always deals with his people in a personal way, fathering his family and overseeing kinship relationships and obligations through each of these covenants. His ultimate purpose, of course, is to reunite the entire human race, which was broken by sin, pride, injustice and violence. Much like Humpty Dumpty after his great fall, the human race cannot mend itself and restore unity through our own efforts alone. No matter how hard we try. Only God can put us back together again and reconcile all of us to himself.

How could such a gigantic task possibly be accomplished? By the coming of Christ, the only begotten Son of God. God himself came to save us. We will see that Christ didn't abolish the Old Testament; rather, he fulfilled and perfected it.

The sixth covenant was made by *Jesus Christ*, with the Eucharist serving as the sign of the New Covenant, making God's family truly *universal* (*katholikos* in Greek), otherwise known as the

Catholic Church. So Christ's kingdom is not restricted to one region or race; nor is it governed by political coercion, military force and human fear, but by spiritual means, sacramental graces and divine mercy and love.

This is the constitution of the New Covenant, and it is actualized within the Catholic Church. All human beings are now called to become members of this universal family of God in order to serve as instruments in the Father's work of reconciliation through the Son and by the Spirit. Human power alone is incapable of such a task.

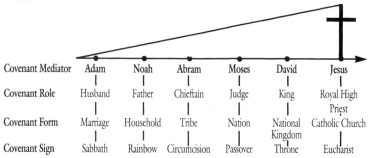

Covenant Mediator	Adam	Noah	Abram	Moses	David	Jesus
Covenant Role	Husband	Father	Chieftain	Judge	King	Royal High Priest
Covenant Form	Marriage	Household	Tribe	Nation	National Kingdom	Catholic Church
Covenant Sign	Sabbath	Rainbow	Circumcision	Passover	Throne	Eucharist

Thus we see how God fathers his family by means of the covenant throughout the various periods of history. At each and every stage, the covenant is what God uses to maintain the spiritual solidarity and structural unity of his family, as it keeps growing from one age to the next, until at last his children form a fully international household of faith.

This is the very thing that our world needs most at the present time: a new vision of real and lasting family unity under God the Father. Western society has become a culture made of people who share in common little more than the commercial freedoms needed to pursue our own private interests as individuals. What we really need—and long for—is the covenant love of a family, God's family.

The Trinity Is the Eternal Covenant Family

What is it that unites people as members of one family? Flesh and blood and a common name. Accordingly, the members of God's universal family, the Church, are united in the sacrificial family banquet we call the Eucharist—Christ's flesh and blood. Similarly, just as a common name unites a family, we as Church are united through baptism, rebirth and adoption into God's family in *the name of the Father, Son and Holy Spirit.*

The sacramental bond of baptism reflects a covenant oath, which Christ has established as the New Adam, the founding father of this new family. And this bond is perfected and strengthened when we receive the *flesh and blood* of the Father's firstborn Son, the Passover Lamb of the New Covenant, in the power of the Spirit.

Thus, the Trinity is the eternal and original covenant family. As Pope John Paul II writes: "God in His deepest mystery is not a solitude, but a family, since He has in Himself fatherhood, sonship and the essence of the family, which is love."[11]

The Trinity is the eternal source and perfect standard of the covenant; when God makes and keeps covenants with his people, he's just being true to himself. In short, "covenant" is *what* God does because "covenant" is *who* God is. From a sinful, shameful couple cast out of paradise, to God's glorious, redeemed worldwide family of saints at home forever in heaven—that miraculous transformation is the covenant story of the Scripture. God's widening circle cannot be confined. God's family covenant has become universal and everlasting in and through his Son, Jesus. From the beginning, the Father planned that Adam and Eve would be the first members of a worldwide family circle, swept up into the eternal love of the Trinity. Now we turn to take a closer look at that initial covenant between God and our race, where the divine love story began.

TWO

Creation Covenant and Cosmic Temple:
God's Habitat for Humanity

The announcement took us kids by surprise: "We're going to build a new house!" As a second-grader and the youngest in my family, even I knew this was big news.

The next day we piled into the car and drove over to see the property. Images of paradise were racing through my mind. We pulled up and I jumped out, not knowing what to expect, and then just stood there with a blank stare and mouth agape.

It was nothing but a tangle of trees and brush and weeds and mud, utterly devoid of any homelike qualities. At least, that's the way it seemed to me. But not to my mother.

From the beginning, Mom visited the property at least once a day to check on progress and to troubleshoot. Her watchful presence was like the Spirit hovering over the face of the water at the beginning of creation (see Gn 1:2): she kept things moving.

It was lots of fun for us kids to watch the process unfold. First, the bulldozers came to clear the ground and dig out the foundation. Concrete blocks, bricks and lumber were then piled in our future yard. The foundation was laid in just two days; then the concrete basement was poured. Next the carpenters came, and from the clouds of sawdust, the skeletal frame of the first story emerged, and then the second. The walls went up, and the plumbing and wiring went in.

Finally, we were allowed to wander around inside. It was strange at first. There was something missing. It was a house but not yet a home.

Then came moving day. The big van pulled up one morning, and the men started carrying out our furniture and all those boxes. They worked fast. The new house was less than two miles away, so by evening the van was empty.

At the end of the day, with much work and unpacking still before us, we celebrated as a family. My dad held up the housekey, then showed us a secret hiding place, under a rock outside, where we'd find it whenever we needed to. It was no longer just a house; it had now become our home.

I look back on that whole building process and wonder if, in this common family experience, God the Father doesn't give us a key to unlock creation. We will test this key in the lock of Genesis 1, to see how God built the world—in stages—to be the holy house where his beloved children could feel at home.

But before testing the lock, we need to make sure that we have the right key: there are other keys in common use, some look-alikes that seem to fit but only jam the lock.

Avoiding Ventriloquism

Did you ever find yourself in a conversation with someone who—you could just tell—didn't really care what *you* thought? Perhaps you got the signal from a glance or some snap reply, but the attitude was clear, "I want your support, not your thoughts." Or worse: "If I want your opinion, I'll give it to you." In any case, you're almost made to feel like their dummy.

I suspect that if the ancient writer of Genesis were alive today, he would feel that way about modern interpreters of his work, especially the Creation account. To put it bluntly, many readers are more interested in figuring out whether or not Genesis can be squared with the theory of evolution than in discovering what the author really meant to say. Our modern preoccupation with science often gets in the way of a fair reading of Genesis.

In fact, the only time Scripture even raises the question of *how* the world was created is in the Book of Job, where God basically says to forget it (see Jb 38-41). It's simply too hard for us even to imagine, much less figure out for ourselves.

Instead, the Creation account seems to address some other— but no less important—questions, such as *what* and *why* God created. To see how these questions are addressed, perhaps it's time we reread Genesis through new eyes, as it were, by looking at it through old eyes. This means going back to the text in search of clues as to what the ancient writer intended to say to his original readers.

For the sake of simplicity, we will consider the author to be Moses, and his original readers to be those ancient Israelites who received this material from him as part of God's law (the five books of Moses). Such a traditional approach may seem out of fashion, but it has certain advantages that commend it. For one thing, it takes its interpretive cues from the biblical text itself. For another, it has greater explanatory power. In sum, it makes better sense of Genesis, and the whole Pentateuch, for that matter. It also faithfully echoes the living Tradition of the Church, as it has been reaffirmed by the Magisterium.[1]

By allowing Genesis to speak for itself, Moses becomes our teacher rather than our dummy; we become his students, instead of ventriloquists. At the same time, we should be aware of how some readers throw a modern voice back into the biblical text.

On the one hand, some readers insist upon six literal twenty-four-hour days and assert that Genesis refutes any form of evolution (theistic or otherwise), almost as if Moses and the Holy Spirit conspired to launch a preemptive first strike against Darwinism several thousand years in advance. While many of their critics reply by branding them as "fundamentalists," like most labels, this one isn't helpful or appropriate.

For one thing, certain versions of the theory of evolution clearly *are* at odds with Genesis, as well as sound reasoning. For another, some of the early fathers and doctors of the Church interpreted Genesis literally in terms of six twenty-four-hour days; yet we wouldn't brand them as fundamentalists, any more than we would call Nebuchadnezzar a Nazi because he persecuted the Jews and sacked their temple back in 586 B.C. Some labels just don't fit.[2]

But there are problems with this kind of literal reading. For instance, how were the first three twenty-four-hour days measured if the sun wasn't made until the fourth day? In addition, there's no end mentioned in connection with the seventh day, because it signifies God's rest, rather than a literal twenty-four-hour period.

Of course, God could have created the world in six days, if he so desired—or six hours or six minutes or six seconds, for that matter. However, "day" (Hebrew *yom*) doesn't always refer to clock-time; so it isn't necessarily used here to refer to how long God took to get the job done.

I realize that "literal" advocates are not unaware of these problems. I raise them merely to point out how they weren't problems for Moses (who was oblivious to them), precisely because they're beside the point, that is, *his* point. However, this form of "literal" interpretation is not the only ventriloquist act around. There's another approach, found at the opposite end of the interpretive spectrum, that would also throw its modern voice back into the ancient text.

Myth Conceptions

It is not uncommon to find readers who wish to reduce the Genesis account to little more than an ancient Hebrew myth. The line of reasoning frequently goes something like this: Since the Creation account is a religious narrative and not a scientific description of secular history, then it must be regarded as ancient Hebrew mythology based upon their primitive superstitions and sacred propaganda.

There's one problem with classifying Genesis as myth: it doesn't fit the facts. A comparative reading of Genesis and other ancient tales of Creation universally recognized to be mythical discloses far greater differences and divergences than parallels or similarities. For instance, the ancient myths all describe the Creation process in terms of a war among the gods, with the winners forming the cosmos out of the carcasses of the losers. Likewise, the myths treat the sun, moon and heavenly bodies as deities. Genesis is clearly cut from different cloth.[3]

Both of these forms of mythical and literal interpretation involve a subtle kind of ventriloquism. The net effect is much the same for both—the ancient text is forced to address modern problems by putting words into Moses' mouth. Although contrary conclusions are drawn, the two approaches build on the same set of premises, drawn not from the ancient text of Genesis but from the categories of modern science. Unfortunately, devout readers who adopt these scientific categories often find themselves fighting an interior battle between science and religion. I'm convinced that this is a false dilemma based on two unsuitable options.

I should add, without getting into a complex discussion of interpretive theory, that the literal meaning of Genesis is not to be disregarded. On the contrary, the Church teaches that it is essential to discern the literal sense of Scripture before delving deeply into its spiritual senses (#116-18). Thus, the literal sense is precisely and primarily what we're after; we just need to look for it in the proper way.[4]

So a proper reading of Genesis may call for disengagement from current debates raging between evolution and religion, in order to apply the tools of literary analysis with balance and detachment. However, this doesn't mean that we detach our-selves from the biblical text. On the contrary, we must adhere to the narrative as closely as possible; it beckons us to read it with great care and with a critical empathy for the culture and time in which it was originally written and transmitted.

If the Creation account is initially approached and studied in this manner, on its own terms, the text will yield a literal sense that remains open to the genuine discoveries of modern science, along with the valid findings of comparative religion and ancient mythology. Indeed, it's my conviction as a Catholic Christian that the results of such an approach will eventually demonstrate a profound complementarity of religion and science, faith and reason.

So without further ado, let's strap on our sandals, gird up our loins and join with ancient Israel in reading Genesis.

From Chaos to Cosmos

The eternal love story of Scripture begins very simply: "In the beginning God created the heavens and the earth" (Gn 1:1). Isn't it striking how easy it sounds? Without any exertion, or gods to fight off, God simply spoke, and ... BOOM (or BANG, if you prefer): the entire universe—space, time, galaxies, solar systems, planets, molecules, subatomic particles—all of it burst into existence out of nothing. That's what I call power.

The Bible's first verse makes it clear, from the outset, that God is absolutely supreme, totally sovereign, all-powerful and, thus, not to be confused in any way with the world he made. He alone is God, and we are not; nor is the vast cosmos his body or house (contrary to New Age teachings). As big and vast as the creation may appear to us, in reality it just isn't big enough to fit the infinite Creator.

If the first verse tells us who God is (the Creator) as well as what he's *not* (the creation), one question remains: what *is* the creation, according to Genesis? This is what the rest of the first chapter explains.

The next verse sets it up: "The earth was *without form and void*" (Gn 1:2). That last phrase, in the original Hebrew, is *tohu wabohu*, two words that describe primordial earth's twofold condition: *formlessness* and *emptiness.*

These words strategically fit between what comes before and after. In the preceding verse, "the heavens and the earth" point to the two main realms within creation, the spiritual and material. The first one refers to the immaterial realm that is occupied by pure spirits, "heavenly hosts" we call angels; while the second one points to the earthly habitat God made for humanity. Unlike the heavens, however, earth was still in an incomplete state of *formlessness* and *emptiness.* After these words, the rest of this chapter narrates God's creative response to, and resolution of, both of these problematic features of the earth's primordial chaotic condition. God transforms earth—from chaos to cosmos—according to his power and plan.

God's power is revealed in the next verse, which describes how "the Spirit of God was moving over the face of the waters" (v. 2b). Like my mother's watchful presence at the site of our future home, the Holy Spirit kept everything moving along in the Creation process, from ground-clearing and foundation-laying to its transformation and sanctification (see Ps 104:5-30; Prv 8:1-31). Along with the power, the plan is then revealed.

How to Build a House in Six Days

The Creation account seems to follow a very orderly format. Careful reading of the narrative shows how the Creator responded to the problem of earth's formlessness in the first three days and then resolved its emptiness in the last three days. Perhaps a diagram will make this easier to see:

	Time	Space	Life	
		DAY 7 **Sabbath**		
Emptiness	DAY 4 **Sun Moon Stars**	DAY 5 **Birds Fish**	DAY 6 **Man Animals**	Rulers
Formlessness	DAY 1 **Day Night**	DAY 2 **Sea Sky**	DAY 3 **Land Vegetation**	Realms

On day one, God called forth light and divided light from darkness to make day and night (see vv. 3-5); that's how earthly time was formed. On the second day, God made the skies and seas by separating the waters above and below (see vv. 6-8); that's how earthly space was formed. On day three, God created land and vegetation (see vv. 9-13); that's how earthly life began. The three basic conditions for earthly existence were now complete: time, space and life. Likewise, the three essential elements for human sustenance were also now in place: light, water and food. Three realms now stood in need of rulers.

On day four, God made the sun, moon and stars, calling them "to rule over the day and over the night" (vv. 14-19), the temporal realm already formed on day one. On day five, God made the fish and birds, calling them to fill the skies and seas (see vv. 20-23), to rule over the spatial realm God made on day two. On the sixth day, God created the animals and man, calling them to rule the land and vegetation, that is, the biotic realm that God had formed on day three.

There's a perfect match between what God did on the first

three days and the second three days. The Lord first created the structure in three days, then filled that structure with living beings on the second three days. First the realms and then the rulers. Is this a mere coincidence? I don't think so.

These parallels reveal the literary framework embedded in the Creation narrative, which Moses employed to describe God's transformation of earth into a suitable habitation for humanity. We've discovered, through a close and careful reading, a simple but profoundly coherent framework, one that offers some valuable clues as to how the original Israelite readers probably understood the Genesis Creation account. More to the point, it helps *us* to understand the meaning and significance of creation. In short, it shows us *what* and *why* God created.

Image Is Everything

As to *what*, God was building a home for his children-to-be. Creation is a big construction project. Good builders work with the end in mind. Aristotle wrote, "What is last in execution is first in intention." God always works with his end in view; so we discern his goal in the last thing that he made, which is us.

"Then God said, 'Let us make man in our image, after our likeness.... So God created man in his own image, in the image of God he created him; male and female he created them" (Gn 1:26-27). Now the plot thickens, as they say. What does it mean for us to be made, male and female, in God's "image and likeness"?

First, it means that human life possesses great sacredness. Society often makes the mistake of ascribing value according to a person's great works, good looks or economic productivity and output. This mistake was made by the Nazis in World War II, and it is at the heart of the tragedy of abortion and euthanasia in our time. The sanctity of human life includes the preborn and aged, the physically infirm and mentally impaired. Every person has this awesome and immeasurable dignity because each human is made in God's image. Even those who sin or commit some heinous crime remain cloaked in this dignity. No human is beyond redemption.

Second, it means that our work has special value. Society gets it backwards. My labor isn't what confers dignity upon me; it is bearing the image of God that invests my work with honor. Work is not a curse, in and of itself, even though it is cursed, because of Adam's sin, with frustrating toil (see Gn 3:17-19). God himself labored to bring creation into existence. We were called to work, before the Fall, in imitation of God our Father.

Third, it means that we are like God. As *persons*, we have reasoning intellects, free wills and a unique capacity to love. Furthermore, God made our nature unlike any other. As human beings, we find ourselves somewhere between the angels and beasts, with physical bodies and rational souls. Angels can love but not reproduce; animals reproduce but without love. However, we humans have a truly unique capacity to do both in the reproductive act of marital love, the covenantal source of interpersonal communion and family life. When we truly love as a spouse, a parent, a sister or brother, we are sharing ultimately in God's very own life and love (they are one and the same in God). As persons-in-family, we are called to live and love like God the Father, the Son and the Holy Spirit. It all begins with the marriage covenant, when interpersonal love is intentionally shared in a life-giving way.

Many talk about the importance of a good self-image these days. Some say it's a false problem, that it doesn't really matter. I disagree. It does matter—a great deal. But we're going about it the wrong way. It's not the problem that is false but the so-called solutions. What we need isn't to create good self-images for everyone but to believe that everyone is created in God's image.

The profound truth about God creating us in his "image and

likeness" first appears in Genesis, but in a very simple way. The original sense of the phrase conveys a down-to-earth truth. This is made plain in the next occurrence of the phrase, in Genesis 5:3, when Adam fathered a son named Seth, "in his own likeness, after his image." There it plainly refers to a father-son relationship. And it carries essentially the same meaning here in the Creation story.

Human Nature Created in a State of Grace

More than a mere creature, Adam was endowed with the grace of divine sonship. From the first moment of his existence, Adam stood in the presence of God, as a son before his loving Father. Many of us have heard this before. In fact, some may even find it boring. That's not good. In fact, it may be dangerous; for the difference between Creator and creature is immeasurably vast. And yet it's often neglected, and sometimes denied.

A little bit of sound philosophy can be a great help here: compared to God's inexhaustible and infinite nature, humans are like little pieces of dust. Even the highest angels are specks of finite spirit when compared with the Almighty One. As one of my Jesuit professors once said, "In and of ourselves, we're more like rocks than we are like God." It's true, even if we don't like to think about it. But we *need* to think about it—frequently and carefully, or else we won't have the proper understanding and appreciation of what God's grace really accomplishes in us, and how much we need it. By nature, we are God's creatures and servants; but by grace, we are elevated to become his beloved children.

It's hard to exaggerate the importance of this point about how God's image relates to nature and grace. Let me summarize two of the most significant points. First, because we are created in God's image, *human nature* possesses three essential qualities: the sanctity of human life, the dignity of human labor and the sacredness of family love. God created man with a *nature* suited for temporal life on earth, which enabled us to live and work and love *like* God, as persons-in-family. This is the classical (and Catholic) notion of the *natural law*,[5] which is the same as the moral law of the covenant. Second, there is a higher mystery connected to God's image that is *divine grace*, which signifies our elevation to share in the glory and love that eternally flow among the three divine Persons of the Triune Family. Man was infused with *grace*, which suited him for eternal life *in* God, which enabled him to live as his adopted son, now and forever. This corresponds to what St. Thomas Aquinas calls the *divine law*.[6]

You might be wondering what all of this has to do with the Genesis account of Creation. The answer is, everything. From the beginning of human existence, the orders of nature and grace were meant to be married. But in our day they've been divorced. The wedding occurred at the dawn of history, with Creation, as Genesis reveals. The seventh day, the holy Sabbath, was the sign of this nuptial covenant, as we'll see, marking the union of heaven and earth, God and man, male and female. The initial separation was triggered by Satan's rebellion, the divorce by Adam's sin. Christ came to renew this nuptial covenant, as the New Adam who sealed the New Covenant with the Church, his bride.

If we allow this biblical vision to sink in, it will change the way we think and live. We'll see creation as it really is: the house that God built to be our temporal and temporary home, a place of pilgrimage where we come to know the Lord through his awesome creation as a loving Father, not just a wise Creator. This covenantal vision of creation is revealed so that we might live as God's children, not just his creatures, in the beautiful palace that the King of Kings made for his royal family.

The Sabbath: Saving the Blest to Last

As to *why* God created, the seventh day reveals the answer: God not only "rested on the seventh day," he "blessed ... and hallowed it" (see Gn 2:2-3). While some modern readers may wonder about God getting tired, no ancient Israelite would have missed the real point of God's action: He made the Sabbath to be the sign of the covenant (see Ex 31:12-17).[7] As such, the seventh day doesn't signify God's exhaustion but rather his exuberance—in calling his children to the end for which he made us: to rest in our Father's blessing and holiness, now and for all eternity.

This is why God gave the Sabbath to his people, and why they had to "remember" and "keep" it (see Ex 20:8); for it was the sign of the covenant between God and creation that God's people were called to mediate. This role as covenant mediator involved two tasks: exercising *royal* dominion (see Gn 1:26-29) and attaining to *priestly* holiness (see Ex 31:16-17). Our work and worship were thus meant to go hand in hand.

As a son of God, Adam was both king and priest. The double action of God on the seventh day was connected to these two roles. God's "blessing" is what made it possible for Adam to be a king; while God's "hallowing" action enabled him to be a holy priest. Because of the Sabbath, man's work could be taken up into worship. Of these two sacred roles, however, the priestly was clearly higher—and holier—than the kingly, at least in ancient Israel.

God also meant the Sabbath to be a joy for Israel, here and now. Isn't it odd that God has to command us to be blessed? Why is that even necessary, except that God knows that we don't know what ultimate blessings he made for us (see 1 Cor 2:9)? From the beginning, God knew what we needed to be fulfilled, and so he provided it, as it were, "in the beginning." The Sabbath thus serves to remind us that our fulfillment requires something more than what we can obtain by our own natural labor or in our earthly life. That's why Israel had to "remember the Sabbath," so that, by renewing the covenant with their Father, they might continually rediscover how much he can be trusted to provide all that is needed, including what it takes to keep his laws.

In marking the end of God's work, the Sabbath also points to the ultimate end of man's royal work and priestly worship: eternal life in heaven. Our goal is to share God's Sabbath rest. Nothing less will do, at least as far as God is concerned. This reflects the family spirit of God's covenant law: the Father mandates our sanctification and blessing. He commands us to be saints in order to enjoy communion with him forever. Thus, we must always do our temporal work with our *eternal* end in view.

The Sabbath:
The First Day of the "Rest" of Man's Life

Since man was created on the sixth day, his first full day would have been the Sabbath. Curious, isn't it, that God called man to rest—even before he began to work? (Similarly, in the New Covenant Christians begin the week by resting on Sunday, the Lord's Day.) Personally, I think God was trying to teach us an important lesson—from the very beginning—about faith.

The danger of unbelief is subtle: we often prefer to labor as slaves rather than work as sons trusting in our Father's grace. We are tempted to reduce the Father's law to a servile code. Jesus thus reminds us, "The Sabbath was made for man, not man for the Sabbath" (Mk 2:27).

This sheds a whole new light on Creation. God's intention is so pure. Everything that he does is for our good, our joy. God could have made everything in an instant, effortlessly. He didn't need six days to create, nor one to recuperate. Truly, God didn't need to make anything at all, period. When he decided to bring the human race into existence, it wasn't due to boredom or loneliness. The Father, the Son and the Spirit have shared the most intimate family life and love from all eternity. They didn't need more fellowship, and God didn't lack any glory.

When history is finished, God will not have any more glory than he had at the start. It is reasonable to conclude that God did not create and redeem to get glory but to *give* it. So it is essential for us, as faithful and obedient children, to *get* it.

God created and redeemed us to share in the grace and glory of divine sonship. The Lord worked for six days and then rested on the seventh for our sake, not his, as a healthy pattern for us to imitate, one that fits our nature perfectly. After all, the Father should know.

Another reason why Moses described God as setting apart the seventh day at the end of his creative work may be related to the ancient Israelite practice of covenant oath-swearing. The Hebrew word for "oath-swearing," *shebà*, is based on the word for seven. In Hebrew, "to swear an oath" means literally "to seven oneself" (see Gn 21:27-32). Since a covenant is formed by oath-swearing, which means "sevening oneself," it may not be unreasonable to see God covenanting himself to the cosmos in the very act of creating it, deliberately in a sevenfold way. In any case, it's significant that the Sabbath was understood by the Jews as the day for Israel to "remember" God's covenant with them and creation. They did so in prayer and worship, to renew the covenant oath that made them God's sacramental family.[8]

The Sabbath: A Sanctuary in Time

Genesis presents Creation as God's grand home-building project for his children. This is reflected elsewhere in Scripture, especially in poetic passages that describe Creation as having a foundation, a cornerstone, a roof, doors, windows and other architectural features (see Jb 38-40; Ps 104). In particular, three architectural images frequently recur: house, palace and temple. Of these three, the temple is the highest and holiest.

The account of Creation teaches the most fundamental truth about the world, that it was formed to be a holy place for God's indwelling presence and man's priestly worship in sacrifice. In other words, God wants us to view the world as a macrotemple.

This ancient Jewish outlook is reflected in select biblical texts: when Moses erected the Tabernacle at Sinai, for instance (see Ex 25-31), or when Solomon built the temple in Jerusalem (see 1 Kgs 5-9). Several parallels show how each shrine was designed and built—as a microcosm—to commemorate and reenact Creation.

When God instructed Moses about the tabernacle (see Ex 25-31), he spoke directly ten times ("The Lord said to Moses..."). And in Genesis 1, God spoke the creative word ten times ("Let there be..."). Also, the first six days of Creation bear a striking resemblance to the building and blessing of the tabernacle:

GENESIS 1-2	EXODUS 39-40
God saw everything that he had made, and behold, it was very good (1:31).	Moses saw the work, and behold, they had done it, as the Lord had commanded it (39:43).
The heavens and earth were finished, and all the host of them (2:1).	All the work of the tabernacle of the tent of meeting was finished (39:32).
God finished his work which He had done (2:2).	So Moses finished the work (40:33).

So God blessed ... it (2:3).	And Moses blessed ... (39:43).
... and hallowed it (2:3).	You shall ... consecrate it (40:9).

Besides these several parallels, the holiness of the Sabbath is declared at the end of both projects (see Gn 2:2-4; Ex 31:12-17).[9]

A similar pattern is evident in the biblical account of the construction of Solomon's temple, which he rushed to complete in seven years and chose to dedicate in the seventh month—during the Feast of Tabernacles, which lasted exactly seven days (see 1 Kgs 6:38; 8:2). To top it off, Solomon's prayer of dedication was composed of seven petitions (see 1 Kgs 8:12-53).

These parallels suggest that the ancient Israelites may have been accustomed to reading the Creation account in view of the erection and dedication of the tabernacle and temple.[10] These parallels also reveal what ancient Jewish readers naturally read as the primary sense or literal meaning of the Creation account: God's erection and dedication of a cosmic temple for his royal-priestly people. As we'll see, this interpretation of creation as macrotemple in chapter one sets the stage for the symbolic meaning of the Garden of Eden in chapter two, as the sanctuary in which Adam is called to serve and minister (see Gn 2:15) as the high priest of humanity.[11]

What's in a Name: From Elohim to Yahweh

Some readers have puzzled over apparent discrepancies in the two Creation accounts in Genesis 1 and 2. However, a close reading of the narrative reveals their profound complementarity. Genesis 1 describes how *Elohim* called the cosmos into existence; while Genesis 2 depicts *Yahweh* acting closely and personally, by forming Adam from the "ground" (*'adamah*) and placing him in the Garden of Eden. The distinction between these two divine names reflects two different types of divine activity. Elohim evokes the infinite power of the Creator, while Yahweh reflects God's covenant love. We make a similar distinction when we switch from the generic term, "God," and speak of "Abba Father," as Jesus did.

How can these two different portraits be reconciled? Once again, the interpretive key is the Sabbath, as the sign of God's covenant with creation. It unlocks the meaning of creation: the cosmos is a temple; we are God's children; the Creator is our Father. This last one explains why God's name in Genesis 1, "Elohim," gives way to "Yahweh" in Genesis 2; because "Yahweh" is only revealed to—and used by—the children in God's covenant family. The name change thus reflects what the sabbath symbolizes, God's covenant with creation. And what a difference that covenant makes: creation becomes a holy temple, the Creator our Father, and we his beloved children.

High Priest of Humanity

God's Sabbath break is also a narrative bridge that carries readers from the earthly temple in Genesis 1 into the sanctuary of the Garden of Eden in Genesis 2. It was the sanctuary that made the temple holy; it would be unnatural for the cosmic temple to be without one. Here again, we need to catch the key parallels that Moses assumed his fellow Israelites would see.

First, God's order for Adam "to *till* [the garden] and *keep* it" (Gn 2:15) uses two Hebrew words (*'abodah* and *shamar*) that only occur together elsewhere in the Pentateuch where priestly duties are assigned to the Levites in the tabernacle (see Nm 3:7-8; 8:26; 18:5-6). The Levitical priests must have seen themselves, then, doing work similar to Adam's in the garden sanctuary of Eden.

Second, certain aspects of the Garden of Eden are described in terms reminiscent of the tabernacle and temple. God revealed himself in the garden (see Gn 3:8), where he "walks" (*hithallek*), as the Lord dwelt in the sanctuary (see Lv 26:11-12; Dt 23:14; 2 Sm 7:6-7). The Garden of Eden and Israel's sanctuaries were all entered from the east. Likewise, the sword-wielding "cherubim" posted by God as angelic guardians at the entrance to the garden closely resemble the two "cherubim" who guarded the inner sanctuary of Solomon's temple (see Gn 3:24; Ex 25:18-22; 26:31; 1 Kgs 6:23-29). Many scholars believe the menorah (a seven-branched candlestick) was viewed as a stylized tree of life, like the one in the garden (see Gn 3:22).

Third, there are parallels between Adam and Aaron, the high priest of Israel. For example, Adam was "clothed with garments" (Gn 3:21), as Moses clothed Aaron (*labas, ketonet*) at God's command (see Ex 28:42; Dt 23:13-14). The gold and onyx inside the Garden of Eden (see Gn 2:11-12) were used extensively to decorate the garments worn by the high priest (see Ex 25:7). Neither Adam nor Aaron could draw near to God with their "nakedness" exposed (see Gn 3:10; Ex 20:26; 28:42).

Adam was called to represent the human race; as high priest, Aaron was called to represent Israel. Adam's task in the garden sanctuary corresponded to that of the high priest, who ministered in the tabernacle and temple. By virtue of Adam's covenant role as the firstborn son of God and the father of God's human family, he was to serve as the guardian of God's holiness. In this role he would be tested, and everything hung in the balance.

THREE

Splitting the Adam:
From Creation to Desecration

One notable feature of the temptation narrative is how short it is. In just seven verses (see Gn 3:1-7), the serpent speaks twice and humanity is ruined. Readers may wonder, how could so much damage result from so little dialogue? There must be something deeper here, something more than a simple tale for children.

Coleridge once wrote: "A Fall of some sort or other ... is the fundamental postulate of the moral history of man. Without this hypothesis, man is unintelligible; with it every phenomenon is explicable."[1] Every phenomenon, that is, but the Fall itself!

What caused two upright and perfect human beings, our first parents, to transgress God's simple command? How was the spark of pride lit and then stoked into the flames of disobedience?

In this chapter, we explore how God formed and tested Adam and Eve, and we examine what factors might explain the seemingly inexplicable Fall. (Warning: it's not as simple as it sounds.)

From the Ground Up—God Raises His Son

God first formed "Adam," which is Hebrew for "man," from "the ground" (*'adamah*, see Gn 2:7). Adam's name points to his role as father of the human race, much as "Israel" initially refers to the founding patriarch who fathered the twelve sons who later raised twelve families, which became the twelve tribes of Israel.

God then "breathed into his nostrils the breath of life" (v. 7).

The word for "breath" (*ruah*) is the same as "spirit." God is depicted as directly breathing his own spirit into Adam. The Church fathers took this to mean that from his first breath, Adam was endowed with the Holy Spirit, not just a rational soul. Opening his eyes, Adam's first glimpse of the creation was thus illuminated by the Holy Spirit. Gazing out through the eyes of faith, he took his first step as a child of God, into the beauty of Eden, fully alive with the Spirit of divine sonship. Not a bad way to begin life, wouldn't you say?

Showing his son around the garden, the Father explained the living arrangements. "There are trees galore, with some of the tastiest fruits in the world, believe me! And all of them right at your fingertips. Hmmm ... well, not quite *all* of them..."

Adam may have noticed the sudden shift in his Father's tone of voice. They were stopped in front of two trees in the middle of the garden. Adam probably knew what was coming next. I know my kids always do, just like I did with my dad. It's rule time!

Rules for the Guardian to Keep the Garden

I still remember how my father would take me aside, look me right in the eye and say, "Scottie, there's no liberty without laws, no rights apart from responsibilities, and no rules makes fools." Naturally, I didn't want to hear it. But years later, I find myself telling *my* kids the same things my father told me.

Yahweh started off by explaining Adam's basic duty "to till and keep" the garden (Gn 2:15). The tilling part was clear enough, since that's what Adam would naturally expect to do in a garden. But the other word, "keep" (*shamar*), carries a distinct meaning, "to guard," implying the need to ward off potential intruders. This was how the word was used to describe the task of the sword-wielding Levites, who were ordered by Moses to keep Israel's sanctuary free of encroachers (see Nm 17:12-18:6).

Perhaps it struck Adam as a curious command, for it seemed to imply not only a need for the sanctity of the garden to be guarded but the existence of a potential intruder to desecrate it. Whatever it meant, Adam now had his priestly orders, to serve guard duty.

We know from experience that a list of restrictions usually comes along with rules. In other words, a list of *don'ts* often follows a list of *do's*. It was no different for Adam, except that only one restriction was given. But it was a very big *don't*.

The Die Is Cast

As far as Adam was concerned, there were two trees of major consequence: the first was the tree of life, which he could eat; the second was the tree of knowledge, which he couldn't (see Gn 2:16-17). Then God added a very ominous warning: "For in the day that you eat of it you shall die" (v. 17, literally "You shall die the death," or "By death you shall die").

The Hebrew word for "die" occurs twice in that last phrase. This emphatic repetition may imply two particular forms of death—spiritual death versus physical—especially since Adam and Eve did not physically die *in the day* they ate the forbidden fruit. But they *did* die spiritually, like the prodigal son in the parable, whose father declared: "He was once dead ... but now he's alive" (see Lk 15:32).

If the "death" threatened by the tree of knowledge seemed a little ambiguous, so is the "life" promised by the other tree. After all, didn't God already give Adam the gift of immortality?[2] What's the use of a tree with fruit to make you live forever if you're already going to anyway? You wouldn't buy fire insurance if you owned a house made of asbestos. So why did God bother to plant a tree that guaranteed immortality for one already immortal, unless the

Father had advance knowledge of a potential threat to his son's immortal existence? The fruit was meant to ensure Adam's human life in the face of mortal danger (or maybe even transform it into divine, eternal life for heaven; see Rv 22:2).

But could Adam even know what death meant before the Fall? After all, nothing had died yet. This is not an easy question. But the answer is clearly yes, necessarily so, since it would be senseless to threaten a man with a meaningless penalty. So while it isn't clear *how* Adam knew, it's reasonably certain *that* he did, at least in some way. In particular, he must have known death would have been dreadfully unpleasant, and hence something to be avoided at any cost. So he knew what he needed to know in order for God's test to be fair: he could eat the tree that promised life, but not the one that threatened death. Could an actor ask for a simpler script?

The stage was now set for the exciting drama that was about to unfold; except the director realized that something more was needed: a beautiful actress to play the female lead. Yahweh knew just what to do.

Alone Again, Unnaturally

Up to this point, you might say, God was really on a roll. After each act of creation he pronounced it "good" (see Gn 1:10, 12, 18, 21, 25). When creation was complete, God pronounced it "very good" (v. 31). But when Yahweh saw his son standing alone in the garden, he reversed himself—by declaring: "It is *not good* that the man should be alone" (Gn 2:18).

Some readers may find those words disconcerting; but rest assured, Adam didn't. In fact, when he heard those words, Adam could finally do just that—rest assured. Then he waited to see what action his Father would take.

Then the Lord God said... "I will make him a helper fit for him." So out of the ground the Lord God formed every beast of the field and every bird of the air, and brought them to the man to see what he would call them.... but for the man there was not found a helper fit for him.

GENESIS 2:18-20

With all due respect, what was the Lord thinking? Did he really suppose that Adam might find enough fellowship from the animals to overcome his loneliness? Hardly. Instead of a gaffe on God's part, we may reasonably infer that Yahweh had something else in mind. But what was it?

God probably wanted the beasts to show Adam what he's *not*, namely, just another animal, although they do share some things in common, including certain bodily appetites. In the process, Yahweh expected that Adam would come to a deeper understanding of what does—and doesn't—bring real fulfillment. As a result, Adam would acquire greater self-knowledge and self-control. It was probably no accident that Yahweh helped his son to find a job first, then a bride. Business before pleasure.

Prime Rib

At the end of that long first day, Adam was tired and lonely after naming all those beasts, and was more than ready for a break. Fortunately, God knew just what Adam needed:

So the Lord God caused a deep sleep to fall upon the man, and while he slept took one of his ribs and closed up its place with flesh ... and made [it] into a woman and brought her to the man.

GENESIS 2:21-22

Talk about having your needs met! As if getting a good night's sleep wasn't enough, Yahweh topped it off by unveiling his most glorious creation yet, his own daughter, and Adam's new bride.

Sages comment on how God formed Adam's covenant partner in the proper way: not from his feet, to be used as a doormat; not from his head, to be put on a pedestal; but from Adam's rib, to be at his side, close to his heart. (Those sages were right!)

Truly, Yahweh had saved his best for last—and Adam knew it. Holding nothing back, Adam let the whole world hear how he felt about this wondrous splendor: "Then the man said, 'This at last is bone of my bones and flesh of my flesh; she shall be called Woman, because she was taken out of Man'" (v. 23).

I love Adam's response. He was simply flabbergasted at all that beauty. An old college friend once paraphrased Adam's last line: "She shall be called Woman, because when I first laid eyes on her, all I could say was, WHOA MAN!" As a modern rendition, this almost captures the essence of Adam's blissful delight.

His line "flesh of my flesh, bone of my bones" echoes the language of covenant solidarity used elsewhere in Scripture (see Gn 29:14; 2 Sm 5:1; 19:12-14). Even more, it is the language of marital love and romantic ecstasy, heard for the first time at the dawn of history.

What a glorious scene. Can you imagine a better opening to the family drama of salvation history? And this little piece of romantic poetry, like a prized family heirloom, has been handed down through the ages so that all of us, as Adam's descendants, might know how greatly beloved was our first mother.

The sights and sounds of Adam's passion that are revealed here, pure and simple, prefigure the future—and even purer—passion of Jesus, the new Adam. As such, Jesus offered the sacrifice of himself for his bride, the Church. In his dying breath he gave us his Spirit (see Jn 19:30; 1 Cor 15:45). From his pierced side there flowed living water and blood (see Jn 19:34; 7:38; 1 Jn 5:6-8). Through the deep sleep of his death came forth the New Eve, who stood at his side, close to his heart (see Jn 19:26-27).[3] But did Adam really love Eve *that* much? If so, how was he to prove it?

The Two Become One

Of course, we don't know exactly when they tied the knot, since Genesis doesn't always narrate events in terms of strict chronology as modern historians do. The events may have been set forth along with symbolic elements—which is not to say that it's not history. Ancient Hebrews would write about historical realities in figurative terms for the purpose of conveying the deeper religious meaning or significance of the events, not just the events themselves.

There's no reason to suppose that Adam lived a long time as a bachelor. In terms of narrative time, his second day began when he woke up from his deep sleep, which also happened to be the Sabbath Day sanctified by God. So Adam's first full day may have been both a day of sabbath rest and betrothal, for Eve and himself, as marriage covenant partners. From a narrative perspective, the Sabbath may be seen as the sign of two closely related covenants: between God and creation, and Adam and Eve.[4]

Trial by Ordeal

In effect, the Father was testing his son in the sanctuary on the Sabbath by allowing him—as high priest and husband— to be confronted with a diabolical threat against his holy bride. Such a threat would demand nothing less than holy obedience and faithful love, calling for Adam's heroic self-sacrifice. However, because he acted as an unfaithful priest and husband, Adam not only transgressed the creation covenant of his Father, he also ruptured his marriage covenant with Eve.

So why *did* he do it? That's the question. The answer that I would like to propose is based on the traditional explanation of Adam's sin in terms of *pride* and *disobedience,* but then it also goes beyond it. In short, the reason why Adam succumbed to pride and disobedience was because of his fear of suffering and unwillingness to die, even for the love of his Father and bride.

Before going further, we should briefly review the relevant narrative facts that we've gathered so far. First, Adam's duty to guard the garden implies a potential intruder. Second, the mortal danger facing Adam refers to a spiritual death beyond the physical; so the threat of death attached to the forbidden fruit was more than what met the eye (notably Eve's eye, which only saw the fruit as "good for food," "a delight to the eyes" and "was to be desired to make one wise," Gn 3:6). Third, the tree of life was Adam's insurance against the potential loss of physical life, although it appears to signify (and confer?) something more than immortality, since Adam already had *that.* Fourth, when Eve came forth from Adam's side, God called him to an even greater duty than work, that is, to love his bride ("Greater love has no man than this, that a man lay down his life for his friends," Jn 15:13; see Eph 5:31-32).

Neither Demons nor Dimwits

In considering why Adam and Eve sinned, we need to avoid two interpretive extremes: demonization and trivialization.

On the one hand, Adam's first sin should not be exaggerated by making it out to be an act of calculated contempt and high-handed rebellion, as though he were an ally of the devil from the start. God created Adam upright and perfect; so his first act of disobedience was hardly motivated by pure malice. That sort of demonic hate usually takes years of practice.

On the other hand, we should not exaggerate Eve's folly by making her out to be a simpleton who couldn't keep things straight. Unfortunately, some take this attitude toward Eve, almost as a matter of course. This assumption was refuted centuries ago by St. Irenaeus:

Why did the serpent not attack the man, rather than the woman? You say he went after her because she was the weaker of the two. On the contrary. In the transgression of the commandment, she showed herself to be the stronger.... For she alone stood up to the serpent. She ate from the tree, but with resistance and dissent and after being dealt with perfidiously. But Adam partook of the fruit given by the woman, without even beginning to make a fight, without a word of contradiction—a perfect demonstration of consummate weakness and a cowardly soul. The woman, moreover, can be excused; she wrestled with a demon and was thrown. But Adam will not be able to find an excuse ... he had personally received the commandment from God.[5]

Whew! Pretty strong language, isn't it? But not inappropriate or inaccurate. St. Irenaeus points us to the golden mean between the two extremes.

So the Edenic stage is set. The lead actor and his leading lady have taken their places. The drama is now ready to unfold.

Enter the Subtle Serpent

The bride and groom soon discover they're no longer alone in the garden, which had been their honeymoon suite. They have a visitor. A serpent. Could this be the potential intruder?

Who or what is the serpent? Since childhood, most of us have pictured a snake, hanging from a tree. (Or perhaps it still had legs. By now, we may have grown a little suspicious of the various renditions of the Fall narrative in those children's Bible storybooks we used to look at in the doctor's office.)

The Hebrew word for serpent, *nahash*, is somewhat ambiguous. It has a wide range of meaning. While it is used most commonly to denote snakes (see Nm 21:6-9), it is also used with reference to evil dragons like Leviathan (see Is 27:1) and the legendary sea monsters, (see Jb 26:13). Across this wide spectrum of usage, the word generally refers to something that bites (see Prv 23:32), often with venom (see Ps 58:4). In any event, at minimum, the serpent here is a life-threatening symbol. And it represents mortal danger.[6]

In this case, the danger was not only (or mainly) physical but spiritual, particularly since the New Testament identifies this "ancient serpent" with Satan himself (see Rv 12:9; 20:2). In fact, this view was widely shared by the ancient Jews.[7]

Some readers are confused by the description of the serpent as being "subtle"; indeed, he's "*more* subtle than any other wild creature" (Gn 3:1). The term employed here (*'arum*) is often used to describe a wise man who is "shrewd" (see Prv 12:16; 13:16) or the "stealth" and "guile" of the wicked (see Jb 5:12; 15:5). It clearly implies the latter here; while it's also a word play on "naked" (*'arom*, Gn 2:25). In other words, Adam and Eve's nakedness is a double sign, which refers *positively* to the intimacy they share alone but *negatively* to their vulnerability in the presence of the serpent. Satan's "subtle" strategy is deliberately aimed at what their "nakedness" symbolizes, their marital union.

Eve of Destruction

The serpent only addressed Eve throughout, but not because Adam wasn't present. (In fact, the serpent's use of Hebrew verbs in the second person plural indicates that *Adam was right there all along.*)[8] By going straight to Eve, Satan was deliberately bypassing the familial structure established by God.

To start the conversation, he asked her a simple question (on the surface), but one loaded with clever ambiguity and evil insinuation: "Did God say, 'You shall not eat of any tree of the garden'?" (Gn 3:1). First of all, he spoke of Elohim, not Yahweh. (He probably was not allowed—or able—to utter that holy name.) Second, he changed the wording of the divine command to distort its meaning. (It can also be rendered, "You shall not eat from every tree.") Third, by emphasizing the negative limits, Satan impugned God's goodwill.

In her response, it becomes clear that Eve didn't memorize her Edenic catechism very carefully. She corrected the serpent, but not quite accurately. First, she dropped the positive tone of the Lord's original statement. ("You may freely eat of *every* tree.") Second, she adopted the serpent's use of Elohim, rather than using his personal name, Yahweh. Finally, Eve altered the original wording of the prohibition by adding "touching" to the divine ban on eating.

She's obviously feeling very defensive, even though Satan was the one who *should* have been on the defensive. After all, he's the intruder, the one who was out of place in the garden, the sanctuary of God. But the serpent was just getting started.

Shamelessly, Satan shot back his answer: "You will *not* die. For God knows that when you eat of it your eyes will be opened, and you will be like God, knowing good and evil" (Gn 3:4-5).

That's it! At last, Satan had crossed the line. He told an outright lie. He contradicted the very word of God. Now was the time for Adam to leap into action, to pronounce judgment on this infernal liar in the name of God. Right?

Adam's Guilty Silence

I can just imagine what Adam was thinking: *Perhaps I should do something, but then again, perhaps not. No need to jump to conclusions or to act rashly—might not be prudent. There may be some more relevant data to be considered.*

But *was* there really anything more to consider? After all, his bride was out there on the firing line! What other data could possibly be relevant?

For one thing, what sounded like bald lies might not really be so bald. After all, the serpent said they wouldn't die; and sure enough, they didn't. For another thing, Satan said their eyes would be opened and that's exactly what occurred: "The eyes of both were opened" (Gn 3:7). And what sounded like the biggest lie of all ("You will be like God, knowing good and evil," v. 5) also came true, as God himself admitted: "Behold, the man has become like one of us, knowing good and evil" (v. 22).

Did the Serpent Get It Right?

What are we to make of this? Did the serpent get it right, while God got it wrong? I don't think so.[9]

For one thing, before the Fall there was no way Adam could have known that what the serpent said was anything but a lie. Apart from eating, how would he have known that they would not die, that their eyes would be opened or that they'd become like God, knowing good and evil? He couldn't have discovered any of these things until he'd already disobeyed. Thus, Adam could not possibly excuse himself on the grounds of conflicting evidence.

For another thing, Adam and Eve *did* die, spiritually. The life of the Spirit was snuffed out in their souls; sanctifying grace was lost. And this was no less of a death than physically dying. Furthermore, their eyes were opened, but to the shame of their own nakedness and sin, not to the glory of God, which they lost. Also, they *did* become like God by exercising their free will; however, the option they chose led them into moral and spiritual bondage.

The Father wasn't threatened by the prospect of Adam and Eve becoming like him, because that's why he made them. "Man was destined to be fully 'divinized' by God in glory. Seduced by the devil, he wanted to 'be like God,' but 'without God.'"[10]

Fear of Suffering

So there must be another reason why Adam kept silent. But what is it? Fear of suffering and death. And how can we know that? By going back and reading between the lines, by carefully listening again not only to what the serpent explicitly stated but also what he meant to imply.

He said, "You will not die." And that defiant contradiction hung in the air until slowly the serpent's meaning became clear: "You will not die—*if* you eat the fruit ..." In other words, Satan used the form of a life-threatening serpent, with his evil stealth, to deliver what Adam rightly took to be a thinly veiled threat to his life, which it was from the outset.[11]

Doing What Comes (Preter)Naturally

This alone explains Adam's silence. As the strategy of the serpent became clear, Adam had to make a dreadful choice. Would he stand up for his bride by engaging the diabolical serpent in mortal combat? Or would he try to cling to his cherished estate in Eden, with its many delights such as earthly dominion, immortality, impassability, and integrity?

Since Adam could not exercise his preternatural gifts apart from faith, without losing them, he really *had* to choose. And his options were greatly narrowed: supernatural grace *or* natural goods; spiritual life *or* spiritual death; physical suffering *or* physical satisfaction; self-sacrifice *or* self-indulgence.

In other words, would Adam avoid sin at all costs? Would he cooperate with God's grace and place all of his love and trust in his Father above everything else? Or would Adam fear death more than offending God, and opt for his created gifts over the Creator and Giver of those gifts? In sum, would Adam sacrifice himself to God, for the sake of Eve, or would he fall back onto his own resources, and succumb to pride and disobedience?

Adam's Options: Proto-Martyr or Apostate?

Of course, we already know what Adam did. Now we are just trying to get a better understanding of *why* he did it. (Please note: explaining Adam's sin is not the same thing as excusing it.) Not only do we know what Adam did, we also know many other relevant details. There are ten underlying factors that need to be added up:

First, we know that *Satan wanted them dead,* and certainly preferred spiritual death, with its everlasting consequences, over mere physical death.

Second, we know that *spiritual death could not be inflicted by the serpent against their will,* since Adam and Eve would only die spiritually if they voluntarily gave consent to mortal sin.

Third, we know that *Adam and Eve dreaded death;* otherwise, the threat against their eating would have been meaningless.

Fourth, we know that *God did not intend the Garden of Eden to be their final state.* He created Adam and Eve for heavenly glory. Earthly paradise was only meant to serve as a foretaste and foreshadowing of heavenly paradise (see Rv 21-22).

Fifth, we know that *God had placed Adam on probation,* and required at least some degree of self-denial and mortification as the condition for his entering into heavenly glory.[12]

Sixth, we know that *Adam's mortification required more than simple self-denial* with respect to the fruit. It called for him to engage Satan in spiritual combat; for if Adam had decided *not* to eat, Satan would not simply have forsaken his project.

Seventh, we know that, left to his own resources, Adam would have been no match against Satan's death-dealing malice and seraphic power.

Eighth, we know that *nothing is said in the narrative about Adam crying out to God in his distress.*

Ninth, we know that *Adam succumbed to pride and fell back upon his own resources,* and thereby fell straight into sin.

Tenth, we know that *the Father would not have forsaken his son in his hour of need, if only Adam had cooperated with grace and called upon God for help.* Either God would have empowered his faithful servant with sufficient grace to destroy the devil, or the Father would have accepted Adam's sacrificial offering of himself as a holy oblation, saving him from death and corruption and rewarding him with eternal glory in heaven.[13]

Not to Decide *Is* to Decide

In the final analysis, this explanation is anything but an argument from silence. Rather, it is an argument *for* silence, that is, an argument that explains why Adam opted for silence, a loud and guilty silence. In fact, it's difficult to imagine any other way to account for Adam's speechless performance.

Ultimately, we should chalk Adam's sin up to a failure of nerve. By not deciding he really decided; since once Eve ate the forbidden fruit, Adam had already failed, even before eating it himself. He should never have allowed things to go that far. If he had intervened from the outset, the entire exchange could have been prevented.

Thus, Adam's failure was virtually complete by the time Eve took her first bite. Besides, what was he to do once Eve ate, condemn *her* and cast *her* out?

When you get right down to it, not only was Adam's failure complete as soon as Eve ate the fruit, but his fate was sealed. Was he expected to forsake his new bride at that point? Was he even capable of getting along without her? I suspect not. In fact, Adam probably couldn't even imagine life without Eve. Once she took a bite, Adam's eating was practically a *fait accompli*.

Eve of Redemption

Their eyes were opened to an altogether different reality, a hostile home and a threatening mate. Fearful of the invisible threat, the man and woman realized they were naked for the first time and made clothes for themselves. And when Adam and Eve heard the sound of the Lord God walking in the garden, they hid themselves from his presence (see Gn 3:1-10).

Our Heavenly Father is no fool. We can't hide under the bed like a small child who has done something naughty. But Adam and Eve began to offer excuses and point the finger of blame: *But we're naked ... and the woman—remember the one who you made to be my helper—gave me the forbidden fruit ... but the serpent beguiled me ...*

They wasted so much time and energy justifying themselves at the expense of their spouse. Sound familiar? Repentance takes much less effort but much more humility.

How did God respond to the temptation and Fall? He decreed severe consequences, including increased pain in childbearing, toilsome tilling of the soil and ultimately death. However, the Father responded to the disobedience of our first parents in the most loving way possible. Even though these human creatures had broken their covenant with him—the sacred family bond of trust—the Father promised a Savior (and a Woman) who would crush the head of Satan.

> Because you have done this, cursed are you above all the cattle, and above all wild animals; upon your belly you shall go, and dust you shall eat all of the days of your life. I will put enmity between you and the woman, and between your seed and her seed; he shall bruise your head, and you shall bruise his heel.
>
> GENESIS 3:14-15

This oracle is known as the "first gospel" (*protoevangelion*). It is the hinge on which the rest of salvation history turns. And it continues to turn, from one covenantal period to the next, as God's people await the fulfillment of this glorious promise.[14]

Suffering: A Punishment That Fits—and Cures—the Crime

Once the nature of Adam's sin is understood to be his refusal to suffer out of love for his Father and bride, three conclusions logically follow. First, the divine curse of suffering imposed on Adam and Eve was perfectly reasonable. Second, their humble acceptance of that punitive suffering would be remedial. Third, Christ's bearing of this curse, in his own sacrificial suffering on the cross, would prove to be redemptive.

God came into the garden immediately after Adam and Eve sinned. He announced the punitive curse, pain in fruit-bearing: for Eve this would mean pain in childbirth, and for Adam, pain in tilling the ground (see Gn 3:16-19). Willingness to give ourselves out of love, even if it entails suffering, is what makes us fruitful. When we refuse to love to this extent, we sterilize ourselves. Our Father still wants us to be fruitful; that is why he imposed the curse of suffering, in order to keep alive our potential to become super-naturally fruitful.

If we think of this curse principally as an act of vengeance, we might easily miss the point. God's wrath is not the opposite of his love, merely the flip side. The Father is not torn between love and wrath. God *is* love (see 1 Jn 4:8); but that love is a consuming fire, which never goes out (see Heb 12:29). That love is also the Trinity's inner life, pure and simple. Thus, self-donating love is the essential law of God's covenant with us, his children, which is designed to make us fiery God-like lovers ourselves.

When we disobey the Father's law, we refuse his fiery love. But we can't escape it; we simply seal ourselves off from it. We're still in it, but it's not in us. So we can't enjoy it; we only feel burned by it until we reopen ourselves to it. That's what repentance does, and that's what God's wrath is for.[15]

Repentance thus involves a change of thinking and living. We no longer view suffering as intrinsically evil; by seeing it as part of God's plan to teach us love, we can embrace suffering as a needed remedy for sin.

In conclusion, the Father who called Adam to life first confronted him with death as a test of sacrificial obedience, a trial by ordeal. If Adam had given consent to death in this situation, by cooperating with God's indwelling grace, he would have realized and perfected faith, hope and love. The earthly gift of grace would have been transformed into heavenly glory.

A Curse-Bearing Death to Undo Adam's Deed

Since the ultimate form of suffering is death, the ultimate moment of love comes at the time of death when we accept it and make it a sacrificial gift of self. Thus, the ultimate form of the curse is death. You encounter sweat, thorns and nakedness "till you return to the ground" (Gn 3:19).

This gives us the key for unlocking the redemptive power of Christ's suffering and death. As the new Adam, Jesus was tested in the garden (of Gethsemane; see Mt 26:36-46), where "his sweat became like great drops of blood" (Lk 22:44). Jesus then had a "crown of thorns" placed upon his head (see Mt 27:29), before he was taken to the "tree" (see Gal 3:13), where he was stripped naked (see Mt 27:31). Then he fell into the deep sleep of death, so that from his side would come forth the New Eve (see Jn 19:26-35; 1 Jn 5:6-8). That is how Christ dealt with sin; he took it out at its source.

We read in Hebrews: "Since therefore the children share in flesh and blood, he himself likewise partook of the same nature, that through death he might destroy him who has the power of death, that is, the devil, and deliver all those who through fear of death were subject to lifelong bondage" (Heb 2:14-15).[16]

Christ undid Adam's deed by doing what he should have done: "Jesus offered up prayers and supplications, with loud cries and tears, to him who was able to save him from death, and he was heard for his godly fear. Although he was a Son, he learned obedience through what he suffered; and being made perfect he became the source of eternal salvation to all who obey him" (Heb 5:7-9).

That is how our eternal salvation was accomplished by the last Adam: "'The first man Adam became a living being'; the last

Adam became a life-giving spirit.... The first man was from the earth, a man of dust; the second man is from heaven.... Just as we have borne the image of the man of dust, we shall also bear the image of the man of heaven" (1 Cor 15:45-49).

Postscript

If Hollywood had made this into an epic movie years ago, we know just how it would look. The background music would build slowly in low ominous tones as the serpent appears. The camera would pan the garden as the interrogation begins. The mounting volume would stop as Satan declares his infernal lie. Suddenly, Adam would leap forward, to the flash of upsurgent music and crashing cymbals, and dispatch the Devil in one fell swoop. He would kiss Eve, sweep her into his arms and carry her off into the sunset to live happily ever after. Roll the credits.

Wouldn't it be nice?

To be honest, I prefer the Book.

FOUR

Shape Up or Ship Out:
A Broken Covenant Renewed With Noah

What images come to mind when you hear the word "family"? Many people may think of Mom, apple pie, bedtime stories and summer vacations; for others it may be in-laws, arguments and mortgage payments. In reality, family includes both sets of images—and everything else in between. And that goes for God's family as well.

Salvation history reveals sin as literally a broken home. Once we see ourselves as members of God's family, we begin to understand that sin is primarily a broken *relationship*, not just broken *rules*. Like rebellious children who want to go their own way, we've all turned away from God many times during our lives. Even as we do, he keeps right on loving us, calling us back to himself, disciplining us in love as only a perfect Father can and keeping his promises nonetheless.

These broken bonds began with the first union of man and woman. By eating the forbidden fruit, Adam and Eve repudiated their trust in the one who made them. What were the consequences for the human family? Look around. We live in a world riddled with fear, shame, anger, murder, pain, depression, isolation, alienation and death. Not a pretty picture.

Raising Cain

Genesis 4 quaintly describes the next major development in the biblical love story between God and humanity: Adam knew his wife and she conceived a child. Eve bore Cain, saying, "I have gotten a man with the help of the Lord" (from *qanah*, "gotten"). Then she bore a second son named Abel, who grew up to be a keeper of sheep (see Gn 4:1-2).

As a tiller of the ground, Cain brought an offering to the Lord of the fruits of the ground, while Abel sacrificed firstlings from his flock. God accepted Abel's gift but rejected Cain's. Cain was furious, and his countenance fell. But God gave him some sound fatherly advice: "If you do well, will you not be accepted? And if you do not do well, sin is couching at the door; its desire is for you, but you must master it" (Gn 4:7).[1]

Did Cain learn a simple lesson, go back to the drawing board, and try a second time? No. Cain apparently preferred an altogether different sort of sacrifice. He lured his brother out to the field and murdered him. In doing so, Cain bore the malicious fruit that Satan had planted as a seed within our human nature.

It is important to see that Eve's firstborn didn't succumb to a little fit of *jealousy;* he succumbed to the deadly sin of *envy.*[2] Technically speaking, jealousy seeks the good that is perceived in another person; whereas envy resents it, and even seeks to destroy it. Jealousy can be good or bad, but envy is only and always evil. Scripture describes God as "jealous" (see Ex 20:5) but never envious; he wants us for himself—since he made us—but only for our good.

I remember watching a movie years ago in which Sissy Spacek played the role of a homecoming queen. Her "friends" resented her beauty so much that they threw pig's blood on her at the homecoming dance. They didn't get her beauty; they just took it away from her. That's the nature of envy. No wonder it (unlike jealousy) has always been counted among the seven deadly sins. Along with pride, envy was the root cause of Satan's rebellion (see Wis 2:24). It's also the source of some of the worst sins, as we see with Cain, who murdered his younger brother out of envy (see 1 Jn 3:4-12).

Perhaps Cain figured he could get away with it. He defensively answered the Lord's query as to Abel's whereabouts: "I do not know; am I my brother's keeper?" (Gn 4:9). Cain's evil didn't diminish or deter the fatherhood of God, who acted swiftly to discipline his unrepentant son. He banished Cain from Eden, making him a fugitive and a wanderer, and then branded him with a mark (see Gn 4:10-16).[3]

We might have expected the nasty fruit of sin to grow slowly, insidiously. Instead, it almost seemed to multiply like a malignant tumor, rapidly destroying a great many healthy cells along the way. How did one bite of the forbidden tree so quickly produce the fruit of murder? We shake our heads and wonder how such violence could be possible. Yet the same destructive power of envy is still at work in families and neighborhoods and workplaces everywhere. The only remedy is to abandon ourselves to God's providence, to trust our Heavenly Father to meet our needs and to keep his promises to us.

We see how much we are called to be our brothers' and sisters' true keepers when we discover the meaning of God's covenant love. The body of Christ is the family of God, with each parish living out one small reflection of that divine love. Are we trying to live out the image and likeness of God? Or are we blaming others, while excusing ourselves, even with the best of motives? As we perceive more clearly the Father's continuing pursuit of his people, we must allow his love to penetrate our hearts more deeply.

Trouble Brews in the Land of Nod

As we saw in the previous chapter, Adam and Eve represented the smallest possible family unit, the married couple. Marriage is the basic covenant relationship through which God fathers the human race. The very next generation suffered the consequences of sin when Cain slew his brother out of envy. And it didn't stop there.

Banished from the Lord's presence, Cain traveled east of Eden and took up residence in the land of Nod, where he built a city and named it after his son (see Gn 4:16-17). Six generations later, Cain's line reached a kind of diabolical fullness in a descendant named Lamech, who took two wives (see Gn 4:17-24). This is the first record of polygamy recorded in Scripture. In view of the primordial marital covenant, Cain's descendant clearly flouted God's standard. Unbridled lust is accompanied by violence; so the arrogant Lamech boasted to his wives, "I have slain a man for wounding me, a young man for striking me. If Cain has avenged sevenfold, truly Lamech seventy-seven-fold" (vv. 23-24). As we've seen, the number seven is a covenant symbol. Here it signifies the maturation of evil over time in the line of Cain.

Meanwhile, God's first family continued to grow. Adam knew his wife again, and she bore a son named Seth (see Gn 4:25). The birth of Seth's son, named Enosh, marks a crucial turning point in human history: "At that time men began to call upon the name of the Lord" (Gn 4:26), a phrase that signifies covenant worship (see Gn 12:8).

Note the important difference here between the two lines of Cain and Seth. Cain was trying to make a name for himself by having a son and naming a city after him. But when Seth had a son, the son's work was not for himself but rather for God—calling "upon the name of the Lord." (The Hebrew word for "name" is *shem*, which takes on a special meaning with the birth of Noah's firstborn son, Shem; we'll say more about this later.) With Seth's generation, the city of God began. God's covenant family finally started to make progress, albeit belatedly.

Genesis 5 lays out the generations of Adam, beginning with the phrase "when God created man, he made him in the likeness of God" (v. 1). Then Adam had a son in his own image and likeness. Just as God fathered a son, so Adam fathered a son, Seth.

These two divergent cultures of Sethites and Cainites provided a ready-made stage for conflict. We see Seth's family line built on the covenant worship of God, calling on the name of the Lord. In the opposing corner, we see Cain's family reaching its tyrannical completeness. These contrary groups had to live on the same earth, preferably in peace. But as long as evil, pride and injustice had a foothold, harmony was out of reach. Could anything but conflict and persecution ensue?

Wayward Sons

Next Genesis 6 describes a puzzling yet ominous development:

When men began to multiply on the face of the ground, and daughters were born to them, the sons of God saw that the daughters of men were fair; and they took to wife such of them as they chose. Then the Lord said, "My spirit shall not abide in man for ever, for he is flesh, but his days shall be a hundred and twenty years." ... [I]n those days, and also afterward ... the sons of God came in to the daughters of men, and they bore children to them. These were the mighty men that were of old, the men of renown.

GENESIS 6:1-4

In Hebrew "the men of renown" means literally the men of the *shem*, the men of the name, wicked tyrants who were making a name for themselves, unjust men who were building a culture of pure evil.

God would have no more of this violence. He waited more than a century after passing sentence on the human race and giving them due warning. God then sent the flood waters as a punishment. We shall consider its dire consequences for the human race shortly.

But what's going on in the first two verses of this chapter? "The sons of God saw that the daughters of men were fair" (v. 2). Some translators see this as mythical language suggesting that the angels (or some other celestial beings) intermarried with earthly women. But nowhere else are angels called "sons of God" in Genesis. In addition, angels cannot reproduce like humans, as Augustine and Aquinas pointed out long ago. Besides, if angels were the primary instigators, why did God punish the entire world? Why not target the wayward angels and their evil offspring instead? The flood punished everyone *but* the angels.[4]

Then who were "the sons of God" mentioned in the preceding chapter? In the opening verses of chapter five, we hear again about God creating Adam in his own image and likeness. Then we read that Adam fathered a son named Seth, "in his own image and likeness" (see Gn 5:1-2). This serves to link Seth and his line directly to the gift of divine sonship that God first gave to Adam.

Then who were the sons of God? The *Sethites,* that family of God that built itself up by calling upon the name of the Lord. In his classic work, *The City of God* (Book XV), Augustine tells how God's family, the Church, was restored in the Sethites after the death of Abel. What we see here is the Church pitted against the world, God's family against the seed of the serpent, which craves power and comfort and luxury.

So a major crisis is described in Genesis 6. In conflict with the wicked Cainites, like Lamech the murderous polygamist, all the godly men of Seth remained steadfast and righteous, right?

Wrong.

When people began to multiply on the face of the earth, "the sons of God," that is, the *Sethite* men, were seduced by the beauty of "the daughters of men," that is, the *Cainite* women. The beauty of the wicked proved stronger than the resolve of the righteous. Sethite men found a new forbidden fruit, the beautiful but ungodly Cainite women, to be irresistible. And they didn't just marry them; "they married as they chose," which might imply that, along with mixed marriages, polygamy had now also entered into the line of Seth, the covenant family of God. And violent men were born.

When left unchecked, sin becomes institutionalized. In every age of salvation history, sexual immorality and violence go hand in hand, triggering the hard remedy of God's judgment in the form of the covenant curses. And nothing institutionalizes sin more than marital infidelity. The whole culture gets clobbered, especially the children. And afterwards only a remnant survives, barely.

This pattern continues throughout Israel's history, even to the Babylonian exile in the sixth century B.C., and beyond. That's why Ezra required the Jews who returned from exile to abandon their foreign wives. His point was clear: your mixed marriages invite a spirit of indifference, compromise and disobedience. God the Father is unwavering in his commitment to the marriage covenant.

In this first instance of judgment, God declared his refusal to allow the seed of the woman, the righteous family of God, to be comingled with and infused with the family of Satan. And so he sent a disastrous flood to wipe out the human family, with the exception of one covenant household, the family of Noah. This was to be the righteous remnant through which God would save the world. Even if the Father had to start all over again from scratch, his promises would surely come to pass.

Flood, Sweat and Tears

As the covenant family of God grew, so did the complexities of life. People gradually developed additional laws and regulations and principles to avoid and resolve disputes. God's sacred family bond with his people had to be enlarged to account for this growth.

The second major covenant by which God fathered his family involved Noah. God called Noah to be the covenant mediator, as a husband, like Adam. Noah was also the father of three sons, each of whom had his own wife and children. At this point in salvation history, God's covenant with the human race grew to be a *household* of several families.

Scripture tells us that God determined to blot out all living creatures because of the immense wickedness in the earth: "Every imagination of the thoughts of his heart was only evil continually" (Gn 6:5). Nevertheless, "Noah found favor in the eyes of the Lord, for he was a righteous man, blameless in his generation" (vv. 8-9).

Chosen by the Father to embody—and deliver—the remnant of the human race, Noah was called to refound God's family, like a new Adam. Interestingly, the description of God's flood-judgment is notably similar to the pattern of divine Creation in the opening chapters of Genesis. In both cases, a new world would emerge from the chaotic waters of "the deep" (see Gn 1:2; 7:11). The number "seven" also stands out prominently in both accounts. As the sign of God's "rest" at Creation, it is closely linked to Noah (whose name means "rest" or "relief," see Gn 5:29). Likewise, Noah was ordered to take seven pairs of clean animals into the ark (see Gn 7:2), which he did, before closing the door: "After seven days the waters of the flood came upon the earth" (Gn 7:10). And in the seventh month, the ark came to "rest" upon Mount Ararat (see Gn 8:4). After a long wait, Noah sent out a dove every seven days (see Gn 8:10-12), until his family was finally able to disembark.

After disembarking, Adam's divine commission was repeated for Noah: "Be fruitful and multiply, and fill the earth" (Gn 9:1). God also restored Noah to Adam's former position of dominion over the beasts (see Gn 9:2). Finally, the Father renewed the creation covenant with Noah (see Gn 9:9), revealing to him the sign of the new covenant: "I set my bow in the cloud, and it shall be a sign of the covenant between me and the earth" (Gn 9:13).[5]

Clearly the flood account is presented as a re-creation event. And not only the flood but perhaps also the Fall, in view of other parallels between Adam and Noah: Both find themselves in a garden or vineyard (see Gn 2:15; 9:20), where they consume a fruit that exposes their sin and nakedness (see Gn 3:6-7; 9:21) and elicits a curse (see Gn 3:14-19; 9:25), which redounds to future progeny (Cain and Canaan).

Deviled Ham

The sons of Noah who went forth from the ark were Shem, Ham and Japheth. From these three sons the whole earth was repeopled. With Cain's line destroyed, righteousness reigned on earth, right? Wrong again. Sin soon reared its ugly head once more.

We read how Noah planted a vineyard and enjoyed the fruits of his labor too much. He consumed so much wine that he became drunk and lay uncovered in his tent. We read that his youngest son, Ham, looked upon "the nakedness of his father" (Gn 9:22).

Our modern translations don't seem to capture all that's going on in this episode. After all, for Ham to "look upon his father's nakedness" just doesn't seem to be that big of a sin to warrant a curse, especially since Noah pronounced it upon Ham's son,

Canaan. As various scholars have noticed, the key is found in the idiomatic meaning of the Hebrew phrase "to look upon his nakedness," since it refers elsewhere to *incest* (see Lev 20:17; 18:6-18).[6]

All cultures use idioms to refer to various sexual acts. So, for instance, in American English we don't take the phrase "making love" literally, as if to conjure up images of a factory assembly line manufacturing love. The words refer to the act of marriage by which husband and wife renew their covenant with one another. But an outsider wouldn't have a clue as to its meaning.

Here in Genesis 9, we see a similar case involving the Hebrew idiom ("to look upon nakedness"), that refers to a very sordid act. Without going into detail, it may suffice to summarize the matter: Ham committed maternal incest, and the accursed fruit of that union was Canaan. Interestingly, an equivalent expression ("to uncover nakedness") is used later on by Moses in warning Israel about the perverse practices of the people of "Canaan" (see Lv 18:6-18; Ex 23:23-24). Not surprisingly, what heads the list of Canaanite vices is maternal incest, followed by various other forms of incest, which were actually practiced as part of the ritual worship in Canaan.

It is also significant that the only other time drunkenness is mentioned in Genesis occurs when Lot's daughters deliberately get him drunk—precisely for the purpose of committing incest with him (see Gn 19:30-35). Like the story of the drunkenness of Noah, this incident of paternal incest is recounted in Genesis for the purpose of revealing the origins of Moab and Amon (see Gn 19:36-38), two of the most perverse enemies of Israel, alongside the evil Canaanites.

After discovering Ham's evil deed, and as a reward for Shem and Japheth foiling their brother, Noah declared:

Cursed be Canaan;
a slave shall he be to his brothers.
Blessed by the Lord my God be Shem;
and let Canaan be his slave.
God enlarge Japheth,
and let him dwell in the tents of Shem;
and let Canaan be his slave.

GENESIS 9:25-27

This cryptic pronouncement contains the rest of biblical history in an encoded nutshell.

According to some ancient rabbinic and patristic interpretive traditions, this oracle points forward to Israel's future conquest and subjugation of Canaan, since the Israelites are the chosen line of the blessed Shem. Likewise, the other part of Noah's blessing ("Let Him dwell in the tents of Shem") is fulfilled when God came to dwell, as the Shekinah glory-cloud, within the sacred tent that Moses and the Israelites erected in the desert (see Ex 35-40).[7]

Covenant Karma

Like father, like son, like grandson and so on. Covenantally speaking—what goes around, comes around. For many centuries the Canaanites practiced the same sexual perversion that had spawned their founding father, Canaan. As we saw with Adam and Eve, the effects of sin don't end with the death of the sinner but travel down through the generations—unless those sins are repudiated through acts of repentance and renunciation.

How can we make sense out of Ham's incestuous union with his mother? We can only speculate. But some scholars point out that Ham was trying to usurp his father's authority by sleeping with his mother. Perhaps that's why he told his brothers what he'd done, rather than keeping it a secret.

This reflects a pattern found elsewhere in the Old Testament, especially where sons resent fathers for showing favor to siblings. For example, Jacob's son Reuben sought to undermine his favored half-brother Joseph by taking his father's concubine—for which he received a paternal curse (see Gn 29:32; 35:22; 49:3-4). Likewise, Absalom resented the plans of his father, King David, to give the throne to one of his younger half-brothers, Solomon. In response, Absalom drove King David out of Jerusalem and then slept with his father's concubines—right in public—to signify his seizure of royal power. This was a defiant gesture of both lust and ambition. Absalom was saying to the people, "I've got the royal harem, so I'm in charge here" (see 2 Sm 16:21-22). Sex and politics were often inseparable, even back then.

This is all spelled out in one of the most popular books from the time of Jesus, a widely read commentary on Genesis which was entitled Jubilees.[8] (At least five copies were found among the Dead Sea Scrolls). Jubilees explicitly shows the political motive behind the adversarial actions of Ham and Noah, as well as Canaan and Shem (see Jub 7-10). In a nutshell: Ham attempted to usurp Noah's power before the father could give it to Shem; so later on, Canaan seized Shem's landed inheritance, "in the middle of the earth" (Jub 8:12).

Naturally, ancient Israelite readers would have interpreted this narrative in terms of three fundamental truths: first, God's call to Abram, as a descendant of Shem's, to go to Canaan (see Gn 12:1-3); second, God's promise to give this land as an inheritance to Abraham's seed (see Gn 17); and third, God's command for Israel—as the "seed" of Abraham in the blessed line of Shem—to conquer the land. (It's very important to remember that Jews are Shemites, hence the term "anti-semitic," refers to anti-Jewish sentiments).

The name, "Canaan," is thus a negatively charged term, a sign of a long-boiling family feud. Perhaps it may be useful to compare it to the episode in the Christmas movie classic *It's a Wonderful Life,* when George Bailey returned to Bedford Falls only to discover that it had been renamed "Pottersville," after the arch-villain of the story. Just the name itself was enough for alarm, since it was highly symbolic of those evils that would have befallen the city, "if George Bailey would have never been born."

The story of Noah's drunkenness is recounted here in Genesis so that ancient Israelites may comprehend why God delivered them from Egypt and sent them to conquer and reclaim Canaan as their own ancestral inheritance. Furthermore, it reinforces the strongly worded laws that God gave to Israel at Sinai, to the effect that they must have nothing to do with Canaanites (see Ex 23:24).

Once we understand more of the family history of these warring peoples, we catch a glimpse of God's dealings with them. Suppose someone drove you out of your own home, and off your own property. Would you be allowed to use force to reclaim it? Of course, if it were necessary. That's apparently how the Shemites, the Israelites, the children of Abraham, were to understand their marching orders from God when they were sent to conquer Canaan centuries later. This land was meant for God's family, from Noah and Shem through Abraham, Isaac and Jacob, all the way to Moses, Joshua and beyond.

The Hall of Shame

In the aftermath of the flood, the human race once again became one big, unhappy family torn apart by sin. As we have seen, sin begets sin. Genesis 10 tells us the names of the sons born to Shem, Ham and Japheth after the flood. Ham had four sons: Cush, Egypt, Put and Canaan. Notice that from Ham's line springs the Philistines as well as the nation of Egypt, which would hold Israel in bondage for centuries (see Gn 10:14). We have only to pick up the latest newspaper to read about how this family feud continues to this very day, with plenty of fault on both sides.

Cush fathered Nimrod, "a mighty hunter before the Lord" (v. 9), who built a kingdom for himself in Babel (later called Babylon, which is present-day Iraq). This tyrant continued into Assyria and built the great city of Nineveh. So Ham's family came to encompass Egypt, Canaan, Philistia, Assyria and Babylon.

The Israelites would look at this list and see a veritable rogues' gallery, an ancient hall of shame, consisting of the most vile characters in history, all of whom raised their families to become Israel's worst foes. Old Testament history offers a blow-by-blow account of Israel's ongoing abuse at the hands of Ham's wicked descendants: Israel was enslaved by Egypt, ensnared by Canaan, oppressed by the Philistines, annihilated by Assyria and exiled by Babylon.

In the face of such opposition, God's chosen people needed to remain strong in faith or else perish. The elect family was growing through Shem. (He was one of the two firstborn sons in Genesis who didn't succumb to pride and end up being passed over for a worthier younger brother; the other was Abram.) Not only did Shem not abuse his power, he even used his favored position as firstborn to serve his father and his family. Because of his righteousness, Shem was elevated and blessed in a unique way. He is said to have lived five hundred years after the flood (see Gn 11:11). Not surprisingly, he was not without enemies, especially within the line of Ham.

Meanwhile, the Hamite king, Nimrod, had settled in the land of Shinar, along with his offspring. They apparently wanted to outdo the architectural feats of the Canaanites: "Come," they said, "let us build ourselves a city, and a tower with its top in the heavens, and let us make a *name* (Hebrew, *shem*) for ourselves, lest we be scattered abroad upon the face of the earth" (Gn 11:4).

God quickly intervened and put a stop to this ill-conceived

project by confusing their speech. He thus scattered the peoples by making it impossible for them to communicate with each other. Why was God so opposed to this tower-building project? The key is to see the subtle way in which the narrative presents their sin.[9]

Apparently, it wasn't just a neutral architectural enterprise. By announcing their intention "to make a *shem* for ourselves," these builders were implementing Nimrod's plan to build a counter-kingdom to the godly line of Shem. It was starting to sound like a repeat performance of the preflood situation. Once again, the ungodly were rejecting the covenant authority structure within the Father's family; only this time Shem was the target, as the firstborn son that Noah had blessed. Presumably, Noah had been grooming Shem to assume leadership as a new father figure after his death.[10]

But the Hamites under Nimrod didn't go for it. They deserved divine judgment. But God had sworn a covenant oath never to wipe out the wicked with another flood. So instead of a clean sweep, build-an-ark rescue mission, God embarked on a plan to reconquer the human race with his love, through a man named Abram.

God went to work, restoring his family's legacy by calling Shem's great-great-great-great-great grandson, Abram. "I will ... make your name (*shem*) great, so that you will be a blessing.... and by you all the families of the earth shall bless themselves" (Gn 12:2-3).

In other words, God was telling Abram: I won't wipe out my family again, not even the wicked. Instead, I'll do the impossible. I will take you—a seventy-five-year-old man—and use you to bless all of the families on earth. In that way, the whole unhappy human family that has been torn apart by sin might be brought back to me, as their Father, even the wicked. In other words, Babel-in-reverse. How could the Father achieve such an impossible goal? Against all odds, as we shall see in the next scene from this biblical love story.

FIVE

How Do You Spell Belief?:
The Faith of Father Abraham

What if God asked you to pack up your belongings, leave your home and your people and travel almost a thousand miles to an unknown destination? I'm sure a host of questions would cross your mind. *How can I be sure this crazy idea is really from God and not just my imagination? Assuming we survive the journey, how will we find a place to live and a new job to provide for our needs? How can I know if the people who live there are hostile or friendly to people of our race?*

And what if you heard this divine message when you were seventy-five years old? God the Father chose that time to speak these words to a man named Abram: "Go from your country and your kindred and your father's house to the land that I will show you" (Gn 12:1).

Actually, seventy seemed to be about middle age in Abram's time. His father, Terah, was seventy before siring his three sons; he lived over two hundred years in all (see Gn 11:26).

We tend to shrug our collective shoulders and think, *So what's the big deal? This old guy was probably living in a tent in the middle of nowhere.* But the reality was far different. Abram lived in Ur, the Las Vegas of the ancient world, a city known for its prosperity. And Abram himself was a rich man. In that case, we might think, *maybe God is finally showing some sense by going to a rich city to find a man of power and wealth to conquer the world by force.* Such a conclusion would miss God's intentions entirely.

The Father essentially told Abram, "Leave this rich, powerful city and go to a land you've never seen. Leave your people. Leave all your real estate holdings." And Abram obeyed. What incredible faith! Through this one faithful man, God was able to father the growing family of God.

Promises, Promises, Promises

Incredible promises seemed to more than compensate for these tangible losses. And although God waited much longer to fulfill them than Abram wanted, he kept every one of his promises. In his consuming desire to father a people to be his own, God patiently worked in the life of this one man of faith, as if tending a garden that would produce abundant fruit for all humankind.

At the time of God's call, even prior to Abram's obedience, the Father gave him three unconditional promises: first, to make of him a great nation; second, to make his "name" great; and third, to bless "all the families of the earth" through him (see Gn 12:1-3). Let's take a look at each one of these divine assurances.

The first promise concerned land and nationhood. Any people who didn't own land could never be a nation, great or otherwise. Without land those people would continue to hold the status of immigrants. God promised to make Abram's descendants the national occupants of a vast amount of land where they would live and serve the one God.

The second promise concerned Abram's name. The Hebrew word for name also refers to a dynasty or kingdom, which carries the notion of political power. God was saying, in effect, "After deposing the tyrants who have usurped the Promised Land, I will give my humble and faithful servant Abram a lasting legacy by raising the nation of his descendants to royal power. I will make them a kingdom that rules other nations."

The third promise concerned God's fatherly blessing of all the nations issuing from the seed of Abram. God didn't explain exactly what form this blessing would take, but we'll see how it represents the climax of God's family plan and purpose for calling Abram.

God Plants a Family Tree

In the next few chapters of Genesis, we discover what God did in giving Abram these three great promises. He planted a seed that would grow—in time—to become a great tree, a family tree. We'll come to know Abram's family tree, by faith, as the family of God; just as we'll come to see its time of growth as salvation history. So Abram's divine call is the acorn, of which salvation history is the oak tree. God planted and then tended these three promises of blessing throughout Abram's life by raising each of the *promises* to a much higher level, as *covenants*, which the Father made on three distinct occasions (see Gn 15, 17, 22; Heb 6:13-19).

God's first promise, that Abram's descendants would become a landed nation, was upgraded to covenant status in Genesis 15, when God appeared in the form of a fiery torch, which passed between the pieces of divided animals (see vv. 7-21). Actually, this was not an uncommon covenant-making ritual in antiquity.

The second divine promise, that of a "great name" or kingdom, was raised to a divine covenant, the covenant of circumcision, when God appeared to Abram in Genesis 17, renamed him Abraham and then promised him a son through Sarah and a future dynasty in the land of Canaan (see vv. 1-16).

God's third promise to Abram, that of a worldwide blessing, was elevated to a covenant in Genesis 22, where it represents the distinct object of God's solemn oath, which he awarded to Abraham after Abraham offered Isaac at Moriah (see vv. 16-18).

Furthermore, careful reading of the rest of Scripture in the light of these three covenants will reveal how all three Abrahamic covenants were gradually fulfilled in the next three major periods of salvation history. First, Abram's seed received its national land and boundaries after the Exodus, through the Mosaic Covenant. Second, Abraham's seed became a kingdom after the conquest of the Promised Land, through the Davidic Covenant. Finally, the seed of Abraham became the source of blessing for the entire world with the Incarnation of Christ, through the New Covenant. The first verse of the New Testament reads: "The book of the genealogy of Jesus, the son of David, the son of Abraham" (Mt 1:1; see Gal 3:6-19).

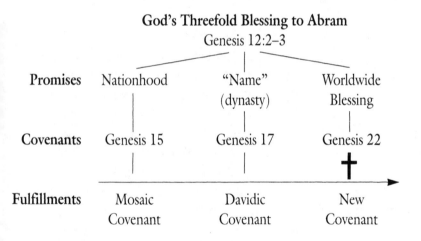

God's Threefold Blessing to Abram
Genesis 12:2–3

Promises	Nationhood	"Name" (dynasty)	Worldwide Blessing
Covenants	Genesis 15	Genesis 17	Genesis 22
Fulfillments	Mosaic Covenant	Davidic Covenant	New Covenant

We see God personally fathering his family of faith through his dealings with Abram, the father of faith. He laid out his grand plan to this one man, but in a rather cryptic way. Only as the drama unfolds through ages of redemptive history do we see the glory emerging before our eyes.

The Rocky Road to Glory

Abram departed from Haran when he was seventy-five years old. He took Sarai his wife and his brother's son Lot and all their possessions and servants—perhaps two hundred people in all, no small group. You can imagine what this would involve if you consider, for example, what it might take to organize a cross-country relocation for your entire church or neighborhood.

When they finally arrived in Canaan, Abram might have said to himself, *Okay God, we've arrived! Let the blessings begin!* And what did God do? Did the Father proceed with a "sensible" plan? Did he tell Abram to marshal all his wealth and weapons and wisdom in order to conquer the Promised Land? Not quite. On the contrary, God welcomed Abram by sending famine to the land—an odd sort of blessing.

The scarcity of food forced Abram and his whole entourage to leave Canaan and travel all the way down to Egypt, another foreign and perverse culture. Can you imagine having to pack up and make a long journey so soon after having arrived at what you thought was your final destination? Wouldn't you have wondered what was wrong with God for sending you on this apparent wild goose chase?

Maybe Abram was feeling a bit grumpy and resentful and resistant to more trouble. Or maybe he was just plain scared. In any case, the father of faith escaped death by telling Pharaoh that Sarai was his sister. (She was in fact his half-sister. But most of all, Sarai was his wife. Abram resorted to a strategy of convenient deception.) The Egyptian king took beautiful Sarai into his harem. In return, Abram managed not only to survive but also to accumulate sheep and oxen, menservants and maidservants, camels and asses.

However, things were not going so well at the palace. God afflicted Pharaoh and his household with several plagues because of this appalling abuse of Sarai. When Pharaoh finally caught on to

Abram's duplicity, the frightened ruler quickly sent them on their way to avoid any more of God's wrath. Abram came up out of Egypt very rich with cattle, gold and silver (see Gn 13). And when he returned to where his tent and altar had been between Bethel and Ai, he called on the name of the Lord.

All's well that ends well, right? Wrong. As soon as they got back to the Promised Land, a family feud erupted. Abram's nephew Lot had also returned from Egypt with flocks and herds and tents. He split the family down the middle by insisting that there wasn't enough land for him and Abram.

Not wanting to foster hard feelings with his kinsman, Abram offered Lot his pick of the land. Seeing that the Jordan valley was well watered, Lot chose the fertile land for himself. Unfortunately for Lot, the valley was also the site of Sodom and Gomorrah. Lot moved his tent as far as Sodom, where the inhabitants were great sinners against the Lord. After Lot had gone his separate way, God renewed his promise with Abram to give him land as far as he could see and descendants as numerous as the dust of the earth.

Can you imagine the scene? Lot, one of the few family members who accompanied Abram on this pilgrimage of faith, split and took the best land. What an ingrate! This young guy was hanging on to the coattails of his uncle, receiving divine blessings through Abram, and then he pulled this stunt. What was Abram to think? *Maybe Lot wasn't part of the whole plan to begin with. But he's the only relative I have for "seed." Okay, God, what's next?*

Then all of a sudden, the Promised Land ignited into a major battle zone. Five kings joined forces against four kings. The victors claimed all the goods and provisions of Sodom and Gomorrah—including Lot and his possessions. Someone who had escaped came to tell Abram, who by then was living by the oaks of Mamre.

If I had been Abram, I would have said, "Serves him right, the rat! Taking the best land and leaving me high and dry." But Abram was a righteous kinsman. His immediate response was to take 318 of his own trained domestic warriors and pursue those who had taken Lot captive. By dividing his forces at night, Abram's men routed the king's armies and retrieved Lot, along with his whole family and all his goods.

Having conquered the conquerors and taken possession of all this booty, Abram's supremacy should have been unquestioned. He could have returned to Mamre and commanded the other kings to bow down to him. Not Abram. Upon his return from battle, he met a mysterious figure, a priest called Melchizedek. His name means "king of righteousness" (see Heb 7:1-3), and he was king of Salem, a city that later became known as Jeru-Salem (see Ps 76:2).

Abram paid homage to Melchizedek by giving to him a tithe, a tenth of everything. Melchizedek in turn offered "bread and wine" to Abram and his men, after which he blessed them (see Gn 14:18-20). Clearly, there was something profoundly symbolic going on here.[1]

Faith Up to the Facts

Now Abram seemed to have it made: a beautiful wife, loyal servants, substantial property, power, wealth. What more could a man ask for?

An heir. Abram remained childless. Promise after promise—even from God—can wear thin. Faith begins to fray around the edges when year after year it fails to deliver what we most desire.

The Lord spoke to Abram in a vision: "Fear not, Abram, I am your shield; your reward shall be very great" (Gn 15:1).

In all due respect, Abram questioned God's promise. How could this plan come to pass since God had slipped up on one key detail: giving him a son? Would one of his domestic servants be his heir?

God assured Abram that his own son would be his heir and then brought him outside to underscore the point. Count the stars, the Father told him; "so shall your descendants be" (Gn 15:5).

Talk about a faith stretcher! But Abram believed the Lord, who "reckoned it to him as righteousness" (Gn 15:6). The Father then renewed another promise with a personal calling card: "I am the Lord who brought you from the land of Ur of the Chaldeans, to give you this land to possess" (Gn 15:7).

But Abram seemed to have his fill of promises. "O Lord God, how am I to *know* that I shall possess it?" (v. 8, emphasis added). Suddenly this giant of faith seemed more like the man who said to Jesus, "I believe, Lord, help my unbelief."

God was not put off; the Father loved his son Abram. So he bolstered his promise with an oath dramatically enacted in a sacrificial ritual. According to the Lord's instructions, Abram brought a three-year-old heifer, a goat, a ram, a turtledove and a young pigeon. He cut the larger animals in half and put each side opposite the other.

As the sun sank to the horizon, a deep sleep fell upon Abram. In Abram's ensuing dream, the Lord filled out a few more details of his plan. Abram's descendants would be sojourners and slaves in a foreign land. After four hundred years of oppression, God announced that he would bring judgment on that nation (Egypt) and deliver his people to this land with great possessions. Meanwhile, Abram himself would die a peaceful death at a ripe old age.

In the darkness of night, Abram then saw a vision of a smoking fire pot and a flaming torch pass between the animal pieces. The fire pot and torch represented God himself. This ritual was an ancient oath saying, "May I be torn in two like these animals if I don't fulfill my promised covenant to you." God was actually telling Abram that even though he was God, he would subject himself to be torn apart if he did not keep his promise to Abram.

"On that day," the story goes on, "the Lord made a covenant with Abram, saying, 'To your *descendants* [literally "seed"] I give this land, from the river of Egypt to the great River, the river Euphrates, the land of the Kenites, the Kenizzites, the Kadmonites, the Hittites, the Perizzites, the Rephaim, the Amorites, the Canaanites, the Girgashites and the Jebusites'" (Gn 15:18-21). In fact, it was enough real estate for all of the nations that were descended from Abram, not just Israel.[2]

Good News, Bad News

I can imagine Abram waking from his sleep and running to tell Sarai, "I've got some good news and some bad news, honey. God has just sworn an oath to give our descendants this land. But during four hundred years, they will be slaves in another land." (With blessings like this, who needs curses?)

Eager to get things rolling, Sarai makes a proposal. Shifting the blame to the Lord, who, she said, had "prevented" her from bearing children (see Gn 16:2), she encouraged her husband to go in to her Egyptian maid, Hagar, in hopes of having a son.

"And Abram hearkened to the voice of Sarai" (16:2). That verse has an ominous ring. Did he think to seek the voice of God in this matter? Perhaps he just mused, God helps those who help themselves. Humanly speaking, Sarai was way beyond the age of fertility. *So why not try her suggestion,* Abram may have rationalized. After all, God's promise of "seed" didn't specify a female individual by name. So Abram took a concubine—an *Egyptian* concubine, no less. Having taken matters into his own hands, Abram only needed to look around the nearest bend to see big-time problems headed his way.

Sarai gave Hagar to her husband after they had dwelt ten years in the land of Canaan. The Egyptian maid immediately conceived, and then proceeded to look with contempt on Sarai, her barren mistress. Justifiably angry at her maid's attitude, Sarai complained to Abram (problem number one coming into view): "May the wrong done to me be on you! I gave my maid to your embrace, and when she saw that she had conceived, she looked on me with contempt. May the Lord judge between you and me!" (Gn 16:5).

What is this man of faith to do? Try to restore peace in his household? Remind Sarai this was all her idea to begin with? Correct Hagar and counsel her on the proper attitude toward a mistress? Separate the two women and care for Hagar, the mother of his child, in another place? After all, a maid could be replaced; a woman pregnant with his seed could not.[3]

Abram opted for the easy way out. "Behold," he told Sarai, "your maid is in your power; do to her as you please" (Gn 16:6).

When Sarai dealt harshly with her, Hagar fled into the desert. God sent an angel to comfort her, with instructions to return to Sarai, her mistress, and submit to her. Promising Hagar a multitude of descendants, the angel told the woman that she would bear a son who would be called Ishmael, "because the Lord has given heed to your affliction" (v. 11). The angel prophesied that he'd be a "wild ass of a man" who would be in continual conflict even with his kinsmen.

Hagar called the name of the Lord who spoke to her: "Thou art a God of seeing" (v. 13). She was definitely impressed; her expression tells us she was amazed she had seen God and lived.

When Abram was eighty-six years old, Hagar bore him a son whom they named Ishmael. He became the founding father of the Arab people. The Arabs and Israelis certainly act like brothers, don't they? Always at each other's throats. Their history is nothing more than an extension of this fraternal rivalry, which has become, arguably, the longest and most volatile family feud in history. Yet God is still faithful to both sides of Abram's family, and then some.

Abraham Makes the Cut

Just fourteen years later, when Abram was ninety-nine years old, the Lord came to him and renewed his covenant promise. "I am God Almighty; walk before me, and be blameless. And I will make my covenant between me and you, and will multiply you exceedingly" (Gn 17:1-2). Abram fell on his face and worshiped.

How long does it take to test a man's soul, to prove his faithfulness to God, to teach him how to walk before God and be blameless? And even when that individual has proven ready, only God knows the surrounding circumstances that dictate the timing of certain actions. Evidently, Abram had passed the test thus far, and the time was ripe. God was finally ready to move ahead with his plan—*twenty-five years after Abram was called to an unknown land.*

To symbolize the next step, God declared two name changes. Abram became Abraham, which means "father of a vast multitude." Sarai became Sarah, which means something like "queen mother," for "she shall be a mother of nations; kings of peoples shall come from her" (Gn 17:16). God went on to promise Abraham that he would have a son by Sarah.

After hearing God pledge that Sarah would give birth in exactly one year, I suspect Abraham may have begun to wonder: *Hmm, that's twelve months, minus nine months for gestation ... that leaves three months to recover from my surgery and resume marital relations; and all of this before my hundredth birthday! And who says that God doesn't have a sense of humor?*

So how did the illustrious father of faith respond? Abraham fell on his face and laughed! He said to himself (not to God), "Shall a child be born to a man who is a hundred years old? Shall Sarah, who is ninety years old, bear a child?" (Gn 17:17). The writer of the story put it even more bluntly: "Now Abraham and Sarah were old, advanced in age; it had ceased to be with Sarah after the manner of women" (Gn 18:11).

Had God lost sight of the practical obstacles to fathering a son through Sarah's barren womb? Abraham graciously offered the Father of the human race a way out of his outrageous promise, an alternative course of action acceptable to him: "Oh that Ishmael might live in thy sight" (Gn 17:18). In other words, "Why not give us all a break and take Ishmael. After all, he is my seed."

This time around, the Lord made his intentions crystal clear. At the same season the following year, *Sarah* would bear a son named Isaac. The Lord also promised to bless Ishmael and make him a great nation, but repeated that he would establish his everlasting covenant with Isaac, whose name means "he laughs." The Father was saying in effect, "I will bring you laughter. I will establish my covenant, my own family with Isaac and his descendants after him."

Can you imagine having to tell Sarah about this encounter? Actually, Abraham had something more pressing on his mind. As a sign of his covenant, God commanded Abraham to circumcise every male in his household: "So shall my covenant be in your flesh an everlasting covenant" (Gn 17:13). Carved into flesh indeed!

Abraham had work to do. Can you picture this revered tribal chieftain coming into the tents of his own domestic servants? "Gentlemen, I've got some good news and some bad news, again. First, the good news: God has renewed his promise with me today, swearing to make us not just a nation but a kingdom."

Imagine the happy but hesitant response of his servants. "That's just great, master. But what about the bad news? And why *do* you have that flint knife in your hand?"

Abraham had to explain that the sign of this new covenant was circumcision. And that it wasn't just for him but for all of the males in his household. This unexpected turn of events undoubtedly provided a supreme test of loyalty for Abraham's servants. It's one thing to be circumcised as a baby, and an altogether different proposition to be circumcised as an adult. Nor could the men of Abraham's household run down to the local clinic, where out-patient surgery could be done under sterile conditions and with proper anesthetics. Evidently, Abraham must have garnered considerable loyalty from the male members of his household over the years. In any case, they submitted to God's covenant ordinance.

At least they all suffered together.

Entertaining Angels Unawares

As Abraham sat at the door of his tent, three men came into view. He ran to meet them and bowed low in greeting, begging them not to pass by. While they rested under the oak trees and washed their feet with the water Abraham provided, their zealous host asked Sarah to whip up a fresh batch of bread. Then he picked out a tender calf from his herd and gave it to his servant to prepare. When all was ready, he laid the food before his heavenly guests and stood by while they ate. Apparently, Abraham knew that these were no ordinary strangers but representatives of the Most High (see Gn 18:1).

After they had eaten their fill, the visitors asked, "Where is Sarah your wife?" In the tent, Abraham replied. "The Lord said, 'I will surely return to you in the spring, and Sarah your wife shall have a son'" (Gn 18:10).

Wanting to hear what these three honored guests had to say, Sarah had her ear glued to the tent door. Just like Abraham, she laughed to herself, saying, "After I have grown old, and my husband is old, shall I have pleasure?" (v. 12)

The Father's ears are ever sensitive to our slightest chuckle or softest whisper. The heavenly visitor asked Abraham why Sarah laughed and questioned his promise, for "is anything too hard for the Lord?" (v. 14).

What Would You Like for Your Hundredth Birthday?

God had been promising to shower Abraham with blessings for so long, he may have been tempted to wonder: *If this is the way you treat your friends, I pity your enemies. When will the good stuff begin?*

At long last, God opened a small window of heaven to pour out his blessings in the form of a baby boy. Isaac was born to Sarah the following spring, just as the Lord had promised—this long-awaited, miraculously conceived son of promise. Can you imagine the ecstasy of two parents who had waited a century for this moment? What bliss! What harmony, right?

Wrong. The birth of Isaac split the family in two. When Sarah saw Hagar's son playing with three-year-old Isaac, a full-fledged family feud ensued. She implored Abraham, "Get those two out of this house. Now that I've got a son, this slave boy isn't going to be co-heir along with my boy!" (see Gn 21:10).

Displeased by this request on account of his son Ishmael, Abraham was instructed by God to do as Sarah wished because this second covenant was with Isaac alone. So Hagar and Ishmael were not only sent away as before (see Gn 16:1-6), they were also disinherited (see Gn 21:9-10). But God had promised to give land and nationhood to the seed of Abram, which also included Ishmael, since he was still in the family at the time that the first divine covenant was made. So God renewed his promised blessing with Ishmael (see Gn 17:13, 18).

The Lord Giveth; the Lord Taketh Away

"After these things," Scripture tells us, "God tested Abraham, and said to him, 'Abraham! ... Take your son, your only son Isaac, whom you love, and go to the land of Moriah, and offer him there as a burnt offering'" (Gn 22:1-2).

Amazingly, Scripture records no questions or bargaining this time on Abraham's part. Maybe he sensed something different in the Father's voice. Perhaps he was just too dumbfounded to utter a peep. Whatever his mental state, Abraham rose early in the morning and cut the wood for the burnt offering. Then he saddled his ass, and taking two of his servants along with his son Isaac, started toward Moriah, where God had told him to go, a three days' journey. When they drew near, Abraham told his servants to wait. "I and the lad will go yonder and worship, and come again to you" (v. 5). More than wishful thinking, these are words of faith.

When Abraham laid the wood for the burnt offering upon his son's shoulders, Isaac asked a sensible question: "Behold the fire and the wood; but where is the lamb for a burnt offering?" (v. 7).

Abraham said, "God will provide himself the lamb for the burnt offering, my son" (v. 8).

"When they came to the place of which God had told him, Abraham built an altar there, and laid the wood in order, and bound Isaac his son, and laid him on the altar, upon the wood. Then Abraham put forth his hand, and took the knife to slay his son" (Gn 22:9-10).

What a dramatic story! Can you imagine? If I had been in Abraham's shoes, I would have been sorely tempted to lay the knife on the altar and say to God, "You do it yourself." And what must have been going through Isaac's head? The boy may have been in his teens, perhaps thirteen or fourteen, maybe even older, certainly able to put up a fight. How much he must have trusted his father to submit to being bound and placed upon an altar.

"But the angel of the Lord called to him from heaven, and said, 'Abraham, Abraham!'" (v. 11).

I'd wager that a quicker "Here am I" has never been spoken.

The angel of the Lord said, "Do not lay your hand on the lad or do anything to him; for now I know that you fear God, seeing you have not withheld your son, your only son, from me" (v. 12).

When Abraham looked up, he saw a ram caught in a nearby thicket, which he offered as a burnt offering instead of Isaac. "So Abraham called the name of that place The Lord will provide; as it is said to this day, 'On the mount of the Lord it shall be provided'" (v. 14).

"The Lord Will Provide"

When the Father provides for us in some special way, our faith is strengthened. We feel more confident that he will care for us down the road as well. Abraham knew that God had already provided a sacrifice on Moriah, but the name he chose also referred to the future. He was prophesying about a much more glorious provision that would come to pass in this very place.

We typically envision Abraham walking way out into the barren wilderness to sacrifice Isaac. Yet 2 Chronicles describes the exact location of Mount Moriah: "Solomon began to build the house of the Lord in Jerusalem on Mount Moriah, where the Lord had appeared to David his father, at the place that David had appointed, at the threshing floor of Ornan the Jebusite" (2 Chr 3:1).

Mount Moriah is the place where Solomon set about building the house of the Lord, the temple that contained the Holy of Holies. Mount Moriah wasn't out in a remote desert; it was located where the city of Salem was situated in Abraham's day, which later became known as Jerusalem (see Ps 76:1-3).

Why the name change? An old rabbinic tradition attributes it to Abraham, based on what he said after sacrificing the ram: "Abraham called the name of that place, The Lord will provide; as it is said to this day, 'On the mount of the Lord it shall be provided'" (Gn 22:14). The Hebrew word for "provide" is *jira,* which was then prefixed to Salem, thus making Jeru-salem.[4]

Abraham knew that somehow God would provide there on Mount Moriah. Did his words refer to the temple that Solomon built? In part, yes, but his statement pointed to something far greater—the sacrifice of Jesus on the cross.

Consider what kind of God Abraham was dealing with. This God promised blessings and then gave the worst hardships you could imagine, heaping one on top of another, making his servant weaker and poorer and more helpless. We ourselves deal with this same God every day. How could he act this way toward those whom he supposedly loves?

I'll tell you how. Two thousand years later, this same God called his only beloved Son to go to that very same place to die on a cross for our sake. Calvary is one of the hills of Moriah. And the Son of God climbed that hill, just like Isaac; for the Lord did "provide himself" the Lamb of God who takes away the sins of the world.

This time it wasn't Isaac carrying the wood; it was Jesus carrying the wooden cross through Jerusalem on the way to Calvary. But this time no angel called from heaven, "Stop! Don't do it!" Instead, the only sound from heaven was complete and utter silence, as the soldiers hammered the nails, then hoisted the cross and dropped it into place. The Father's only beloved Son was thus sacrificed like a lamb for our sins.

God blesses us in a way that many people are not able to recognize. By swearing an oath, he voluntarily put himself under a curse. God thus declared his intention to do whatever it takes to bless us, even if that means bearing the curse of death for our sin. This may help us to understand the Father's purpose in commanding Abraham to offer Isaac. In effect, he called Abraham to show the world what was needed to take away our sin, that is, a faithful father who offers his only beloved son as a holocaust atop Moriah. This also clarifies why God prevented Abraham from carrying out the sacrifice, since the world's salvation required nothing less than the offering of the God-man, Jesus Christ, the "seed of Abraham" (see Gal 3:14-19).

When God saw that Abraham had not withheld his only son, he

swore to bless all nations through Abraham's seed (see Gn 22:15-22). Since the blessing of a father is reserved for his family, this oath is nothing less than God's pledge to restore the human race as his own worldwide family. That is why the establishment of the Catholic Church must be attributed to God's faithfulness and power. It represents nothing less than the historic fulfillment of God's sworn covenant to Abraham.

A fast tour through the rest of Genesis shows the early stages of the long process in which God's covenant is gradually fulfilled, beginning in the lives of Abraham's descendants. In considering Isaac and Rebecca, Jacob and Rachel and Leah, and then Joseph, it is abundantly clear that God works through real people with real lives—like us—in the ongoing plan to father his covenant family.

"The Elder Shall Serve the Younger":
Firstborn Failures and Family Feuds

Just when God's family seemed bound for glory, the rest of the story in Genesis begins to read like a biblical soap opera. Yet through all of the turns and twists and turmoil, God the Father kept all of his promises, often turning misfortune and tragedy into bounty and blessing for his chosen people.

Advanced in years and fearful that his son might marry a Canaanite, Abraham dispatched his most trusted servant to the land of Ur, Abraham's hometown. The assignment: find a wife for Isaac from among his own people. God the Father led this servant to Rebekah, the daughter of Abraham's brother. This woman of unusual faith and courage agreed to leave her family and hastily set off for a distant land.

Happily, it was love at first sight; but sadly, Rebekah was barren. In due time, however, God granted Isaac's prayer, and his wife conceived twins. When the two sons struggled together within her womb, the Lord told Rebekah, "Two nations are in your womb, and two peoples, born of you, shall be divided; the one shall be stronger than the other, the elder shall serve the younger" (Gn 25:23).

Even though God had already earmarked the younger son, Jacob, to be Isaac's heir apparent, Isaac loved his older son the best. Esau was a manly hunter who could also cook up a mean batch of stew. Rebekah favored Jacob, a quiet man who enjoyed being home more than in the fields. Isaac wanted to bless his elder son, while God intended to bless the younger.

Once again God would pass over the prideful firstborn son and continue his blessing through a worthier younger brother. In fact, this pattern runs as a major subplot throughout Genesis, from the earlier chapters (Cain and Abel, Ishmael and Isaac), to the later ones (Jacob and Esau, Reuben and Joseph, Manasseh and Ephraim). This subplot will also emerge as one of the central themes in Exodus, where Israel is called to serve as the "firstborn son" (see Ex 4:22) in the family of nations, just as the firstborn sons of Israel were redeemed by the Passover lamb's blood for priestly service in the twelve tribes.

Pulling the Fur Over Isaac's Eyes

When Isaac was old and his eyes too dim to see, he called for his son Esau: "Go into the field to hunt and bring back some savory game which I so love, so I can eat it and bless you before I die" (see Gn 27:3-4).

Enter Rebekah, the wily wife who eavesdropped and then made plans to outsmart her aging husband. She instructed Jacob to dress up in Esau's best garments and a fur skin so that he looked and smelled like his hairy older brother. Meanwhile, she used two kids from the flock to prepare Isaac's favorite savory stew.

The old man fell for their trick and gave his blessing to Jacob:

"May God give you of the dew of heaven, and of the fatness
of the earth, and plenty of grain and wine.
Let peoples serve you,
and nations bow down to you.
Be lord over your brothers, and may your mother's sons
bow down to you.
Cursed be every one who curses you,
and blessed be every one who blesses you!" GENESIS 27:28-29

The younger son had scarcely left his father's presence when Esau returned from the hunt. Fully expecting to receive the coveted blessing, Esau also prepared the savory food and brought it to his father. Isaac began to tremble violently when he realized he'd been tricked. Esau, the rightful heir of the blessing, cried out bitterly, "Bless me, even me also, O my father!" (v. 34).

Isaac could have said, "Sure, I'll bless you anyway," but he knew that the blessing had gone forth and couldn't be retrieved—even though Jacob had won it by trickery. During Old Testament times, the father's benediction played a huge role in a son's life. The one who got the blessing got all the marbles. Thus, as heir apparent, Jacob was first in line to gain the double portion of the father's power, which included standing as father figure in relation to his older brother Esau.

Esau knew all this, and he was furious. He pointed out that the name "Jacob" literally means "he supplants or undermines." Having been seriously "jacobed" by his brother, Esau swore to take revenge by killing him.

The aggrieved son once more besought his father. Didn't he have just one blessing left for him? Isaac gave what he could:

"Behold, away from the fatness of the earth
shall your dwelling be,
and away from the dew of heaven on high.
By your sword you shall live,
and you shall serve your brother;
but when you break loose
you shall break his yoke from your neck."   GENESIS 27:39-40

What a dramatic difference from the first blessing! How can we understand this sort of treachery on the part of Jacob?

A previous incident provides an important backdrop (see Gn 25:29-34). Once when Jacob was cooking a pot of stew, Esau came in from the field. He was famished and wanted something to eat. The food must have smelled awfully good to the hungry man.

Jacob seized his opportunity for gain. "First," he said, "sell me your birthright"—that is, the family privileges to which Esau was entitled as the firstborn.

The famished hunter didn't even put up a fight. Maybe he figured he was about to die anyway, which would negate any value a birthright might have. So Esau legally sold to his younger brother the family birthright that normally belonged to the eldest son. Because he was willing to sell something so precious for a pot of lentils, we might surmise that Esau never really wanted the birthright in the first place. In fact, Scripture says that he "despised his birthright" (Gn 25:34).

Nevertheless, then as now, older brothers don't like to be bossed around by an upstart younger brother, much less to be tricked by one. Esau plotted to take his revenge after his father died.

A Taste of His Own Medicine

Aware of Esau's anger against Jacob, Rebekah hastily arranged for her younger son to flee the country and live in Haran with her brother Laban until things cooled off at home. Besides, lamented Rebekah, her life would be worthless if Jacob married one of those Hittite women (which Esau soon proceeded to do).

Isaac agreed with Rebekah and expressly charged his younger son not to marry a Canaanite but to take as wife one of Laban's daughters. He then bid his son farewell with a final blessing invoking his family heritage: "God Almighty bless you and make you fruitful and multiply you, that you may become a company of peoples. May he give the blessing of Abraham to you and to your descendants with you, that you may take possession of the land of your sojournings which God gave to Abraham!" (Gn 28:3-4).

Jacob obeyed his father and set out toward Haran. As he camped out under the stars one night, he encountered the Lord in a dream. Jacob saw a ladder standing upon the earth and reaching up to heaven, with the angels of God ascending and descending on it. The Lord spoke to Jacob:

> I am the Lord, the God of Abraham your father and the God of Isaac; the land on which you lie I will give to you and to your descendants; and your descendants shall be like the dust of the earth, and you shall spread abroad to the west and to the east and to the north and to the south; and by you and your descendants shall all the families of the earth bless themselves. Behold, I am with you and will keep you wherever you go, and will bring you back to this land; for I will not leave you until I have done that of which I have spoken to you.

GENESIS 28:13-15

Sound familiar? God the Father evidently wanted to communicate his promises directly to the next generation.

Jacob's response is classic: "Surely the Lord is in this place; and I did not know it" (v. 16). He named the place Bethel, which means the house of God, and made a vow that if God kept all these promises, then the Lord would be his God.

Notice Jacob's escape clause? I take it he wasn't fully convinced that these farfetched pledges would come to pass. The trickster's faith wavered a bit, perhaps from a bad conscience for his dealings with his father and brother.

In any case, faith seemed to overrule skepticism. Having experienced a life-changing encounter with the Lord of the universe, Jacob responded in several practical ways. He set up a stone for a pillar and declared that if he returned to his father's house in peace, that stone would become God's house. He also promised to give

God a tenth of everything he received. Of course, a tenth of nothing is nothing, so maybe he didn't have anything to lose.

Jacob continued east to seek his wife and his fortune. You have to remember that travelers in those days had no access to road maps. Jacob probably used the stars and landmarks to find Haran. Neither, of course, were addresses affixed to houses nor telephone numbers listed in a directory. How to find his kinsmen?

When Jacob came to the "land of the people of the east," he spotted a well where three flocks of sheep were being watered. He asked the shepherds where they came from. When they replied Haran, the visitor asked if they knew Laban. Not only did they know him, but Laban's daughter Rachel happened to be coming with her father's sheep.

After rolling back the stone that covered the well and watering Laban's flock, the dusty traveler greeted Rachel with a brotherly kiss and wept aloud. After Jacob told her who he was, she ran off to tell her father the news. Laban warmly welcomed his sister's son.

After a month's time, Laban asked his nephew what wages he would like to receive for his work. It didn't take the young bachelor long to reply: "I will serve you seven years for your younger daughter Rachel." Laban readily accepted Jacob's proposal. And we read that it seemed but a few days to one so much in love (see Gn 29:20).

After seven years had passed, Jacob asked for his wife. Laban prepared a feast to celebrate, but on the wedding night he slipped his older daughter Leah into the darkened honeymoon tent. Oblivious to the change in personnel, Jacob slept with the wrong woman. According to ancient customs, sexual consummation marked the point of no return in a marriage relationship. Jacob had just been "jacobed" by Laban, thereby receiving a dose of his own medicine.

Jacob was furious when the light of day revealed his uncle's treachery. "I wanted Rachel! What have you done to me?"

Laban was cool. "Well, it's our custom always to marry the oldest daughter first. Work for me another seven years and you can wed Rachel as well." As agreed, Jacob completed the marriage week of seven days with Leah. He then went back to work for Laban—for seven more years—before he got Rachel.

No doubt God the Father was displeased by his children's long string of jealousies, deceptions and marital irregularities. Jacob and the others were making a terrible mess of their family relations, a tangle worthy of any soap opera plot. Nevertheless, God's purposes would not be stopped. Once again, out of the threads of sin he spun a strategy to fulfill his promises.

More Than One Wife Spells Trouble

Needless to say, Jacob loved Rachel more than Leah. God the Father, however, often has a soft spot for the underdog. "When the Lord saw that Leah was hated, he opened her womb; but Rachel was barren" (Gn 29:31). The slighted wife proceeded to conceive four sons in succession: Reuben, Simeon, Levi and Judah—the four patriarchs of the most prominent tribes of Israel. God's plan to fashion a family for himself now had a firm foundation.

Intensely jealous, Rachel blamed her husband. "Give me children, or I shall die!" (Gn 30:1). Jacob, who no doubt had been trying as hard as he could, threw up his hands in anger.

In my experience, confrontation and conflict don't usually promote togetherness. Rachel became so desperate that she pulled a "Sarah." She approached Jacob with a proposal: "Why don't you sleep with my maidservant, Bilhah, so that I may have children through her?"

God's people never seem to learn their lessons, do they? (But then, we too are often slow learners.) Jacob took Bilhah as a concubine, who immediately conceived (of course) and bore a son, Dan, and then a second son, Naphtali.

Meanwhile, back in the other tent, Leah realized that she had ceased bearing sons. Since this was her primary source of esteem and influence, she gave Jacob a second concubine, her maid Zilpah, who bore Gad and Asher. When Leah's son Reuben found some mandrakes (a natural fertility enhancer), Rachel bartered with her sister: a night of Jacob's company in exchange for some of the "miracle root."

A miracle happened, all right—Leah conceived first Issachar, then Zebulun.

Imagine Rachel's bitter disappointment! At last God intervened. "Then God remembered Rachel, and God hearkened to her and opened her womb" (Gn 30:22). Rachel conceived and bore a son named Joseph, with the prayer that the Lord would help her to bear a second son. Some years later, she died giving birth to Benjamin. These twelve sons were to be the heads of the twelve tribes of the nation of Israel.

After twenty long years, Jacob finally found a way to leave dear Uncle Laban, who turned out to be harder to escape than flypaper. The trickery employed by these two men is quite humorous, as each tried to corner more than his fair share of the wealth. Jacob proved to be the wilier of the two and grew exceedingly rich in large flocks, maidservants and menservants and camels and asses—not to mention wives and children.

When Laban's duplicity approached the danger zone, the Lord appeared to Jacob in a dream and warned him to set out for his homeland. He even presented a calling card: "I am the God of Bethel, where you anointed a pillar and made a vow to me" (Gn 31:13). Rachel and Leah readily agreed to leave, since Laban was taking property away from their children as well. While Laban was away shearing his sheep, Jacob fled with all of his wives, concubines, children and livestock, and set his face toward Gilead. God's family was heading home again.

Homecoming

Jacob was escaping trouble on one end of the journey but heading into a potential beehive on the other. Esau, the avenging brother, still awaited the return of the one who had cheated him out of his blessing. Jacob could only hope that twenty years would have been enough to cool Esau's ire.

Wily as ever, Jacob sent messengers ahead of him with a humble and solicitous greeting for his older brother. Esau sent back a message of his own: "I'm coming to meet you, with four hundred men" (see Gn 32:6).

Four hundred men! "Greatly afraid and distressed," Jacob created an extravagant buffer zone between him and Esau. He divided all of his company and livestock into two groups. Then Jacob sent the first ahead of his own, in hopes of appeasing Esau's temper. If his older brother destroyed them, then he and those most dear to him could still escape.

Jacob also prayed for deliverance and reminded God of his promises. He was returning to his own country a wealthy man, which would do him no good if Esau killed him and his wives and children. "But remember, God, you *did* say, 'I will do you good, and make your descendants as the sand of the sea,' didn't you?" Jacob still hoped to receive the divinely promised blessings, even though he knew that he didn't deserve them.

But just to play it safe, Jacob sent his servants on ahead with hundreds of livestock. When Esau asked to whom the animals belonged, the servants were instructed to say: "They belong to your servant Jacob; they are a present sent to my lord Esau; and moreover he is behind us" (Gn 32:18).

You'd think Jacob had enough on his mind at this point, but

God heightened the drama by a personal encounter (see Gn 32:22-32). During the night, Jacob arose and sent all that he had out of harm's way across the stream. While he was alone, a stranger wrestled with him until dawn. When the man saw that he could not prevail against Jacob, he said, "Let me go, for the day is breaking." But Jacob refused to let the stranger go without a blessing.

The man asked, "What is your name?"

"Jacob."

"Your name shall no more be called Jacob, but Israel, for you have striven with God and with men, and have prevailed."

Jacob, henceforth called Israel, asked, "Tell me your name."

To which the man replied, "Why is it that you ask my name?" And then he blessed Israel.

Israel called the place Peniel, for he had "seen God face to face," and yet his life was preserved.

As it turned out, Israel need not have feared the wrath of Esau, who tearfully embraced his long-lost brother. Only under protest did he accept Israel's gifts. Having found favor in Esau's sight, the son of promise then built a house in the land of Canaan and settled down to raise a family.

Brotherly Love in Reaction

After many intervening years filled with illicit sex, violence and intrigue, we pick up the story of salvation with Genesis 37. Seventeen-year-old Joseph, the son of Israel's old age and the first-born son of Rachel, was clearly his father's favorite. Israel's favoritism provoked strong resentment and envy in the much older sons of Leah; they became even angrier when this juvenile upstart tried to lay claim to the family birthright.

Joseph's half-brothers hated him all the more when their father gave him a long robe with sleeves. Why? Because they saw it as something like a coat of arms, the mantle of the father's authority. And Joseph did little to endear himself, especially when he told his half-brothers about two dreams in which they bowed down to him. Even Israel rebuked his favorite son when he heard about the dream in which the sun, the moon and eleven stars were bowing down to Joseph.

One day, Israel sent Joseph from the valley of Hebron to Shechem, where his brothers were pasturing the flock. "Go now, see if it is well with your brothers, and with the flock; and bring me word again" (Gn 37:14). Joseph reached Shechem only to discover that his brothers had taken the flock to Dothan. When they saw him coming, they conspired to kill "this dreamer" and throw him into a pit. "Then ... we shall see what will become of his dreams" (v. 20).

Planning to rescue his younger brother later, Reuben persuaded the others not to shed any blood but simply to leave him to die. And so they stripped Joseph of his many-colored robe and cast him into the pit. Then these callous fellows sat down to eat!

When they saw a passing caravan of traders, Joseph's brothers realized they could get rid of Joseph and turn a profit at the same time. Judah said to his brothers, "What profit is it if we slay our brother and conceal his blood? Come, let us sell him to the Ishmaelites, and let not our hand be upon him, for he is our brother, our own flesh" (vv. 26-27). For twenty shekels of silver, they sold Joseph into slavery to the Ishmaelites, half-Egyptians through Hagar, and their kinsmen from Ishmael. In order to cover their tracks, Joseph's brothers dipped his torn coat into goat's blood. When they showed it to their father, Israel wailed and mourned his son's death.

God's family had once again taken a very wrong turn. How could the Father possibly turn this betrayal to good?

The traders sold Joseph to Potiphar, the captain of the guard and one of the most powerful men in Egypt. "The Lord was with Joseph, and he became a successful man" (Gn 39:2); so successful that Potiphar put him in charge of all that he had. And the Lord blessed the Egyptian's house and land for the sake of Joseph.

From Prisoner to Prime Minister in a Day

Unfortunately, at this point a new episode in our biblical soap opera began to unfold. Potiphar was not the only one to notice Joseph; the master's wife gazed upon the handsome young man as well, and not with honorable motives. She repeatedly tried to lure Joseph into her bed, but he steadfastly refused to sin against God and his master. Potiphar's wife finally became so adamant that she ripped off the Hebrew's outer garment and begged him to lie with her. When Joseph fled the house without his garment, the spurned woman accused him of attempted rape. Furious over this presumed treachery, Potiphar threw Joseph into prison.

Difficult circumstances never seem to deter the Father from carrying out his plans and keeping his promises. He is especially creative whenever adversity strikes, even showing a flair for the dramatic. Stories like this one make me wonder whether God doesn't sometimes arrange severe obstacle courses in order to make his divine power more unmistakable.

Scripture tells us that the Lord was with Joseph in prison, showing him his steadfast love. He also gave Joseph favor in the sight of the prison guard, who entrusted him with the day-to-day responsibility for the prison. Although a few notches lower on the social ladder, Joseph ended up playing essentially the same administrative role as he had in Potiphar's household.

Some time later, Pharaoh became angry with his chief butler and chief baker and sent them to the same prison where Joseph was confined. One night they both had vivid dreams, which allowed Joseph to demonstrate his God-given gift of interpretation. Two years later, Pharaoh could find no one to tell him the meaning of his own haunting dream. The chief butler (who had long since been restored to his position) told him about the imprisoned Hebrew who had interpreted his dream.

Hastily called to appear before the king, Joseph reassured Pharaoh that the dream had been sent by God to let him know what would surely come to pass. Seven years of bumper crops would be followed by seven years of famine. Joseph further displayed his wisdom by suggesting a way to deal with the situation. His proposal so impressed Pharaoh and all his servants that the king immediately set Joseph over all the land of Egypt, second in command only to Pharaoh himself.

Joseph was thirty years old when he entered into the king's service. Pharaoh gave him in marriage Asenath, the daughter of Potiphera priest of On, who bore him two sons. The first Joseph named Manasseh, for "God has made me forget all my hardship and all my father's house." The second he called Ephraim, "for God has made me fruitful in the land of my affliction" (see Gn 41:51-52).

Turnabout Is Fair Play

All that Joseph predicted came true. During the seven years of extraordinary harvest, he directed the storage of grain to prepare for the coming famine. When famine struck and the need for food became acute, Joseph opened the storehouses and sold grain to the Egyptians. In fact, we read that the famine was severe over all the earth. Food could be found in only one place: Egypt.

Meanwhile, since food was scarce in Canaan as well, Israel's family was in danger of starving. So Israel eventually sent his ten older sons to buy grain in Egypt. (He held back Benjamin for fear any harm should come to him.)

And so it came to pass that Joseph's ten half-brothers came and bowed down before him, just as the dream had prophesied. When they fell on their faces before Egypt's prime minister to beg for bread, none of them recognized the grown-up Joseph arrayed in splendor. (The irony in this story is delicious.)

Joseph recognized them immediately but showed no sign of it. Instead, he pulled all kinds of mean tricks on them, turning them every which way but loose. As a result of their troubles, they uttered among themselves a heartfelt repentance for their sin against Joseph so many years before.

We finally come to one of the most poignant scenes in all literature, when Joseph broke down in tears and revealed himself to his brothers. The young man's wisdom and compassion were confirmed later on when he told them: "Fear not, for am I in the place of God? As for you, you meant evil against me; but God meant it for good, to bring it about that many people should be kept alive, as they are today. So do not fear; I will provide for you and your little ones" (Gn 50:19-21).

When Israel heard that his son was not only alive but living in splendor, he brought all of his family to Egypt. Pharaoh directed Joseph to give them the best land. So the Israelites settled in Goshen, the prime piece of real estate in Egypt.

Once again, God's people seemed to be going in circles: from Ur to Canaan, from Canaan to Ur, from Ur to Canaan again, and now from Canaan to Egypt. We almost begin to wonder whether God knows how to draw straight lines. But then again, he was dealing with human beings, creatures made in his own image but faulty creatures nonetheless.

Genesis ends with a deathbed scene, where Israel blesses his twelve sons, along with his two grandsons through Joseph, Manasseh and Ephraim, whom Israel took and blessed as his own.

Like his father Isaac, old, dim-eyed Jacob gave the blessing of the eldest son to the youngest—except in this case, it was his youngest *grandson*, Ephraim.

Joseph protested. He thought the special favor ought to be given to his oldest son, Manasseh. But his father Israel said, "I know, my son, I know; he also shall become a people, and he also shall be great; nevertheless his younger brother shall be greater than he, and his descendants shall become a multitude of nations" (Gn 48:19). Israel then proceeded to bless his other sons, counseling them regarding their strengths and weaknesses, and charging them concerning his burial place. Finally, this venerable patriarch breathed his last and was gathered to his people.

Joseph lived in Egypt to the ripe age of 110, and bounced Ephraim's children upon his knee to the third generation. On his deathbed Joseph reassured his brothers that God would visit them and bring them out of Egypt to the land that he had sworn to Abraham, to Isaac and to Jacob. His last request was that they carry his bones with them.

The Father had kept his promises to provide for his people and to prosper them in the midst of plenty or poverty. Would he also keep his promise to bring them out of Egypt and give them a land of their own? As before, we shall see that God's timetable rarely corresponds to our own.

"Let My People Go!":
Israel's Exodus From Egypt

After Joseph's generation had gone the way of all human flesh, the descendants of Israel continued to be fruitful and multiply greatly, "so that the land was filled with them" (Ex 1:7). In a matter of centuries, Jacob's twelve sons had grown to become the twelve tribes of Israel. But they weren't a unified nation yet, and things went from bad to worse.

A new Pharaoh eventually came to power "who did not know Joseph" (v. 8). This doesn't mean that he had never heard of Joseph. The Hebrew word for "know" (*yada'*) is often used with reference to the covenant bonds of *family members* (such as Adam "knew" Eve and she conceived) or *treaty partners* (as Joseph and Israel had been "known" by the previous Egyptian administration).

Here the term marks a sudden shift in the political winds affecting Israel's fortunes in Egypt. The new Pharaoh's message to Israel may be paraphrased: "I repudiate any former covenant treaty made by my dethroned predecessor with the Israelites, you who sit so fat and pretty in Goshen, the best land in Egypt."

In short, a contender for the throne orchestrated a palace coup to overthrow the dynasty of a previous Pharaoh and begin a new one. All former treaties were thus invalidated as a matter of course. And the new Pharaoh naturally viewed former allies as a potential threat to his own political power.

"Look," Pharaoh said to his people, "the Israelites have become much too numerous for us." This new Pharaoh set heavy taskmasters over the Israelites, but the more they were oppressed, the more they multiplied and spread abroad. In dread of them, the Egyptians made their lives miserable with all kinds of hard work. Then the king implemented an even more aggressive plan, almost a precursor to Hitler's "final solution" in Nazi Germany: Pharaoh ordered the midwives to kill all of the Hebrew male children at birth (see Ex 1:9-16).

No doubt the king promised to reward the Hebrew midwives for their obedience, but these women feared God and refused to kill the male infants. When Pharaoh found out his commands were not being carried out, he questioned the midwives. They gave him a clever answer: the Hebrew women were so much more vigorous than the Egyptians that they delivered before a midwife could even arrive. And God blessed the midwives and gave them families of their own (vv. 17-20).

We can only speculate as to why Pharaoh didn't order the killing of female babies. Perhaps he thought that without any males in the next generation, the Hebrew women would have no one to marry but Egyptian men. And then to whom would ownership of Goshen pass? To the Egyptians. So with a few ruthless behind-the-scenes moves, Pharaoh hoped to manipulate the inheritance laws to retrieve all that prime real estate in Goshen and put the Hebrews in their place: as serfs.

Recall how the Lord had warned Abraham in a dream that his descendants would be enslaved for four hundred years (see Gn 15:13-16). Yet the Father didn't see this as a serious obstacle for the realization of his family plans. In fact, the biblical drama shows how God always uses adversity to demonstrate his love and power, to prove that he keeps his promises no matter what—or who—stands in the way.

A Boat Over Troubled Waters

In the midst of these tough times, a certain Levite's wife conceived and bore a son. When she could hide him no longer, she placed the three-month-old baby into a basket made of bulrushes and placed it in the reeds along the edge of the Nile. The child's older sister watched from a distance to see what would happen (see Ex 2:1-4).

The daughter of Pharaoh, who happened to be bathing in the river, found the basket and took pity on the Hebrew child. The baby's quick-thinking older sister offered to fetch a Hebrew wet nurse, who happened to be his mother. After the baby was weaned, Pharaoh's daughter adopted him as her own son and named him Moses, "because [she] drew him out of the water" (see Ex 2:5-10).

Raised as a member of the royal court, Moses received the best clothes, the best education, the best food, the best everything. But one day this favored young man was visiting Goshen when he happened to see an Egyptian beating a Hebrew, one of his own people. In a fit of fury Moses killed the taskmaster, then hid the body in the sand.

The next day Moses came across two Hebrews fighting each other and admonished the one who seemed to be in the wrong. The man turned on Moses with a stinging rebuke: "Who made you a prince and a judge over us? Do you mean to kill me as you killed the Egyptian?" (v. 14).

Perhaps Moses expected a warm welcome as Pharaoh's boy returning home to Goshen. But he soon discovered that the Israelites weren't impressed with his credentials. They probably viewed him as a fair-haired, spoiled brat raised on the lap of Egyptian luxury, who had come to lord it over them. They wanted no part of him. And when Pharaoh learned that Moses had murdered an Egyptian, he sought to kill the Hebrew upstart (see v. 15).

Rejected by the Israelites and hunted by the Egyptians, like a man without a country, Moses fled. Even so, the fugitive was nestled securely in the hands of a Father who would guide his footsteps, patiently biding his time until his son was ready for the task ahead: the rescue of God's family from bondage.

God's Covenant With Moses

Moses escaped from Pharaoh into the desert and stayed in the land of Midian. One day he helped the seven daughters of the priest of Midian, who had come to draw water for their father's flocks. When Jethro learned of the Egyptian's kindness to his daughters, he invited Moses for supper. They must have hit it off rather well, because Moses stayed on with this prominent Midianite family (who happened to be relatives of Abraham). Jethro gave him his daughter Zipporah as wife, who bore him a son named Gershom (see Ex 2:16-22).

Meanwhile, back in Egypt, God heard the groaning of the Israelite slaves and remembered his covenant with Abraham (see vv. 23-25). It almost sounds as if God had gotten too busy with some other project and stopped listening or had too much on his mind and forgot his people. But on the contrary, the Lord had been working behind the scenes all along to accomplish his purposes. This is just a scriptural way of saying that the time had come when God would act decisively, that all the pieces were in place. And Moses, a man without a country, was to play a crucial role in God's plan to deliver Israel from bondage.

One day when Moses was tending Jethro's flock, he drew near to Mount Horeb on the far side of the desert. God appeared to him in a burning bush and said, "Moses! Moses!"

Moses answered, "Here am I."

"Don't come any closer. Take off your sandals, for the place where you are standing is holy ground. I am the God of your father, the God of Abraham" (see Ex 3:1-6).

If the voice speaking from the burning bush had stopped there, Moses might not have known which god he faced. As direct descendants of Abraham, Midianites and Ishmaelites worshiped the same God. And the Edomites who descended from Esau could have said, "He is our God." Even the Egyptians could lay some claim to this God because the first one to bear Abraham a child was Hagar, the Egyptian.

But the voice continued: *"I am the God of Abraham, the God of Isaac, and the God of Jacob"* (v. 6). He narrowed down the family line so that Moses could follow it from Shem to Abraham to Isaac to Jacob and to the twelve tribes of Israel enslaved in Egypt. God had worked in Moses' life to prepare him for this very time, for the time when the promise of deliverance would be fulfilled in the lives of his people.

"I have seen the misery of my people in Egypt and I am going to do something about it. I want to bring them out" (see vv. 7-9).

Having revealed his intentions, the Lord proceeded to tell Moses what all of this had to do with him. "Come, I will send you to Pharaoh that you may bring forth my people, the sons of Israel, out of Egypt" (see Ex 3:10).

Do you remember the old television program called *Mission Impossible*? "Your mission, should you choose to accept it ..." Like some of the difficult assignments in that TV series, I'm sure this sounded like a suicide mission to Moses. After all, the last he knew, the Egyptians wanted to execute him for murder, and the Israelites wanted nothing to do with him. And now he was supposed to waltz right into the palace empty-handed and ask Pharaoh to let him waltz right out with thousands of Hebrew slaves? Right!

Whatever thoughts might have been stampeding through his mind, Moses respectfully asked, "Who am I that I should go to Pharaoh, and bring the sons of Israel out of Egypt?" (v. 11)

God the Father assured Moses (who had demonstrated a strong tendency to proceed in his own power): "But I will be with you; and this shall be the sign for you, that I have sent you: when you have brought forth the people out of Egypt, you shall serve God upon this mountain" (v. 12).

We often forget that God's initial request of Pharaoh did not entail total and permanent liberation of the Hebrews. He did not send Moses to deliver a celestial imperative, "Let my people go." He simply asked Pharaoh to release Israel for a three-day journey into the wilderness to offer sacrifice to the Lord on Mount Horeb.

If the Egyptian ruler had cooperated, the Israelites presumably would have returned to slavery. But God said, "I know Pharaoh won't let you go unless compelled, so I'll have to send ruinous plagues his way."

"Who, Me?"

Our unlikely hero wasn't exactly filled with enthusiasm. Moses tried to "but" his way out of this impossible mission. "But they won't listen to me or believe you appeared to me."

The Father understood Moses' misgivings and gave his fearful son some signs that might help to convince the Egyptians (see Ex 4:1-9). "Throw your shepherd's staff on the ground," said the Lord. Moses did, and the staff became a snake.

God said, "Now reach out your hand and take it by the tail." When Moses did, it became a staff again.

"Now put your hand into your cloak." Moses did, and when he pulled it out again, his hand was white with advanced leprosy.

"Now put it back," God said. Moses did, and when he brought it out yet again, his hand had the flesh of a baby.

Was God showing off? No, these various signs were symbols. The staff was a sign of Moses' authority. When he threw it down, it became a serpent, a symbol of evil. In other words, God was giving this man dominion over the natural order, including evil. When Moses grabbed the serpent by the tail, it again became his staff of authority.

The leprosy of Moses' hand was also an important symbol. In Scripture, leprosy is often associated with sin and its harmful consequences (see Nm 12:10). Thus it may serve here as a sign of Israel's bondage, which God planned to lift at the hands of Moses. In any case, the restoration of Moses' hand was meant to increase Israel's faith in God and enkindle hope for healing.

Even having witnessed these signs and wonders, Moses still balked at his assignment. In fact, he was downright scared. "Oh, Lord, I've never been eloquent," he said. "I even stutter. Why send me?" (see Ex 4:10).

The Father didn't see his son's limitations as an obstacle. After all, the power of God himself would win the victory through this human instrument of salvation. "Who has made man's mouth?" God asked Moses. "Who makes him dumb, or deaf, or seeing, or blind? Is it not I, the Lord? Now therefore go, and I will be with your mouth and teach you what you shall speak" (see vv. 11-12).

Can you picture this dialogue between a patient father and a recalcitrant son? Moses was really pressing his luck when he offered one last objection. "Oh my Lord, can't you find someone else for this job?" (see v. 13).

Evidently God's patience was beginning to wear thin. Scripture tells us that the Lord's anger burned against Moses. "What about your brother Aaron? He's already on his way to meet you. Speak to him and put words in his mouth, and I'll help both of you speak and know what to do. Aaron will speak to the people for you and it will be as if he were your mouth and as if you were God to him" (see vv. 14-16). Thus Aaron the Levite assumed the role of intermediary between Moses and Pharaoh, parallel to the role of Moses as mediator between God and Aaron (and all Israel).

Going Home Again

When his audience with God had drawn to a close, Moses returned to his family. Breaking this sort of news to his father-in-law and especially to his spouse wouldn't have been easy, as you can well imagine. "Guess who I just met over by Mount Horeb!"

Actually, Moses used a bit more discretion. He said to Jethro, "Let me go back to my kinsmen in Egypt and see whether they are still alive." With his father-in-law's blessing, Moses took his wife and his sons and set off for Egypt—with the staff of God the Father firmly in hand.

While still in the land of Midian, Moses learned from the Lord that all those who had been seeking his life were dead. The Father also gave him further instructions about how to proceed once he arrived at the royal court. But God warned Moses that Pharaoh would refuse to let the Israelites go.

Then God dictated a message for Pharaoh that resounds with the covenant language of family and commitment: "Thus says the Lord, Israel is my firstborn son, and I say to you, 'Let my son go that he may serve me'; if you refuse to let him go, behold, I will slay your firstborn son" (Ex 4:22-23).

What was the Father saying through Moses? Did "firstborn son" mean that Israel was God's only child? Not necessarily. It meant that the other nations were like God's younger children, Israel's younger siblings. But as the firstborn son, Israel was to be the covenant mediator in God's worldwide family, the role model and pacesetter who would lead the other nations back to their divine Father.

God was saying in effect, "Israel is my firstborn son. Egypt, you are potentially my child, but only if you let your older brother go to worship me so that you will learn how to serve me by watching him." God's plan was to raise up Israel as a royal priest to serve all the other nations if only the nations would cooperate.

Bridegroom of Blood

In the grandeur of God's plan, we can easily miss one little verse: "At a lodging place on the way the Lord met him [Moses] and sought to kill him" (Ex 4:24). But Zipporah, his wife, took out a flint knife, cut off her son's foreskin, touched Moses' feet with it and said, "You are a bridegroom of blood to me!" So the Lord relented (v. 25).

God, the assassin? So which way is it? We had the impression that you wanted to use Moses to liberate your people, and now you're trying to exterminate him before he ever crosses the border? What was going on? Once again, we need to understand Scripture from the perspective of Hebrew signs and symbols, their family heritage. Moses was in fact a covenant breaker because Gershom, his firstborn, was uncircumcised. When God had instituted circumcision in his covenant with Abraham several generations before, he had told Abraham, "If any man refuses to circumcise his son in eight days, I shall cut him off like so much foreskin" (Gn 17:10-14).

Why hadn't Moses kept the covenant? The Midianites *did* practice circumcision, but like the Ishmaelites, they followed the custom that many Arabs practice down to the present time. Arabs perform circumcision around the age of thirteen (as with Ishmael), as a rite of passage from boyhood to manhood. On the other hand, the Israelites were to follow God's command given to Abraham concerning Isaac, by circumcising their male infants on the eighth day, a statement of acceptance by God into the family covenant that did not depend upon their future "manliness."

Maybe Moses excused himself by saying, *When in Midian, do as the Midianites do. After all, I don't want to offend Jethro, my father-in-law, who also happens to be a priest of Midian.*

Evidently, Moses had offended his *Father*, so seriously that God tried to kill him. He was showing Moses that he meant business when he talked about breaking the covenant: "When you break the covenant, you rupture my family."

Moses is spared only because his Midianite wife circumcised Gershom and touched her husband's feet with the bloody foreskin. Since Zipporah knew exactly what to do, we may suppose that she was aware of the specific obligation her husband had neglected. In short, the severity of God's response may indicate sufficient knowledge on both their parts. In any case, Zipporah's response averted disaster; her important role in God's redemptive plan for his family should not be overlooked.

"Let My People Go"

God the Father, just as he had promised, sent Aaron into the wilderness to meet his younger brother at the mountain of God. Moses gave Aaron the details, then they returned together to Egypt, where they spoke to all the elders of Israel. Hearing the words of the Lord and seeing the signs of power, the people believed that God had heard their cries. They bowed their heads and worshiped. Moses had apparently cleared the first hurdle (see Ex 4:27-31).

Moses and Aaron then visited Pharaoh and delivered this message: "Thus says the Lord, the God of Israel, 'Let my people go, that they may hold a feast to me in the wilderness'" (Ex 5:1).

Pharaoh was in no mood for dealing with unknown deities. "Who is the Lord, that I should heed his voice and let Israel go? I do not know the Lord, and moreover I will not let Israel go" (v. 2).

Do you detect a hint of arrogance in Pharaoh's response?

Moses and Aaron tried rephrasing the request: "The God of the Hebrews has met with us; let us go, we pray, a three days' journey into the wilderness, and sacrifice to the Lord our God, lest he fall upon us with pestilence or with the sword" (v. 3).

Pharaoh had no intention of taking the people away from their work. If these lazy Hebrews wanted to offer sacrifices to their God, evidently they didn't have enough work to do. So the Egyptian ruler decided to make their burdens even heavier by ordering the taskmasters not to provide straw for making bricks. The Israelites now had to gather the straw themselves—with no reduction in their quota of bricks. The weary people in turn blamed Moses and Aaron for stirring up trouble.

Lest his son admit defeat, the Father repeated his promises to deliver Israel with his own mighty hand. God issued this declaration to the people of Israel:

> I will bring you out from under the burdens of the Egyptians, and I will deliver you from their bondage, and I will redeem you with an outstretched arm and with great acts of judgment, and I will take you for my people, and I will be your God; and you shall know that I am the Lord your God, who has brought you out from under the burdens of the Egyptians. And I will bring you into the land which I swore to give to Abraham, to Isaac, and to Jacob; I will give it to you for a possession. I am the Lord.
> EXODUS 6:6-8

The Israelites didn't listen to Moses, "because of their broken spirit and their cruel bondage" (v. 9). Nonetheless, the Father would keep his promises.

God then directed Moses to use various signs and to unleash one plague after another, all designed to change Pharaoh's mind (see Ex 7:14-8:24).

The first of the ten plagues turned the Nile to blood. God wasn't just flexing his muscles and saying, "Here, watch this. I'll turn the river to blood." The Egyptians worshiped the Nile as a divine entity, identified with the god Hapi. Turning the river to blood meant, for all practical purposes, the slaying of this god.

Next came the plague of frogs. As they died and began to stink,

God was thereby passing judgment on the Egyptian goddess Heket, often worshiped in the form of a frog. Meanwhile, with each plague, God protected his people in Goshen from harm or loss.

Pharaoh softened just a bit. After all, the national economy would soon be in ruins at the rate things were going. So the ruler of Egypt summoned the Levite brothers and said, "Go, sacrifice to your God within the land" (Ex 8:25). He consented to the proposed religious festival, but with one unacceptable stipulation: Israel was not to venture off too far. If they didn't return, as the king probably feared, who'd complete all their construction projects?

Moses refused to compromise on the grounds that Israel's sacrifices would be detestable in the eyes of the Egyptians. "The sacrifices we offer to the Lord our God," he replied, "would be an abomination to the Egyptians. The people would stone us if we did it in their sight. We must take a three-day journey into the desert to worship the Lord as he commands" (see vv. 22-23). Why didn't Moses accept the Pharaoh's seemingly reasonable compromise?

False Idols in the Land

Why did God require Israel to come out of Egypt to worship and sacrifice at Mount Horeb? The Father wanted his people to sacrifice cattle, goats and rams.

Sounds harmless enough. We tend to view these bloody offerings as legalistic rituals, as if God were appeased simply by the smell of burnt flesh. Yet the Egyptians worshiped these types of animals as divinities. To sacrifice just one of them in the midst of Egypt would have been like killing a sacred cow in India. Such acts could seriously endanger a person's life.[1]

Was God saying that these animals were intrinsically demonic? Of course not. But as Ezekiel 20 tells us, Israel had been in Egypt so long that it had already begun to absorb the idolatrous ways of the Egyptians, a religion of nature, fertility, power and wealth. Through these gods, the powers of darkness promised to give earthly treasures and influence in exchange for a person's eternal destiny.

The Father commanded his people to sacrifice these animals because the Israelites were becoming addicted to these false gods. He was essentially saying, "You can't hear my voice because you're worshiping animals." God acted for the sake of his name, because he had sworn an oath to Abraham to give his descendants the land of Canaan. But how could God lead his people out of bondage and into the Promised Land until they had done away with these false gods? The idols had to go (see Ez 20:7-8).

God wanted the Israelites to come out of Egypt and sacrifice these false idols as an act of worship. Then they could return to Egypt and resume their work as slaves. Given a cooperative Pharaoh, God's objective was more spiritual than political: to liberate his people from bondage to false idols and addictions to earthly goods. Then they would be free regardless of their earthly circumstances. After all, as it turned out, the Israelites weren't headed for any picnic in the Promised Land.

Creating a Power Vacuum

Through Moses, God sent a chilling message to Pharaoh: "These plagues will ruin the gods of Egypt to show Israel that I'm the God of the universe and to break them of their addiction to power, to wealth and to pleasure." The ten plagues then symbolically judged, condemned and slaughtered all of these false deities, including Apis, the bull god; Hathor, the cow goddess; and Khnum, the ram god. The plague of darkness was a judgment on Re, the Egyptian sun god.

The tenth plague, which took the lives of the firstborn, was the worst of all—not merely because humans were slaughtered, but because Pharaoh was considered to be divine, and his firstborn was actually divinized in a special ceremony. All fathers and firstborn sons were called to share in a quasi-divine power and wealth. In a sense, the firstborn represented the political gods of Egypt (see Nm 33:4).

By destroying all the firstborn in a culture that depended upon family relations and tribal structures, God created an immense power vacuum. The Israelites could finally escape from bondage. Even more importantly, they would no longer be seduced or even attracted to a broken culture and a barren way of life.

God the Father took special action to protect his people during the Passover. He gave specific instructions to Moses: "Take a lamb without any broken bones. Slay it and sprinkle its blood on the doorpost. That night, eat the lamb. If you do this, your firstborn will be alive when you wake up in the morning. If you don't, your firstborn will be dead, along with all the firstborn in your flocks" (see Ex 12:1-23). The elders made sure that all the people were prepared as instructed.

The Jewish Passover commemorates that night of terror when the destroyer, the angel of death, passed over Egypt and killed all the firstborn in the land. A great wailing and mourning arose throughout Egypt as every Egyptian family felt the mighty hand of God. Having lost his own firstborn, Pharaoh finally summoned Moses and delivered a terse directive: "Get out!" As God had foretold, the Israelites were able to plunder the Egyptians of their gold and silver in exchange for their years of slave labor.

Having been in Egypt 430 years, Israel now numbered about six hundred thousand men, not counting women and children.

This multitude set out on foot along with a great number of live-stock. And because the ravaged Egyptians forced them to leave in such haste, the Israelites had few provisions for the journey. They did go equipped for battle, however, and Moses did remember to bring along the bones of Joseph as promised.

Suddenly and surprisingly, Pharaoh changed his mind. He gathered his army, with hundreds of chariots and horses, and hastily pursued the Hebrews. Can you imagine what a maniac this man must have been? Egypt's livestock, flocks and crops had been completely destroyed. His country lay in ruins, and he still refused to let God's people go. His humiliation had been too great; Pharaoh's pride refused to admit defeat.

The dramatic crossing of the Red Sea described in Exodus 13 and 14 paints a vivid picture of God's love and power as expressed on behalf of those he had come to save. Having embarked on a rescue mission, the Father would not be stopped. Against all odds, he freed the Hebrews from their slavery. Whether or not the Israelites would be liberated from the deeper bondage of sin, represented by Egypt's false idols, remained to be seen.

Short-Lived Jubilation

But God the Father now had his children in tow, with Moses in the lead. They had just witnessed one awesome demonstration of divine power after another as the plagues descended upon Egypt. In every affliction, the Israelites were miraculously protected from harm. Going before them in a pillar of cloud by day and of fire by night, the Lord had then ushered this ragtag assembly across the Red Sea on dry ground, even as the Egyptians perished in their wake. Surely the Israelites were now convinced that the God of Abraham, Isaac and Jacob would meet their every need and keep every one of his promises.

Scripture tells us that "the people feared the Lord; and they believed in the Lord and in his servant Moses" (Ex 14:31). They celebrated by singing a rousing song of victory, giving tribute to the God of their fathers who had granted them salvation (see Ex 15:1-18). Miriam, the prophetess and sister of Aaron, led all the women in singing with timbrels and dance: "Sing to the Lord, for he has triumphed gloriously; the horse and his rider he has thrown into the sea" (v. 1).

Unfortunately, their jubilation was short-lived. After three days' journey into the wilderness, the Israelites could find no water and began to murmur against Moses. But the Father heard their cry and provided water.

After six weeks, their stomachs rumbled with hunger so that the whole nation murmured against Moses and Aaron. Already they were tempted to return to Egypt, the land of former bondage. "Would that we had died by the hand of the Lord in the land of Egypt," they complained, "when we sat by the fleshpots and ate bread to the full; for you have brought us out into this wilderness to kill this whole assembly with hunger" (Ex 16:3).

Not exactly words of faith or gratitude. Nonetheless, the Father satisfied Israel's hunger by covering the ground each morning with manna (waferlike bread that remained edible for just one day) and sending quail every evening—enough to feed hundreds of thousands of men, women and children (see Ex 16).

Poor Moses. I remember vacations with my dad driving cross-country—trying to keep his cool—with three whining kids in the back seat. I can't imagine how Moses kept the entire nation of Israel moving forward.

Once again the people complained against their appointed leader because they could find no water to drink. An exasperated Moses cried to the Lord, "What shall I do with this people? They're ready to stone me." Once again the Father mercifully provided them water from the rock at Horeb. And when they were heaping up complaints to Moses, seventy elders were appointed—and anointed—to exercise judgment in lesser disputes. Otherwise Moses would not have been able to endure much longer.

Through each of these crises of faith, we see God the Father patiently lifting his people up and carrying them one step farther. We see him full of compassion and ever ready to meet their needs. We see him faithful to his promises, even when his human family is ready to turn back to slavery. Like most of us, Israel had to learn about God's love the hard way.

Consequently, divine compassion often came in the form of those hard mercies that some fathers like to call tough love. God wasn't content with liberating Israel from mere physical slavery in Egypt. Instead of a cosmetic surgery that only deals with the externals, the Father saw the need for radical surgery, without which Israel would have remained forever enslaved—internally—to the idols of Egypt. His goal was not simply to bring them into the Promised Land but to make them reliant on him alone. That's a lesson we're always learning, that God loves us just as we are, but he loves us too much to leave us that way.

EIGHT

Israel's Calf-Hearted Response:
The Mosaic Covenant at Mount Sinai

Three months after Israel's harrowing escape from Egypt, they came to the wilderness of Sinai and encamped before the holy mountain. Moses received far more than he bargained for when he ascended the peak to pray. There God declared his intention to transform this complaining bunch into a kingdom of priests.

> Thus you shall say to the house of Jacob, and tell the people of Israel: You have seen what I did to the Egyptians, and how I bore you on eagles' wings and brought you to myself. Now therefore, **if** you will obey my voice and keep my covenant, you shall be my own possession among all people; for all the earth is mine, and you shall be to me a *kingdom of priests* and a *holy nation*. These are the words which you shall speak to the children of Israel.
>
> EXODUS 19:3-6

Israel's future identity hung upon the biggest "if" in history: "**If** you obey my voice and keep my covenant ..."

When Moses delivered the word of the Lord, the people seemed ready to get with the plan. They all answered Moses in chorus, "All that the Lord has spoken we will do" (v. 8). Little did they know what they were getting themselves into.

They might have been wondering, What exactly did God mean when he spoke of "my covenant"? Since the Sinai covenant wasn't made yet, they probably thought back to the Abrahamic covenant; after all, God had already spoken to them about keeping that one himself (see Ex 6:1-8). Now he seemed to be calling Israel, as the natural "seed" of Abraham, to accept that covenant as their own. This meant that Israel was expected to collaborate with God in ful-filling his pledge to bless "all the nations," which he had sworn to Abraham to do through his "seed" (see Gn 22:16-18).

No wonder God singled out Israel from all the nations. As a father, he wasn't playing favorites; he was just working with his "firstborn son" (see Ex 4:22) so that together they might reach all the other nations—as Israel's younger brothers in the family of God. That is also what he had in mind in calling them to become "a kingdom of priests and a holy nation" (v. 6). They were to extend the Father's unifying and universal rule to the whole world. Thus, Israel would fulfill a royal-priestly role—as the oldest brother amidst the other, younger-brother nations.[1]

Now that sounds good, but what exactly did God have in mind in calling this newly liberated nation of ex-slaves to become a "kingdom of priests"? What political shape would it take?

The Declaration of Dependence

The laws given in the next few chapters reveal the unique design that God apparently had in mind in calling Israel to this "con-stitutional convention" at Mount Sinai. First, the Ten Command-ments, listed in the next chapter (see Ex 20:1-17), gave this ragtag outfit of twelve loosely knit tribes a new identity. The Decalogue revealed to Israel a radically new way of living under the lordship of Yahweh.

The Ten Commandments are sometimes described as Israel's Declaration of Independence from Egyptian slavery. That's fine, as long as we recall that these laws were meant to serve—more accu-rately—as Israel's formal Declaration of Dependence on God. The laws in the next three chapters (see Ex 21-23) formed the "Book of the Covenant" and—to extend the political analogy—served a purpose very similar to the Articles of Confederation, which transformed thirteen colonies into the United States: for the Israelites, this was accomplished by turning the twelve former slave-tribes of Israel into God's national family.

There's another parallel: the Articles of Confederation proved to be inadequate for maintaining the union of thirteen decentralized states, making it necessary to ratify a stronger document, the Constitution. In a similar way, the "Book of the Covenant" was eventually superceded by the "Book of the Law" (otherwise known as Deuteronomy), which Moses gave to the second generation at Moab, forty years after Sinai (see Dt 29:1).

The Deuteronomic Covenant thus served for many centuries as Israel's constitution, having been ratified exactly when they needed to become a strong unified country, that is, at the time of their conquest of Canaan, where they were destined to become a landed nation and eventually a kingdom. Israel was never to live again as a mere confederation of nomadic tribes wandering in the desert. But we're getting ahead of ourselves.

Before God could expect Israel to unify the other nations, he first had to unify them as his own "holy nation." We can imagine that God the Father spoke to them of an awesome calling: "You will be a kingdom of priests. You won't rule through political power or military strength, as the Egyptians do, but through wisdom and righteousness and holiness. Through holy lives and prayer and sacrifice, you will earn the right to be heard and believed and followed. You will draw the nations to return to me freely, but only if you put all your trust in me and meet me face-to-face and hear me speak my law of love."

To establish this intimate father-son relationship with Israel, God had to manifest himself to all the people—but only after appropriate preparations had been made for such a close encounter with the Creator of the universe. The Lord commanded them to consecrate themselves, to wash their clothes and to abstain from sexual relations for three days.

How Close Is Too Close?

On the morning of the third day, a thick cloud blanketed the mountain, along with the special effects of thunder and lightning accompanied by a loud trumpet blast, which made everyone tremble. When Moses brought the people to the foot of Mount Sinai to meet God, they saw that it was wrapped in smoke because the Lord had descended upon it in fire. The mountain quaked. As the trumpet grew louder and louder, God answered Moses in a thunderous voice, repeating his stern warning that no one touch the consecrated summit. Then Moses went up Mount Sinai to meet with God, to receive his word and to prepare Israel for their reunion with the Father.

Moses returned to find the people trembling with fear at the sights and sounds surrounding Mount Sinai. They all pleaded with Moses to speak to God alone, "but let not God speak to us, lest we die" (Ex 20:19). Moses tried to reassure them that they needn't fear their Father, who loved them as his own children. He had come only to test them that they might not sin. The special effects were simply meant as a reminder to God's children that nobody draws near to the Holy One of Israel—in safety—if they don't approach him in reverence and awe. But still the people stood at a distance and trembled in fear.

Why were the Israelites so frightened? All they basically had to do was shower and wait three days and abstain from sexual relations. Why the holy terror? Because they were frail human beings. Apparently they hadn't followed orders. Perhaps it was that Moses commanded them to forego sex, making it irresistible, like forbidden fruit. In any case, the trembling people fell back and said to

Moses, "You go up the mountain alone." And they stood afar off while Moses drew near to the loud roar and thick darkness of God's presence. Once again, God's infinite respect for human freedom was manifest: if Israel won't accept the gift of his presence, they must learn how to live with his distance, or else face the accursed prospect of his absence. The fact is, Israel wanted God, but on their own terms: at a safe distance.

A wise man once defined diplomacy as the art of letting someone else have your own way—which makes God the consummate diplomat. He would not abandon his children; he only backed as far away as Israel thought safe. As a wise and loving Father, he gave them only what they were ready and willing to receive. In effect, he gave them what *they* thought was necessary—to keep them open to eventually receive what he knew they really needed.

Israel Must Be Sworn Again

The next four chapters (see Ex 20-23) reveal what is basically a household code for Israel to live as God's family. These laws were primarily given to govern relationships within this growing national household: how to resolve disputes, how to deal with slaves, how to treat acts of violence, how to make restitution for theft or property damage, how to handle any other breach of trust and how to relate to God and human authority.

Having made his expectations clear, the Father then entered into a solemn and sacred bond with Israel; we call it the Sinai covenant (see Ex 24:1-11). First, he had the people sacrifice burnt offerings and peace offerings to the Lord. Next Moses took the blood from the sacrifices and used it as the ritual sign of the covenant oath which bound Israel to God:

And Moses took half of the blood and put it in basins, and half of the blood he threw against the altar. Then he took the book of the covenant, and read it in the hearing of the people; and they said, "All that the Lord has spoken we will do, and we will be obedient." And Moses took the blood and threw it upon the people, and said, "Behold the blood of the covenant which the Lord has made with you in accordance with all these words."

EXODUS 24:6-8

According to the ancient Hebrew outlook, the symbolic meaning of the blood-sprinkling upon both altar and people was twofold: positively, it symbolized the blood covenant between God and Israel; negatively, the shed blood signified a solemn curse that Israel placed itself under by swearing the covenant oath. Through this ritual, in effect, Israel declared to God, "Amen, we will share family life with you; you will be our Father, we will be your sons—or else we'll be damned!"[2]

At the Father's invitation, Moses then accompanied Aaron, Nadab, Abihu and the seventy elders up the mountain. Despite the sin of the people, Scripture says that the Lord didn't raise his hand against these leaders as they saw God and ate and drank before him (see Ex 24:10).

From the ancient Hebrew perspective, covenant meals like this conveyed a twofold symbolic meaning: of the intimate family ties between covenant parties, and the awesome responsibilities that both parties assumed.[3] The meal was a sign of the covenant blessing of communion, while the sacrificial victims signified the covenant curse that would befall Israel if they went back on their sworn oath. A similar twofold meaning is also present in the Holy Eucharist, which Jesus instituted to be the sign of the New Covenant—as both a sacrifice and a meal—which the Passover and the Sinai covenant ritual both foreshadow (see 1 Cor 10:1-22; 11:26-32).

The message at Sinai was clear: Throughout all of Israel, God wanted every tent to be a tabernacle, every hearth an altar, every father a priest, every firstborn son a deacon, and every family a domestic church. And the nation was to be a kingdom of priests ...if only they would forsake the idols of Egypt and place their wholehearted trust in God.[4]

Moses' Fast Action

After partaking of this ritual meal with the elders, Moses ascended the mountain again, this time to fast for forty days and forty nights. There the Father spoke to Moses about many important family matters.

The ark, the tabernacle and the altar were to be built according to precise specifications. Aaron was to be consecrated for the priesthood and provided with priestly garments rich with symbolic meaning. Whenever a census of the people was taken, they were to make a sacrifice to the Lord of their valuables. The importance of keeping the Sabbath was underscored as a sign of Israel's special relationship with God. At the end of his extended fast, Moses received the two tablets of the testimony, tablets of stone, inscribed by the finger of God.

Unfortunately, things weren't going so well at the foot of the mountain. Impatient with Moses' delay, the Israelites took matters into their own hands. They besieged Aaron with an urgent request: "Up, make us gods who will go before us. As for this fellow Moses who brought us up out of the land of Egypt, we don't know what's become of him" (see Ex 32:1).

Notice that it was no longer *God* who had brought them out, but *Moses!* And the people were all too ready to cast their erstwhile leader aside. Not to worry.

Moses had left his brother to cover for him. Surely Aaron would rebuke these unruly ingrates, right?

Wrong.

Can you imagine standing against hundreds of thousands of determined idol worshipers? Maybe Aaron thought he could somehow pull this one out of the fire if he just went along with the crowd. Sometimes it's easier to be a lemming than a leader.

Whatever thoughts raced through his mind, Aaron instructed the people to bring all their fine jewelry. Then he proceeded to melt the gold and fashion an idol in the shape of a bull calf, just like the idol worshiped in the form of a bull calf by the Apis cult in Egypt. It also was just like the bullocks Moses had required Israel to sacrifice—and eat—a short time ago. So much for renouncing the idols of Egypt.

At one level, it's hard to understand how Israel could have reverted so quickly. Yet at another level it shouldn't be that difficult. Think about it. How do you explain the powerful fascination people have always had with gold, from ancient times to the present? Gold is a timeless symbol of wealth and beauty. And what about the sign value of the bull calf? Even today we can see it as a sign connoting youthful power and sexual virility. If you put it all together, what do you get? In effect, Israel reverted to the idols of money, sex and power—in their Egyptian form.

The people were delighted. They proclaimed, "These are your gods, O Israel, who brought you up out of the land of Egypt!" (Ex 32:4). So Aaron built an altar in front of the calf and announced that a festival would be held the next day in honor of Yahweh (see v. 6). (Notice the slight shift in Aaron's words as to which god was to be worshiped.)

The next day Israel rose early to sacrifice burnt offerings and present peace offerings to their idol. Then they sat down to eat and drink and "rose up to play." The last phrase is a Hebrew euphemism for the impure behavior associated with ancient fertility cults, namely a sexual orgy such as the Egyptians had while worshiping their bull idol, Apis.

We sometimes dismiss the insidious evil of the golden calf, as if it were some innocent plaything of the moment or else an unfortunate lapse to which this ancient people were somehow more prone. But this graven image represented nothing less than Israel's total betrayal of Yahweh and their return to the idols of Egypt. What the forbidden fruit was for Adam, the golden calf was for Israel: a fall from grace, an act of covenant apostasy.[5]

We wonder how they could have done such a thing, especially after God had just finished doing so much for them. However, it's vital to recall that this was the first time Israel had any direct dealings with an invisible deity, after centuries of living in Egypt—where the gods were (more easily) venerated in visible forms meant to evoke a strong sense of power and fertility. And Moses himself had not been seen for forty days, since vanishing into the fiery cloud atop Sinai. Who was to say whether or not he was even still alive?

Sin Always Complicates Things

But we can't excuse Israel for turning to idols, for God had clearly revealed himself to Israel—again and again. Unfortunately, Israel evidently figured "while the cat's away, the mice will play." And Moses was way out of earshot. But God was not. He said to Moses, "Go down; for *your* people, whom *you* brought up out of the land of Egypt, have corrupted themselves" (Ex 32:7).

Do these words strike you as language somewhat out of character for God? It sounds more like one parent pointing an accusing finger at the other about a disobedient child: "*your* daughter" or "*your* son." God was not dodging blame, however. Rather, he was actually threatening to disown his people.

How could God even imagine doing such a thing? In fact, Israel didn't leave him any choice. God's response was dictated by two factors: an immovable object and an irresistible force.

The immovable object was Israel's hard heart and stubborn will. God calls for a free response of love from his people. He will not force our wills or coerce our hearts. Instead, he always respects our freedom—to an eternal degree—and so abides by our decisions, including the bad ones. Like us, Israel had to learn this lesson the hard way.

The irresistible force was Israel's previously sworn oath. Recall how Israel, by offering—and eating—sacrificial victims in God's presence, placed themselves under a solemn conditional curse that would be necessarily triggered once their oath was violated. Israel had perjured itself, and God could not let it go unpunished.

> I have seen [or witnessed] this people, and behold, it is a stiff-necked people; now therefore let me alone, that my wrath may burn hot against them and I may consume them; but of you I will make a great nation.
>
> EXODUS 32:9-10

Many readers misunderstand God's response. And it certainly does sound erratic, almost explosive, especially for a God who wants to be known as a just judge, not to mention a loving Father.

Some readers might be tempted to resign themselves and piously accept that God can act quite arbitrarily: "After all, he is God, so he can do anything he wants." But that is to miss the point of the covenant almost entirely, which is that God can only *want* what is righteous and good. We'll first look at what was righteous, before considering what was good.

What was righteous here was for God to enforce the oath that Israel had freely and solemnly sworn—and then violated— by fulfilling his role as faithful witness, judge and executor of the covenant. But that spelled Israel's doom; for once they spurned the blessings, they triggered the curses. By invoking God's name, they placed him under the grave obligation to uphold his holy character (which his name signifies) by meting out the curses; otherwise, the covenant would have been invalidated and God's name profaned—by himself.

In considering what goodness called for, we discover how God moved Israel above—but not against—the strict dictates of covenant justice, up to the higher level of his covenant mercy. What this involved was no simple process; sin always complicates things. The legal procedure for renewing Israel's broken covenant—while temporarily suspending their sentence—takes up the rest of Exodus (chapters 33-40), all of Leviticus and the first ten chapters of Numbers! (I'll show mercyby briefly summarizing the three phases of the renewal procedure.)

Blest Be the Bind That Ties

In phase one, Moses is highly exalted as Israel's mediator. Imagine if you were Moses, how would you have responded to God's anger? No doubt his wrathful verdict would have frightened you; but what would you have done with the last part of God's decree: "Then I will make *you* into a great nation" (see Ex 32:10). I don't know about you, but I think I would have been tempted to answer God: "Hey, not bad! You destroy all those scoundrels and start all over again with me. So now it'll be the twelve tribes of ... Moses! You know, God, that definitely has a nicer ring to it: *Moses* instead of *Israel*." After all, Israel had been nothing but trouble for Moses as well as God. Who could blame Moses if he washed his hands of them altogether? But he did nothing of the sort.

Instead, Moses besought the Lord, negotiating on behalf of his wayward brothers and sisters. He started out with a subtle reminder to God that Israel belonged to him, sensitively stated in the form of a question: "O Lord, why does thy wrath burn hot against thy people, whom thou hast brought forth out of the land of Egypt?" (Ex 32:11).

Moses then spoke of the confusing signal that would be sent to Egypt if God destroyed his people: "Why should the Egyptians say, 'With evil intent did he bring them forth, to slay them in the mountain'?" (v. 12). Egypt was also destined to be restored to God's family. But how could God's younger sons (the heathen nations) ever learn to trust their Father once they saw him slay their oldest brother (Israel), especially if they knew God destroyed him for acting like them?

Finally, Moses laid down trump by recalling the covenant oath God himself had previously sworn—four centuries earlier—to bless the nations of the world through the "seed" of Abraham, Isaac and Israel (see v. 13; Gn 22:16-18). How would it look if God executed the curse that would destroy the very "seed" he himself swore to bless, causing him to violate his own oath?

Now it may appear on the surface that Moses got the better of God in this exchange, especially since the next verse states, "And the Lord repented of the evil which he thought to do to his people" (v. 14). However, before concluding that God somehow got himself stuck in a "Catch 22" situation, we might consider the possibility that a deeper rationale may have underwritten God's dealings with Moses. God the Father is not fickle but faithful, wise and merciful—especially when it comes to meeting the needs of his children and in fashioning the mind and heart of their mediator.

Moses, a Christlike Mediator

Here's what I think the narrative is driving at: Moses did not really change God's mind; rather, it was God who changed the mind—and heart—of Moses! After all, God knows the future. He must have foreseen Israel's idolatry at Sinai and the potential problem it might pose for the fulfillment of his covenant plan for them and the nations. What better way to forestall Israel's self-destruction than for God to bind himself to them—by means of his covenant oath to their forefathers—even before they came into existence? This pattern of fatherly foresight and merciful ingenuity is the trademark of God's covenant dealings throughout salvation history.

The net effect of God's faithfulness can be seen in Moses, who was transformed by this exchange to a new level of Christlike mediation. This is evident in his astonishing plea to God:

> Alas, this people have sinned a great sin; they made for themselves gods of gold. But now, if thou wilt forgive their sin—and if not, blot me, I pray thee, out of thy book which thou has written.
>
> EXODUS 32:31-32

He was willing to become accursed for the sake of his brethren! Through the negotiation process, then, Moses not only discovered the saving power of God's covenant oath and the firmness of his commitment to bless Israel and the nations; even more, he came to share the very essence of the Father's self-giving love. (In fact, several other important parallels between Moses and Jesus are to be found in the biblical narrative, as we'll see.)

The elevation of Moses to a higher level of mediation didn't come without personal cost, however, as a careful reading of the next chapter shows. After the calf incident, but before the renewal process got under way, Moses enjoyed the unique (but short-lived) privilege of entering his own tent—at any time—and conversing with God "face-to-face, as a man speaks to his friend" (Ex 33:7-11).

A few verses later, God withdrew the privilege, when he

declared to Moses, "You cannot see my face ... and live" (v. 20). Instead, Moses had to hide behind a rock, where he was allowed to catch a glimpse of the tail end of God's glory only after it passed by (see vv. 21-23).

Why did God suddenly revoke the privilege he had granted Moses earlier in the same chapter? What caused God to reverse himself, by refusing to allow Moses to see his face?

Rock of Ages, Cleft for Moses

The clue for solving this mystery may be buried within the intervening section (see vv. 12-19), which recounts a curious exchange between God and Moses, where they jockeyed back and forth over their mutual relationship with Israel. Moses began by reminding God of his many past favors, and then closed with a strategic remark, meant as a subtle reminder to God about Israel still being his people:

> Moses said to the Lord, "You, indeed, are telling me to lead this people on; but you have not let me know whom you will send with me. Yet you have said, 'You are my intimate friend,' and also, 'You have found favor with me.' Now if I have found favor let me know your ways so that in knowing you, I may continue to find favor with you; and consider too, that this nation is, after all, your own people."
>
> EXODUS 33:12-13, NAB

Did you catch that last line? Apparently God did too, because he aimed his reply exclusively at Moses: "My presence will go before you, and I will give you rest" (v. 14).

Both times that God addressed Moses as "you," he used the second person singular, as if God's "presence" and "rest" were promised only to Moses, not Israel. It is clear that Moses took it that way from the deliberate shift in his counterproposal:

Moses replied, "If thy presence will not go with *me*, do not carry *us* up from here. For how shall it be known that *I* have found favor in your sight, *I and thy people*? Is it not in thy going with *us.... I and thy people?*"

EXODUS 33:15-16

Moses was not about to budge—not until God saw just how intent he was on reconciling the two estranged parties, God and Israel. As a mediator, Moses identified himself inseparably with his own people and called on God to do the same. And in fact God did: "The Lord said to Moses, 'This very thing that you have spoken I will do; for you have found favor in my sight'" (v. 18).

Moses had risked everything, including his own friendship with God. But he got his one request. Now Moses just wanted to find out what it would cost. That's when the Father turned down his other request—to see his face again. Moses was too closely united to sinful Israel to enjoy that privilege any longer. And Moses, like Christ, accepted that loss and humiliation—for the sake of sinners—without complaint.

Mercy Me!

Did Moses end up with less intimacy with God than when he started? It might look that way, judging from his apparent loss of face-to-face access with Yahweh. Upon closer examination, however, the narrative may lead us to the opposite conclusion.

Before the collective bargaining session had begun, Moses was able to enjoy very close encounters with God on a regular basis—he beheld Yahweh with his own eyes. But whatever natural capacity

Moses possessed that enabled him to see the glory of God physically manifest, still it was just that, a *natural* capacity. And that is all that he lost.

In exchange, Moses was ordered to hide his face "in the cleft of the rock," so that the Lord could pass by and proclaim his name (see Ex 33:17-23): "I will be gracious to whom I will be gracious, and will show mercy on whom I will show mercy" (v. 19). So "Grace and Mercy" are God's very name, his own identity. According to St. Thomas Aquinas, divine grace and mercy combine to form the single greatest attribute of God.

Thus, the Lord more than compensated Moses for whatever he lost by way of a natural vision of divine glory; for in return, Moses received a far greater revelation of God's supernatural glory, as it is revealed in his covenant grace and mercy. This is the deepest and most glorious mystery of all, unknowable by the human mind and invisible to the natural eye. It is the essence of God's inner life and the heart of the covenant. We may be sure, then, that Moses came out a winner that day, not a loser; for he gained much more than he lost, infinitely more.

Substitute Teachers: The Priestly Caste of Levi

In phase two of the covenant renewal process, the Levites assumed the Israelite priesthood, replacing the firstborn sons from all of the other tribes.

Having spent forty days and nights in the presence of the Holy One of Israel, Moses descended Mount Sinai and went into action. Carrying the two stone tablets of the law, Moses came near the camp and beheld the graven idol, along with the immoral revelry, and his anger burned hot. He smashed the stone tablets into pebbles against the foot of the mountain—symbolic of what the people had in fact done to the covenant by their rebellion. Then he burned the golden calf, ground it into powder, scattered it upon the water and made the people of Israel drink it. So much for worldly wealth!

Moses demanded an explanation from his brother Aaron, who had brought this great sin upon Israel. Aaron sounded a lot like Adam. *Who, me? It's all their fault.* "You know that this people is set on sin," he whined. "When they demanded gods to go before them, I asked for their gold jewelry. I threw it into the fire, and out came this calf" (see Ex 32:22-24). Aaron spoke as if the graven image had jumped out of the fire by itself, fully formed!

A Loud and Guilty Silence

Moses stood in the gate of the camp, calling for volunteers to stand with him: "Whoever is for the Lord, let him come to me" (Ex 32:26).

You would think that the firstborn sons would be the first to say, "Count us in. After all, we'd be dead if God hadn't been on our side in Egypt. He was the one who gave us the Passover lamb, by whose blood we were redeemed—and consecrated to priestly service." Yet they were conspicuously quiet—a loud and guilty silence.

In any case, it was actually the Levites who said to Moses, their fellow tribesman, "We are on the Lord's side" (see v. 26).

Being on the Lord's side carried a heavy price. Moses commanded every man to take his sword and go through the camp. "Slay every man his brother, and every man his companion, and every man his neighbor" (v. 27). In one day the sons of Levi slew about three thousand Israelite kinsmen.

Then Moses said to the tribe of Levi, "Today you have ordained yourselves for the service of the Lord, each one at the cost of his son and of his brother, that he might bestow a blessing upon you this day" (vv. 29).

That blessing turned out to be the priestly ministry that the firstborn sons had formerly exercised—by virtue of their natural birthright and their consecration through the blood of the Passover lambs, which had redeemed them in Egypt (see Ex 13:2).

Israel Comes to Its Census

The first four chapters of Numbers clarify the nature and significance of this transfer of priestly authority. There we find an elaborate description of the complex threefold census that Moses took of Israel at Sinai right after the golden calf incident: first, every male was counted from among all the twelve tribes, excluding Levi (see Nm 1:47-49); second, all the Levite males old enough for priestly service were numbered (see Nm 3:14-39); third, all the firstborn sons from the other twelve tribes were counted—and replaced by the Levites: "Take the Levites instead of all the firstborn among the people of Israel" (v. 45).

The other tribes were thereby instantly and systematically defrocked and laicized, dispensed from the priesthood. In truth, they had repudiated that priesthood in favor of old-fashioned lust for money, sex and power.

In worshiping the golden calf, the Israelites once again pledged their allegiance to the Egyptian idolatry they had been brought out of. They chose the lesser goods of this world rather than the highest good offered by God—the gift of himself to his people in covenant communion forever.

A Sworded Affair

Perhaps we wonder why the Levites were allowed—much less ordered—to take up the sword against their own kinsmen. Or why God would bless them for doing so. Once again, the inner logic of the covenant is the key. Israel had solemnly sworn an oath to do God's will, voluntarily placing themselves under a curse of death, which now dangled over their heads—like the sword of Damocles that hung by a hair.

By worshiping the golden calf, Israel committed a heinous crime, a desecrating sacrilege, an act of covenant apostasy that profaned the holy name of God and released the dreaded curses. By ordering the Levites to slay with the sword, Moses called Israel to account for spurning the holy God of the universe. In wielding their swords, the Levites began the process of administering the curse that Israel had freely put itself under. For holding their Heavenly Father in contempt, Israel could not go unpunished—or else the seeds of terrible confusion would have been sown. God does not spoil his children; nor does he misinform them. "Do not be deceived. God is not mocked; for whatever a man sows, that he will also reap" (Gal 6:7).

So the Levites became the sole priests in Israel, replacing the firstborn sons from all the other tribes. Why had they been granted such a privilege? Because of their burning zeal for the glory of God, zeal that enabled them to choose the Father above their human blood relatives.

Idol Time for Sacrifice

In phase three of the renewal procedure, God mandated the newly ordained Levites to offer animal sacrifices on a periodic basis in the tabernacle on behalf of the other tribes of Israel.

Before the golden calf incident, daily animal sacrifice was nowhere commanded. Instead, the biblical narrative describes it as a discretionary activity. So those Israelites who wished to make votive offerings to God could do so for whatever reasons they might have: adoration, contrition, thanksgiving, petition. Only *after* the golden calf incident (following the priestly installation of Aaron and the Levites) did God require Israel to offer animal sacrifice on a continuous basis, as set forth in gory detail in Leviticus. The sacrificial slaughter of cattle, sheep and goats then became an everyday ritual.[6]

Why the dramatic shift?

A friend of mine is a recovering alcoholic who sees himself as having been held in bondage for years by the power of drink. And he did not experience instant freedom by rising one morning and smashing his bottle of Jack Daniels in the sink. That would not have been enough. Like so many others, the only way he beat his addiction was by finally admitting that it was beating him and that he could not conquer it alone. Even then, one simple heartfelt prayer of renunciation didn't suffice. As he says, he had to learn to "let go and let God," and not just once but over and over again. Now he realizes that he can only maintain real freedom by taking one day at a time, which he's done now for almost two decades.

For a similar reason, Israel was commanded to offer daily sacrifices. After centuries of living in Egypt, as we've seen, God knew that Israel was hopelessly ensnared in the idolatrous ways of their host country. Even after the plagues "took out" their false gods, the Father saw that Israel was still holding on.

And I said to them, Cast away the detestable things your eyes feast on ... and do not defile yourselves with the idols of Egypt; I am the Lord your God. But they rebelled against me and would not listen to me.... So I led them out of the land of Egypt and brought them into the wilderness. I gave them my statutes and showed them my ordinances, by whose obser-vance man shall live.... But the house of Israel rebelled against me in the wilderness.

EZEKIEL 20:7-8, 10-13

For the Israelites, like my friend, true freedom had to come the hard way. It wasn't enough for them to make a one-time offering at Sinai (see Ex 24:3-11) by slaughtering the animals the Egyptians venerated as gods (see Ex 8:26), as though a single sacrifice would suffice to excise the malignant cancer of idolatry from Israel. With the golden calf it became painfully clear, at least to God and Moses, that something far more radical was needed to cut out this defiling disease.

But was the patient ready to undergo such radical surgery? After centuries of Egyptian slavery and idolatry, would Israel even be able to survive the procedure? Judging from the biblical narrative, and the three phases of the covenant renewal process that we've been summarizing, God's answer was No, not yet. The Great Physician decided to postpone surgery—for over four-teen centuries, to be exact—until "the fullness of time" when "God sent forth his Son ... born under the law" (Gal 4:4), that is, under its "curse" (see Gal 3:10), which Christ alone could bear redemptively.

In the meantime, Israel was placed on life support, so to speak, an image that truly captures the basic purpose and design of the covenant renewal procedure of ritual sacrifices that God mercifully instituted through Moses, Aaron and the Levites. They were responsible to look after Israel's spiritual needs, which required regular reminders of Israel's accursed condition.

Once again, God showed Israel his fatherly foresight and merci-ful ingenuity. By a holy mixture of justice and goodness, God elected certain figures to bear Israel's curse *symbolically*, until he sent the One who was both willing and worthy to bear it *redemp-*

tively. (This idea is also developed in detail in Hebrews 5-10, where Christ's curse-bearing death renews Israel's broken covenant, while his self-offering represents the sacrifice that fulfills the vocation that Israel spurned, to serve the nations as God's royal-priestly firstborn Son.)

In effect, the Father was challenging his children: "I want to set you free from all your earthly addictions. But you keep going back." We know that the Israelites didn't turn around and physically march back into Egypt, but they did return to Egypt's corrupt religious practices. Therefore, the Israelites had to fight a protracted war against idolatry, which they were commanded now to wage by daily animal sacrifice, among other things.

Within the Father's remedial program lay a subtle strategy. On the one hand, Israel couldn't slaughter—or eat—the animals that the Egyptians sacrificed to their gods; they were declared unclean. On the other hand, Israel had to slaughter and eat the animals that the Egyptians venerated but never sacrificed; they were clean. A good explanation of God's purpose was offered by Moses Maimonides, arguably the greatest rabbi in Jewish history:

> The very act which was considered by the heathen [Egypt] as the greatest crime, became the means of approaching God and obtaining pardon for sins.... The very act which was then considered as being the cause of death would become the cause of our deliverance from death.[7]

I find this perspective to be very helpful. It explains why God commanded the ritual slaughter of hundreds and thousands of cattle, sheep and goats for so many centuries. This particular type of animal sacrifice was a continual reminder to the Israelites that their former ways of idolatry would never be their means to redemption. As a wise and loving Father, God had designed the perfect punishment for Israel, one that would not only fit their crime but cure it. God's strategy was subtle but profound, ironic yet effective.

There was also a deeper purpose for the animal sacrifices, one that points beyond the rehabilitation of Israel from idolatry to the redemption of the world from sin by the sacrificial self-offering of Christ. This is what all the sacrifices were meant to prefigure. To renounce idolatry is not the same as to remove sin, much less to replace it with righteousness. Animal sacrifices could effect the former but not the latter. Therefore, only after the self-offering of Jesus, and the outpouring of the Holy Spirit, could the sacrifice of animals cease.

Beloved Backsliders:
Israel in the Wilderness

As a result of the golden calf episode, Israel was detained at Sinai for an entire year. Most of that time was spent going through the complicated process of renewing the broken covenant. First, God had to give Moses a new body of adjusted ritual laws, statutes and ordinances (see Ex 34). Moses then had to teach them to Aaron, in order to get the high priesthood up and running in the newly erected tabernacle (see Ex 35-40). Next, the Levites had to be trained in their new official priestly duties (see Lv 1-16). They in turn had to show the twelve lay tribes—the ten trives descended from the sons of Jacob, plus the tribes of Ephraim and Manasseh—their new path of holiness (see Lv 17-26). Finally, the national census was taken, and the twelve tribes of Israel assumed their places around the tabernacle, which was now surrounded—and cordoned off—by four Levitical clans (see Nm 1-10). No wonder a whole year was needed: "For when there is a change of the priesthood, there is necessarily a change of the law" (Heb 7:12).

This multilayered pyramid represented a new bureaucratic structure for Israel, a bicovenantal order of mediation between God, the clergy and the laity: Moses was God's mediator for Aaron and the Levites; Aaron and the Levites served as Moses' mediator for the twelve tribes. And Israel was still expected to mediate God to the nations.

Talk about complexity. Perhaps this is what Paul had in mind when he asked, "Why then the law? It was added because of transgressions, till the offspring [Christ] should come" (Gal 3:19). In any case, God and Moses both had their hands full.

Aaron: Israel's Altar Ego

After breaking camp at Sinai, Israel spent the next couple of weeks marching across the desert, headed straight for Canaan. It wasn't long, however, before Israel's new order underwent a series of severe trials, starting close to the top with Aaron and working all the way down through the various layers of authority.

It must not have been easy for Aaron to follow his younger brother, Moses. But orders are orders, especially when they're issued by God Almighty. So you'd think that Aaron would do his best to stay in line, right? Wrong.

A few days into the journey to Canaan, Aaron had a bone to pick with Moses (see Nm 12:1-16), and so did Moses' older sister, Miriam, who was probably the one who kept watch over the ark of bulrushes that carried Moses as a fugitive infant on the Nile (see Ex 2:4). Ostensibly, they were both miffed at Moses for his bad choice of a wife, since he had married a Cushite (probably a black Ethiopian) during the desert years he lived in Midian, before the Exodus. It's funny how the private family matters of political leaders always seem to spill over into the public eye, just as they often tend to mask deeper currents of discontent.

It was no different with Aaron and Miriam, who went on to expose their own repressed feelings of sibling rivalry:

Miriam and Aaron spoke against Moses because of the Cushite woman whom he had married ... and they said, "Has the Lord indeed spoken only through Moses? Has he not spoken through us also?"

NUMBERS 12:1-2

Silent in the face of his detractors, Moses' measured response was a study in meekness and a summons to God for vindication, which he enacted—against Miriam especially—with fitting irony:

> The Lord came down in a pillar of cloud ... and called Aaron and Miriam; and they both came forward. And he said, "Hear my words: If there is a prophet among you, I the Lord make myself known to him in a vision.... Not so with my servant Moses; he is entrusted with all my house. With him I speak mouth to mouth, clearly, and not in dark speech.... Why then were you not afraid to speak against my servant Moses?" And the anger of the Lord was kindled against them, and he departed; and when the cloud withdrew from the tent, behold, Miriam was leprous, as white as snow.
>
> Numbers 12:5-10

God's punishment declared to Miriam, in effect, "So you're put off by your younger brother's interracial marriage? What is it, you don't like black skin? Then you can have the whitest skin around, as white as snow." The leprosy was also a sign of the defiling force of their dissent, which was carefully couched in pious terms, but which only masked their own rivalrous envy.

Aaron repented in the humblest possible way, addressing his younger brother: "Oh, my lord ... we have done foolishly and have sinned" (v. 11). After Moses prayed for his siblings, they were both forgiven, and Miriam was healed (vv. 13-15).

Having learned his lesson the hard way, Aaron found himself standing with Moses—on the receiving end—the next time around. They both soon discovered just how contagious the revolutionary spirit of dissent can be. Rather predictably, it spread to the next level down on Israel's hierarchical pyramid.

Rebel Princes Get Just Desert

In the next chapter, Moses chose twelve chief princes, one "from each tribe ... every one a leader" (Nm 13:2). Then he sent them as spies into the Promised Land in order to develop a strategy for invading Canaan (vv. 17-20). As the top leaders of Israel, they were presumably selected as military commanders for the purpose of leading twelve tribal divisions into battle. But upon returning from their spy mission, what ten of them did was worse than dodging the draft, or burning their draft cards.

They utterly demoralized Israel with an "evil report," which described their enemies as giants who lived in "a land that devours its inhabitants" (v. 32). Not surprisingly, the people followed the ten spies and their counsel of despair.

All the people of Israel murmured against Moses and Aaron; the whole congregation said to them, "Would that we had died in the land of Egypt! Or would that we had died in this wilderness! Why does the Lord bring us into this land, to fall by the sword? Our wives and our little ones will become a prey; would it not be better for us to go back to Egypt?"

NUMBERS 14:2-3

Their ingratitude and unbelief would end up costing them dearly. Once again, Moses played trump by reminding God of his oath to the patriarchs, and so won divine pardon for Israel (see vv. 13-20). But a father's forgiveness never precludes a proper punishment, so God handed Israel a stiff penance along with his pardon.

The Father's penalty was severe yet just. Once again, he showed his infinite respect for human freedom by taking Israel totally at its word, which he matched with an oath of his own: "As I live," says the Lord, "what you have said in my hearing I will do to you: your dead bodies shall fall in this wilderness" (vv. 28-29). The other part of the verdict was just as fitting: Israel would wander in the wilderness forty years—corresponding to the forty days that the spies were in Canaan—until the last adult perished, except the courageous spies, Caleb and Joshua. God then had Moses stipulate several new penitential rituals to act as a ceremonial memorial of Israel's sin and their Father's mercy (see Nm 15:1-41).

Korah, the Rebel Priest: He Dissented Into Hades

Dissent kept spreading infectiously downward, until one of the Levitical leaders named Korah caught an unusually virulent strain. He transmitted it to Dathan and Abiram, two rebels from Reuben (the disenfranchised firstborn tribe of Israel, named for their ancestor, the oldest son of Jacob-Israel), and finally to "two hundred and fifty leaders of the congregation, chosen from the assembly, well-known men" (Nm 16:2). We read how all of them masked their envy with the same kind of pious rhetoric as the previous dissenters:

> They assembled themselves together against Moses and against Aaron, and said to them, "You have gone too far! For all the congregation are holy, every one of them, and the Lord is among them; why then do you exalt yourselves above the assembly of the Lord?"

> NUMBERS 16:3

Sound familiar? Like so many modern-day rebels, they insisted that their revolution was launched in the name of "the people," for democracy's sake, and for liberty, equality and fraternity. Korah and company were out to politicize the family of God. So they denounced the distinction between clergy and laity as an unjust imposition of an ecclesiastical hierarchy "out of touch" with the people.

As the shepherd elected by God to guard his beloved sheep, Moses saw right through the sanctimonious smoke screen put up by these dissenting Levites, egalitarian wolves in sheep's clothing. And he wasted neither time nor energy:

> When Moses heard it, he fell on his face; and he said to Korah and all his company, "In the morning the Lord will show who is his, and who is holy...." And Moses said to Korah, "Hear now, you sons of Levi: is it too small a thing for you that the God of Israel has separated you from the congregation of Israel ... to do service in the tabernacle of the Lord, and to stand before the congregation to minister to them.... And would you seek the priesthood also? Therefore it is against the Lord that you and all your company have gathered together."
>
> NUMBERS 16:4-11

True to form, the men turned up their revolutionary rhetoric and inflammatory innuendo against Moses: "We will not come up. Is it a small thing that you have brought us up out of a land flowing with milk and honey, to kill us in the wilderness, that you must also make yourself a prince over us?" (vv. 12-13).

Can you believe it? Korah spoke as if Egypt was really the Promised Land for Israel, and so the Exodus became some sort of Mosaic murder plot. The mind boggles at such brazen arrogance.

But what is even more mind-boggling is that the people fell for it. God had to order Moses, "Say to the congregation, Get away from about the dwelling of Korah, Dathan, and Abiram" (v. 23). What supposedly started as a sincere protest movement was now being fanned into the flames of a full-blown revolution that threatened to consume many simple but confused people. For

God and Moses, it was time to take action. They had to "fight fire with fire," now or never.

> Moses said, "Hereby you shall know that the Lord has sent me to do all these works, and that it has not been of my own accord. If these men die the common death of all men ... then the Lord has not sent me. But if the Lord creates something new, and the ground opens its mouth, and swallows them up, with all that belongs to them, and they go down alive into Sheol, then you will know that these men have despised the Lord." And as he finished speaking all these words, the ground under them split asunder; and the earth opened its mouth and swallowed them up.... And fire came forth from the Lord, and consumed the two hundred and fifty men.
>
> NUMBERS 16:28-35

Surely that must have settled the matter, right? Wrong again. With infectious dissent now spreading among the people, Moses and Aaron found themselves confronted by an angry mob, and accused by members of the "people's church": "You have killed the people of the Lord" (v. 41). One plague and 14,700 victims later, could it be that Israel had still not learned its lesson?

Operation Desert Storm:
Moab's Campaign Against Israel

After forty long years, the first generation had died off, except for Moses and the two courageous spies, Joshua and Caleb. During this time, the second generation was being taught by their Levitical tutors and hopefully rehabilitated from the sinful ways of their parents. But patterns of bad behavior die hard, especially when they're transmitted from parent to child; so the outcome of their probationary period remained something of an unanswered question: Would the second generation succeed where the first had failed?

Israel finally reached the eastern border of the Promised Land on the plains of Moab. This was to be the place where God put the second generation to the test, just as he had done with the first at Sinai. They didn't know it, but the entire future of Israel was hanging in the balance.

Things looked good at first. The initial test consisted of a series of attempts made by a mercenary prophet named Balaam, hired by the prince of Moab, to place the people of Israel under a solemn curse in the name of God. But all four times he tried to curse them, he wound up blessing them instead (see Nm 22-24). God's blessing was simply too strong to be overcome by sorcery. So Israel passed the initial test with flying colors. But what else would you expect? A false prophet's curse was no match for the power of the Father's sworn blessing. Israel was safe under God's protection.

There was a very important lesson to be learned from this sign, if only Israel had eyes to see. But they became blinded by pride; taking credit for Balaam's failure, they imagined that they were invincible and set themselves up like bowling pins. As Scripture says, "Pride goes before destruction" (Prv 16:18).

Before packing up and heading out, Balaam decided he'd try once more; only this time he'd use a totally different strategy. His advice was quite simple: If you can't beat them, join them— or rather, join them to your own pretty daughters who are cult prostitutes in the idolatrous service of Baal-Peor (see Nm 31:16). And so they did (see Nm 25:1-9). Who can guess what happened?

To make a long (and sordid) story short, the second generation fell into idolatry at Beth-peor about as hard as their parents did at Sinai. Only one thing was different: the Levites didn't lift a finger. In fact, nobody did, except for Phinehas, and he lifted more than a finger:

> Behold, one of the people of Israel came and brought a Midianite woman to his family ... in the sight of the whole congregation.... When Phinehas the son of Eleazar, son of Aaron the priest, saw it, he rose and left the congregation, and took a spear in his hand and went after the man ... into the inner room, and pierced both of them ... through her body.
>
> NUMBERS 25:6-8

Shades of Sinai! This time around, however, only one Levite, Phinehas, received the blessing. But what a blessing he got:

> The Lord said to Moses, "Phinehas ... has turned back my wrath from the people of Israel, in that he was jealous with my jealousy among them, so that I did not consume the people of Israel in my jealousy. Therefore say, 'Behold, I give to him my covenant of peace; and it shall be to him, and to his descendants ... the covenant of a perpetual priesthood.'"
>
> NUMBERS 25:10-13

Perhaps Phinehas is not exactly our idea of a pastoral priest, but, no matter, the blessing of the official high priesthood was now destined to be (eventually) established in Phinehas' line.

What the golden calf incident was to the first generation at Sinai, the Baal-Peor episode was to the second on the plains of Moab. Both events involved the worship of idols and sexual immorality. While the Levites received a share of the priestly blessing for their avenging action, Phinehas was awarded an even greater blessing for his, in the office of the high priesthood.

But what changes were effected by the second generation's act of apostasy? And how would those changes affect the shape of

Israel's covenant with God in the future? Both questions were answered when Moses ratified the Deuteronomic covenant.

Raising a Rebel Son With a Strong Will

Moses knew it was his time to go the way of all flesh. But what a hard way to go out, having just witnessed his last forty years of labor seemingly undone by the idolatry of Israel with Baal-Peor. What was left for him to do now, except to sit down and dictate his last will and testament? So he did. We call it Deuteronomy (see Dt 31-33).

Deuteronomy is to the five books of Moses what John is to the four Gospels: the last, yet deepest. All we can give here is a brief summary of its multifaceted character: as testament, treaty, constitution, probation, prescription and prophecy.

Deuteronomy reads like the final legacy of Moses, his last will and testament, but with an interesting twist. The overall structure of Deuteronomy reflects the ancient literary form of the treaty-covenants commonly used by the Hittites (and others) in the second millennium B.C. Besides the similar literary form, there are other curious parallels. For one thing, these ancient treaty-covenants were imposed by kings (or suzerains) upon their potentially rebellious colonies (or vassals), usually by placing the inferior party under sworn oath-curses, as God had Moses do with Israel (see Dt 27-28). Another parallel is that suzerains and vassals *always* addressed each other as father and son (e.g., "I am your servant and son," "I am your king and father"), as God does with Israel in Deuteronomy (see Dt 8:5; 14:1; 32:5-6, 19-20).

Why is this so important? Because it shows how Deuteronomy served as the covenant rule for regulating God's rebellious son, Israel, and its national constitution ("the book of the Torah"), which is how it functioned for centuries, until Jesus' coming.[1]

Deuteronomy also served to validate Joshua as Moses' official successor and the secular head of state (see Dt 31:7-23; 34:9-12); just as it subordinated him to Phinehas, the high priest over the Levites and spiritual head of Israel.

The covenant of Deuteronomy must be distinguished from the Sinai covenant, at least in some sense. Deuteronomy itself makes this clear: "These are the words of the covenant which the Lord commanded Moses to make with the people of Israel in the land of Moab, besides the covenant he made with them at Horeb [Sinai]" (Dt 29:1).

The two covenants were made at different times and places: first at Sinai, then forty years later in Moab; and in distinct ways: God made the one by speaking directly to Israel, while he commanded Moses to make the other. So God appeared to Israel at Sinai in fire and smoke, but was silent and absent at Moab. God had not spoken directly with Israel for forty years, back when many of the second generation were still in diapers.

Since then, they had defiled themselves by worshiping Baal-Peor, a sin that stained the pages of Deuteronomy, "the book of the law," which Moses declared to Israel on the plains of Moab, immediately after—and because of—their apostasy.[2]

After the golden calf incident, Israel deserved to die, as we've seen. Instead, they were placed on probation, as it were, under the strict legal supervision of the Levites, with Moses as the court-appointed guardian and probation officer. After many probationary violations, Israel was resentenced to forty years of detention and hard labor in the desert. At the release date, you might say, a parole hearing was held on the plains of Moab, where it was determined that Israel was not truly rehabilitated. They were found to be—and so were held—in contempt of court. What would you have done if you were Israel's judge and father?

In Deuteronomy God retained many of the original terms of Israel's initial probation. They had to remain under Levitical supervision, while Joshua replaced Moses as Israel's guardian. However, before allowing his son to go free, the judge realized the need to add three new sets of conditions for living at home: legal concessions, ritual stipulations and redemptive curses.[3] These all contain distinctive elements peculiar to Deuteronomy, which were given, for the most part, because of the hardness of Israel's heart (see Mt 19:8).

A Father Who Keeps His (Com)Promises

The first set of conditions came in the form of a series of moral compromises and legal concessions in which Moses permitted such things as divorce and remarriage (see Dt 24:1), foreign slave-wives (see Dt 21:10-14), genocidal warfare against Canaanites (see Dt 20:16-17) and other similar matters. Many of the distinctive laws in Deuteronomy reflect a downward adjustment on God's part to a more realistic level of expectations for sinful Israel. Previously, God had accommodated Israel's sin and weakness in many ways, but without writing it into his holy law. However, since *Moses* had now become Israel's lawgiver, some of the laws stipulated in Deuteronomy might condone certain lesser evils, but without implicating God's justice. Aristotle could have had Moses in mind when he described the wise and prudent lawgiver as one who must be willing to tolerate—and regulate—lesser evils in order to avoid greater ones. In any event, Moses was the one Ezekiel had in mind when the prophet described the Deuteronomic laws that Moses delivered to the second generation:

But the children rebelled against me; they did not walk in my statutes, and were not careful to observe my ordinances, by whose observance man shall live.... Then I thought I would pour out my wrath upon them and spend my anger against them in the wilderness. But I withheld my hand, and acted for the sake of my name, that it should not be profaned in the sight of the nations.... Moreover I gave them statutes that were not good and ordinances by which they could not have life.

EZEKIEL 20:21-25

We will have reason to return shortly to consider what else the prophet Ezekiel had to say about Deuteronomy's laws and rituals.

One of the clear cases of a concessionary Deuteronomic law that is "not good" is the tacit permission given for divorce and remarriage. For one thing, the moral code that God himself gave at Sinai had nothing to say about divorce, much less remarriage. Now for the first time, Deuteronomy tolerated and regulated both (see Dt 24:1-4). As Jesus said: "For your hardness of heart Moses allowed you to divorce your wives, but from the beginning it was not so" (Mt 19:8). Deuteronomy loosened some of the laws concerning polygamy and marriage to foreigners and slave women (or concubines). At the same time, however, priests and Levites had to follow a much stricter marital morality: they were not permitted to marry nonvirgins or divorcees (see Lv 21:7-14; Ez 44:22); nor presumably was divorce and remarriage allowed (see Mal 2:1-16).

Another example would be the contrasting policies against the Canaanites. At Sinai covenants or mixed unions with Canaanites were forbidden (see Ex 23:23-32), whereas in Deuteronomy Moses ordered genocidal warfare (*herem*) be conducted by Israel against their men, women and children (Dt 20:16-17). Jesus addressed this sort of double standard: "You have heard that it was said, 'You shall love your neighbor and hate your enemy.' But I say to you, Love your enemies" (Mt 5:43-44).

Moses Reads Israel Its Rites

The second set of conditions dealt with ritual stipulations requiring the sacrificial offering of firstlings from the herds and flocks (see Dt 15:19-20) at a central sanctuary (see Dt 12:5-18). These laws may be seen as a counterbalance to the first, since the second set served to remind Israel of its call to holiness, though to a lesser degree than the Levites.

Recall how periodic animal sacrifices were only commanded after the golden calf incident. During the forty years in the desert, each time an Israelite family wanted to have some meat with their meal they had to bring the animal(s) to the tabernacle for the Levitical priests to slaughter in ritual sacrifice. No exceptions were made until Israel prepared to enter and settle in the Promised Land, where this law would have been practically impossible to keep.

In Deuteronomy Moses gave permission for Israelites to slaughter animals (nonsacrificially) to be eaten in their lands (see Dt 12:15-24). However, the firstlings of the "clean" animals were to be set apart and then carried annually to the central sanctuary, where the priests would offer them as a holy sacrifice to God. Israel was continuously humbled by God through this constant reminder of their sin and their need for atonement. Once again, Ezekiel seems to have had Deuteronomy's distinctive laws—and peculiar ritual—in mind when he declared: "I gave them statutes that were not good ... and I defiled them through their very gifts in making them offer by fire all their first-born.... I did it that they might know that I am the Lord" (Ez 20:25-26). The purpose of the second set of (ritual) conditions is twofold: It kept Israel from the high places scattered throughout Canaan, where idols were worshiped by means of animal sacrifice. It also offered to Israel a positive way to serve God (and his priests) by bringing their sacrifices to his central sanctuary, that is, the future Jerusalem temple.[4]

(This is related to the "law of the king" [see Dt 17:14-20], which we'll examine in the next chapter.)

The Curse That Cures

The third set of conditions came at the end of Deuteronomy, where Moses solemnly declared with certitude that all the curses of the covenant would inevitably befall Israel at some point in the distant future (see Dt 30:1-10; 31:16-29). Previously, he had placed Israel under the curses conditionally, in a formal oath-swearing ceremony (see Dt 27:1-26). He went on in the next chapter to describe the appalling horror of these curses in graphic detail: disease, defeat, destruction and exile (see Dt 28:15-68).

But wait, didn't Moses announce these terrible things only as hypothetical possibilities? In other words, *if* Israel sins, they'll be cursed; but *if* Israel obeys, they'll be blessed. Right? Not so fast. You've got to keep reading because the next three chapters present the blessings and curses no longer as alternate prospects but as successive realities.

And *when* all these things come upon you, the blessing and the curse, which I have set before you, and you call them to mind among all the nations where the Lord your God has driven you, and return to the Lord your God ... with all your heart and with all your soul; then the Lord your God will restore your fortunes, and have compassion upon you, and he will gather you again from all the peoples where the Lord your God scattered you.

DEUTERONOMY 30:1-3 (emphasis added)

Take note of what follows those fated curses: definitely certain blessings of Israel's future repentance, return and restoration. So the covenant curses were not only punitive but remedial and redemptive.

But after forty years of defiance, how could God be so sure that his son would finally come around? Maybe it was just wishful thinking on God's part. That might be the case, except for one enormous promise that God added just three verses later: "*And the Lord your God will circumcise your heart*... so that you will love the Lord your God with all your heart and with all your soul, that you may live" (Dt 30:6, emphasis added).

What a daring promise, especially in view of the earlier command given to Israel: "Circumcise ... your heart" (Dt 10:16). The shift from the divine command ("You must circumcise") to the divine promise ("I will circumcise") was significant. It underscored the main point of the covenant: God can and must be trusted to meet all of Israel's needs, especially their deepest ones. In particular, it shows that God will have to intervene, decisively and redemptively, for Israel to be delivered from the curses of the Deuteronomic covenant. Israel will be saved, but only by a unilateral act of the Father some time in the future.

Even more than a mixed metaphor, a circumcised heart was a shocking image, no matter how you slice it, so to speak. As a surgical act, circumcision is not meant to be self-administered; how much truer of the interior circumcision of a heart, if such can even be imagined. Besides drawing the implication that God must be the one to do the circumcising, how was Israel meant to interpret the symbolism of the heart needing to be *circumcised*? After all, other verbs could have been used instead of *that* one.

If God has to do something to Israel's heart, why not feed it, cleanse it, strengthen it, enlighten it or clothe it? Why *circumcise* it? Doesn't that seem to indicate Israel's need to be "cut off" at the heart from sin and other carnal attachments? Easier said than done. Such an interior work was something the Father had to do for—and to—his son. Since the Father was also a physician,

Deuteronomy announced just what the doctor had ordered: heart surgery. Deuteronomy showed the patient, Israel, how the prescription was a promise and prophecy, the fulfillment of which would require nothing less than a divine cardiologist.

Ezekiel probably had this part of Deuteronomy in mind when he delivered his most famous and glorious prophetic oracle:

> Thus says the Lord God "… I am about to act … for the sake of my holy name, which you have profaned among the nations to which you came…. The nations will know that I am the Lord, says the Lord God, when through you I vindicate my holiness before their eyes. For I will take you from the nations, and gather you from all the countries, and bring you into your own land. I will sprinkle clean water upon you and you shall be clean from all your uncleannesses, and from all your idols I will cleanse you. *A new heart I will give you,* and a new spirit I will put within you; and *I will take out of your flesh the heart of stone and give you a heart of flesh.* And I will put my spirit within you, and cause you to walk in my statutes…. You shall be my people, and I will be your God."
>
> EZEKIEL 36:22-28 (emphasis added)
> see also ROMANS 2:29; COLOSSIANS 2:11-13

Ezekiel saw a "new Exodus" awaiting Israel in the future. He also saw how the covenant curses in Deuteronomy were intended to serve a redemptive purpose: by delivering the Israelites over to the nations whose gods they worshiped, the Father let his rebel son go his own way, for a time, until he'd come to his senses.

In the meantime, Deuteronomy was the prescribed regimen used to isolate the patient and to inoculate him against any other infections. Israel's subsequent history shows, however, that the quarantine and vaccination never really accomplished their purpose. Nothing less than a heart transplant would do. And that's exactly what Ezekiel announced: "A new heart I will give you.... I will take out of your flesh the heart of stone and give you a heart of flesh" (v. 26).

You might ask: why didn't God just give Israel a new heart from the outset? After all, Moses knew the problem because God had explained it to him. God even ordered Moses to tell Israel: "The Lord has not given you a mind to understand, or eyes to see, or ears to hear" (Dt 29:4). Pray tell, Moses, why not?

The answer is plain: "You do not have, because you do not ask" (Jas 4:2). God would not spoil his children. So he knew better than to impart his gifts to those who didn't ask for them. That would have only encouraged even more ingratitude in Israel. And that was one area where Israel didn't need any help. So why didn't the Israelites ask for a new heart? Because they didn't think they needed one. And that gets to the heart of Israel's problem, so to speak, which was the problem of Israel's heart.

Convincing Israel of their need for a new heart represented the essential purpose behind Deuteronomy. As Augustine states: "The law was given that grace might be sought; grace was given so that the law might be fulfilled."[5] A similar point is made in the Gospel of John: "For the law was given through Moses; grace and truth came through Jesus Christ" (Jn 1:17).

Moses: A Mirror of Christ

This helps us to understand what kind of deity Moses was dealing with. After all, what God would give a command to slay an innocent lamb and sprinkle the blood and then make the people eat the lamb—or else lose your firstborn son to the Destroyer? What kind of God is that?

The same God that we have in Jesus Christ.

In fact, Jesus came as a new Moses. Just as baby Moses was almost slaughtered after birth by imperial edict, so the infant Jesus had to escape Herod's royal decree that all male children under two years of age must die. And where did Joseph and Mary flee for safety? Down into Egypt. Matthew quotes Hosea on the Exodus in saying, "Out of Egypt have I called my son" (see Hos 11:1; Mt 2:15).

If Israel was God's firstborn son, how much more was Jesus Christ. If Israel was brought up out of Egypt, so was Christ. If Israel was delivered through the waters, so Jesus passed through the Jordan River in baptism. Just as Israel was tempted for forty years in the wilderness and Moses fasted forty days on Mount Sinai, so Jesus fasted for forty days in the wilderness.

Moses ascended the mountain to get God's Old Covenant law, whereas Jesus went up the mountain to give the New Covenant law, the Sermon on the Mount. Moses delivered the Ten Commandments to the people, along with curse threats, while Christ gave a law full of God's promised blessings (the Beatitudes). Moses offered himself as a substitute to take away Israel's temporal penalty, while Jesus died on the cross to remove our eternal punishment by reconciling us to the Father and filling us with his Spirit.

Moses fashioned a national church government from twelve chiefs of the twelve tribes, along with the seventy elders. Jesus took twelve disciples and told them they would sit on the twelve thrones and rule the twelve tribes of Israel. He also appointed seventy other disciples to share in his authority (see Lk 10:1-20).

Mere coincidence? Not at all. Jesus saw himself as the new Moses, giving a New Covenant to reconstitute a new Israel. After the feeding of the five thousand, the people cried out, "This is indeed the prophet who is to come into the world" (Jn 6:14).

Only through Christ would the family of God finally be set free from bondage to sin and idolatry. Jesus leads his people out of the bondage of sin just as Moses led the Israelites out of the bondage of Pharaoh in Egypt. Jesus taught his disciples that just as Moses gave their ancestors manna from heaven, so his Father gave them the heavenly manna, the true bread of life. "I am the bread of life; he who comes to me shall not hunger, and he who believes in me shall never thirst" (Jn 6:35).

As for the Passover, Christ is the firstborn Son who is slain. He is also the Lamb without blemish or broken bones, the Lamb who is slaughtered, whose blood is sprinkled and whose body must be eaten (see 1 Cor 5:7). The purpose of our sharing the holy sacrifice of the Eucharist is to unite us as God's family. Our communion is actualized by eating the Passover Lamb of the New Covenant, which we receive every Sunday or, when possible, even every day.

A Lesson for All to Learn

Thanks be to God the Father, who set this glorious plan of salvation into action. When we look back from the vantage point of Christ, we see that the entire Mosaic covenant, starting with the Passover and Exodus and extending through their wanderings in the wilderness up to the plains of Moab, was a powerful preenactment of, and preparation for, the final demonstration of God's mercy in Christ and the Spirit.

Against all odds and by the Father's grace, Moses succeeded in transforming Abraham's tribal family into the national family of God. Through this reluctant leader, the Lord reorganized and cared for his people. Despite their ongoing rebellions in the desert, they were eventually united behind a common purpose: to reclaim the ancestral inheritance that God had promised them.

Again, easier said than done. As we'll see, the nation of Israel had a hard time just finding their way out of the desert. But then all of God's children, to this very day, experience the same struggle to see the promises of God the Father fulfilled in their lives. May God give us the strength and courage to move forward, one step at a time.

"Choose This Day Whom You Will Serve!":
From Conquest to Kingdom

Every parent knows the feeling. Your beautiful little baby is growing and learning to talk. Then suddenly he discovers the word that changes everything: NO!

It may seem cute at first. However, by the hundredth time, which usually occurs by the second day, it's not so enjoyable. In fact, it can get pretty irritating. I recall my own frustration when I was a first-time father. For a toddler, he sounded so willful and defiant. How do you quell domestic revolt?

Later, when our second son started doing the same thing, I realized that it's just a stage of individual assertiveness that most kids pass through. Still, it wasn't easy, until one night at the dinner table.

He wouldn't eat his food, and parental urgings fell upon deaf ears. The wrong words suddenly slipped out of my mouth. "Would you like some applesauce?" He didn't hesitate. Looking up, he bellowed his new favorite word. "NO!"

But this time I was ready. "Would you say No for Daddy?" In a split second, his second "NO!" came back. "Good boy. Can you say No for Daddy again?" This time he hesitated, but said it again. His face told me that he knew something had changed. The tables were turned. After repeating the procedure five more times, he had mellowed. The thrill was gone.

Little did he know that this piece of paternal wisdom was brought to me by studying the fatherly ways of God with sinful Israel, and how he wrote straight with their crooked lines. This was particularly true after Moses' death, from the time of Joshua and the Judges until the establishment of the Davidic kingdom.

From Joshua to the Judges

Moses lived only long enough to see the Promised Land at a distance, from atop Mount Nebo, where he died (see Dt 34:1-6). But he had taken great care in grooming Joshua to be his successor: "And Joshua ... was full of the spirit of wisdom, for Moses had laid his hands upon him; so the people of Israel obeyed him" (Dt 34:9).

Joshua led the people of Israel across the Jordan River into the land of Canaan. The conquest had begun. First, Joshua had all of the males circumcised, so that Israel could celebrate Passover (see Jos 5). Then he prepared them to besiege the city of Jericho, a Canaanite stronghold with virtually impregnable walls (see Jos 6).

Following the Lord's instructions, Joshua implemented a most unusual battle plan. Instead of following the ancient custom of deploying soldiers equipped with the weapons of siege warfare, Joshua ordered the priests to lead the armies. He commanded them to carry the ark of the covenant out in front, with the twelve tribes following behind. After six days of silently marching one time around the city, they were to march around it seven times on the seventh day, and then the priests had to blow their trumpets while the people shouted.

Talk about unorthodox strategies. But it worked perfectly, because the battle belonged to the Lord. What better way to help Israel find their strength in God and his holy priests.

The Father issued explicit instructions: drive out the inhabitants of the land; destroy all their idols and graven images; demolish all their high places; and take possession of the land (see Nm 33:51-53). He also added a stern warning: "But if you do not drive out the inhabitants of the land from before you, then those of them whom you let remain shall be as pricks in your eyes and thorns in your sides, and they shall trouble you in the land where you dwell. And I will do to you as I thought to do to them" (vv. 55-56).

After defeating Jericho, the Israelites went on to conquer much but not *all* of the Promised Land. They did not drive out *all* the inhabitants, and they did not destroy *all* the devoted things. Their early successes went to their heads. Israel became flabby. Even worse, the Israelites began to intermarry with Canaanites, who led them to worship their false idols, just as Moses warned. Evil can be very patient.

A Transition

"A long time afterward," Scripture tells us, "when ... Joshua was old and well advanced in years, [he] summoned all Israel" (Jos 23:1-2). Having just parceled out the Promised Land among the twelve tribes, Joshua feared that Israel would soon stray from the Lord. So he performed a covenant renewal ceremony to remind them of all that God had done for them. When he charged them to be steadfast in keeping the law of Moses and loving God, all the people cried, "Amen!" But Joshua knew that Israel's heart was still divided; so it would be easier said than done (see Jos 24:19-27).

Then followed the period of the judges, when we find Israel falling into one crisis after another. It makes for fascinating reading, but it gets a bit repetitious after a while. Israel kept following the same vicious cycle: sin, slavery, supplication, salvation and surplus.

This up-and-down pattern is manifest throughout the Book of Judges. First, the people fell into sin. Then the Father allowed them to be defeated and sent into slavery. This downward spiral from sin to slavery led the people to supplication. When the Israelites cried out for help, God heard their voice and sent a judge to deliver them from their bondage.

This righteous rescuer brought temporary political freedom, which enabled the people to serve God faithfully again ... for a while. Then the Father blessed them again with prosperity. And they would start another downhill descent. So faithfulness begot fullness, which in turn begot flabbiness and forgetfulness. Then came the fall, followed by forgiveness and freedom. When it came to divine testing, Israel would have earned straight Fs!

This cycle continued through a lengthy chain of twelve judges. Israel just never seemed to learn, which always meant one more time around the mountain. But then are we any better or more proficient at following the ways of God?

Enough Already! Give Us a King!

The chain of twelve judges eventually ended, not because Israel ended the vicious cycle but because of the shortcomings of the judges (like Samson) and the corruption of the Levites (see Jgs 17-19). The problem of corrupt clergy haunts God's family in every age. Priests who misuse and abuse their authority inflict untold damage upon the people of God.

A pivotal example of a priest who misled Israel was Eli (see 1 Sm 1-4). As the officiating minister of the altar, Eli offered sacrifices to the Lord at Shiloh. Each year people came from all around for the holy feasts. On one occasion, Hannah accompanied her husband, Elkanah, on the annual pilgrimage to Shiloh. Along the way, his other wife cruelly mocked Hannah for her barrenness. Hannah wept bitterly and sought the Lord for a child, whom she vowed to dedicate to his service.

God heard Hannah's plea and granted her a baby boy, whom

she named Samuel. After the child was weaned, Hannah brought him back to Eli, who adopted him and trained him for the priesthood alongside his own two wicked sons, Hophni and Phineas. These two boys were nothing but trouble because their father refused to discipline them, and they grew worse over time (see 1 Sm 2:12-17).

As Eli grew older, the people grew concerned lest his wicked sons succeed him to the position of high priest. One night, God visited young Samuel with woeful tidings: he intended to punish the iniquity of Eli's house. The Lord also stated his intention of establishing a new priestly dynasty through Samuel. The boy reluctantly shared this prophetic word with his foster father, Eli, who then had to "sit back" and watch the tragedy unfold.

After bringing the ark of the covenant into battle against the Philistines, Hophni and Phineas were slain. When Eli learned that the ark had been captured and his own sons were dead, he fell off his seat and died of a broken neck. The wife of Phineas died during childbirth when she heard what had happened to her husband and father-in-law. Before her death she mourned the loss of the ark: "The glory has departed from Israel, for the ark of God had been captured" (1 Sm 4:22).

But the Almighty was able to defend himself quite well. After the Philistines had carried the ark into the house of Dagon, their god, the Lord knocked their chief idol on its face a few times. Then he afflicted the people of Ashdod with deadly tumors until they could no longer bear the heavy hand of God. With appropriate gifts of appeasement, the Philistines hastily sent the ark back to Israel.

At this point Samuel began his reign as a righteous judge by calling the people to repent and put away their foreign gods. He judged all their complaints and set up a memorial stone to remind them of God's help. When Samuel became old, he intended to appoint his sons judges over Israel. Apparently, he assumed there was no other way for the Lord to fulfill his promise to establish a priestly dynasty except through Samuel. But there was just one problem: "His sons did not walk in his ways, but turned aside after gain; they took bribes and perverted justice" (1 Sm 8:3).

When the elders envisioned the aging Samuel being replaced by his crooked sons, they at last showed a flicker of insight. "Oh, no, it's like Eli revisited. We've had enough of this! We want a king like all the nations. We don't want these weak priests who don't know how to raise up good sons. We've had enough of worrying about the next generation when we ourselves wield no political power and are threatened by hostile enemies on every side." (Of course, they remained blind to the fact that kings would be subject to the very same problem.)

Their request displeased Samuel. In a sense, he must have felt rejected. He was also wise enough to see their folly; for clamoring for a monarchy was no real solution. It was a move guaranteed simply to compound Israel's troubles.

The Lord encouraged Samuel not to take it personally. In effect he said to Samuel, "They aren't rejecting you. They're rejecting me as king over them. Now go tell them that they're going to get what they want. They want a king, they'll get a king. That's my punishment. And now instead of paying one tithe to the priesthood, they'll end up paying a double tithe, to the church and to the state. The king will take a tithe of everything: flocks, crops, sons, daughters, property, everything. Warn them so that they'll know."

When Samuel carried this message to the people, they refused to heed God's warning. "We *will* have a king over us, that we also may be like all the nations, and that our king may govern us and go out before us and fight our battles" (1 Sm 8:19-20, emphasis added).

Israel seemed to be in the throes of adolescence with peer pressure pushing all their panic buttons. Granted, the people were surrounded by hostile nations, a few of which must have looked like the biggest bully on the block. And each of these military powers was led by an impressive king in regal attire.

After the last of the judges, Israel had only plain old brown-wrapper priests—and crooked ones at that—to lead them into battle. The Israelites were certain that a king would raise them above all this petty jealousy and greed. And royal blood would surely guarantee worthy offspring. Yes, Israel wanted a king so they could be just like all the other nations.

So God said to Samuel, "Hearken to their voice, and make them a king" (v. 22).

If you're a parent, you must know the feeling. Your children just keep pushing until finally you let them have what they want. Sometimes the wisest punishment involves doing just that, giving them what they want and then letting them learn the hard way.

Royal Flush

We've seen how God allowed Moses to frame the Deutero-nomic covenant with various concessions: polygamy, concubinage, divorce and remarriage, slavery, usury, *herem* warfare. Along with these pastoral accommodations, Moses also introduced two additional laws in Deuteronomy for regulating Israel during its adolescent phase: the law of the king and the central sanctuary.

Both laws offer important keys for unlocking God's hidden plan for Israel. They would also be eventually fulfilled in the Father's covenant with the son of David. God's plan, in effect, was to build an earthly model of his heavenly throne and temple.

The law of the king is stated in a very concessionary tone: "When you come to the land which the Lord your God gives you, and you possess it and dwell in it, and then say, 'I will set a king over me, like all the nations that are round about me'; you may indeed set as king over you him whom the Lord your God will choose. One from among your brethren you shall set as king over you" (Dt 17:14-15).

Moses issued three warnings to fence in the future monarchs: a prohibition against accumulating three things "for himself": *weapons* (in the form of chariot horses), *wives* (as a royal harem) and *wealth* (in the form of gold). Knowing that Israel's kings would be tempted to imitate the pattern followed by all ancient Near Eastern kingdoms, God warned against what would destroy his own family.

These three warnings were a formula prescription containing all of the divine statutes for Israel's monarchy. If a king kept these rules, God promised that his kingdom would endure through many generations. Unfortunately, we see these laws systematically violated by practically every king in a way that meant ruin—not only for the monarchy, but also for God's covenant family.

Moses also issued one positive mandate concerning the king: when he sat upon the throne of his kingdom, he was to write for himself a copy of "this law" and read it all the days of his life (see Dt 17:18-20). "This law" refers to "the book of the law," which is Deuteronomy.[1] By strictly keeping the Deuteronomic covenant, the king would be more likely to learn to fear the Lord and be humble before his brethren. It didn't usually work out that way.[2]

This hardly sounds like a mandate for a monarchy. God simply granted permission to Israel in advance. After all, there were no laws about kingship in Israel's original covenant at Sinai. There it was simple enough: God was Israel's king, and he called all of Israel to be a "kingdom of priests" (see Ex 19:5-6). Not until Deuteronomy did God give consent for a human dynasty. And God only permitted it at Moab because he knew his people might otherwise rebel, and be seduced—and reduced to servility—by foreign kings.

On the other hand, Scripture nowhere condemns monarchy, as

such. God promised kings to Abraham and Sarah (see Gn 17:16), just as Jacob predicted a royal destiny for his son Judah (see Gn 49:8-10). For Israel, kingship was a sign of blessing, at least in some sense. So it wasn't wrong to want a king, as much as it was wrong to want it *for the wrong reason*, "to govern us like all the nations" (1 Sm 8:5). By granting Israel a king, God channeled a lower motive in order to lift his people to a higher plane.

Sanctuary Granted

We already touched upon the Deuteronomic law of the central sanctuary in the previous chapter; so we'll keep our remarks here brief and to the point. Moses laid down this command:

> But when you go over the Jordan, and live in the land which the Lord your God gives you to inherit, and *when he gives you rest from all your enemies round about*, so that you live in safety, then to the place which the Lord your God will choose, to make his name dwell there, thither you shall bring ... your burnt offerings and your sacrifices, your tithes and the offering that you present.... Take heed that you do not offer your burnt offerings at every place that you see; but at the place which the Lord will choose in one of your tribes.
>
> DEUTERONOMY 12:10-14

First, the condition for building the sanctuary is total "rest," which God later granted to David (see 2 Sm 7:1).[3] Second, the exact place is nowhere stipulated, though Jerusalem was clearly meant. Third, the achievement of "rest" and the construction of a temple were seen in Israel (and the entire ancient Near East) as a royal accomplishment. Thus, Israel needed to find a righteous king who met the Deuteronomic criteria of the "law of the king," to whom God could give "rest" and the authorization to build a temple.

That's how God who is Spirit responds to the human desire for visible signs of his presence. In this instance, we see how the Father stoops down to his children's level in order to raise them up to his. However, at this point in Israel's history, God still had some more stooping to do.

The Rise and Fall of a Ruler

At God's direction Samuel anointed Saul to reign as a father figure over this unruly family, a tall and handsome youth anointed with a spirit of prophecy and a new heart (see 1 Sm 10:6). Saul was eventually accepted by all the people and crowned as king of Israel. Samuel handed over his authority to Saul by laying down his office as judge.

Things went well in the beginning, with victories in battle and progress on the home front. Then during a military campaign against the Philistines, Saul made a seemingly minor mistake that turned out to be an enormous blunder, one that would cost him his dynasty (see 1 Sm 13). Samuel, who still exercised his priestly function, instructed the king to wait until he appeared to offer sacrifice. Saul waited and waited, but became so impatient that he went ahead and sacrificed on his own. He thereby intruded into the priestly office and acted like a priest-king out of turn.

Just then, Samuel arrived at the camp, only to discover Saul's disobedience. The priest chastised the king with an ominous warning:

You have done foolishly; you have not kept the commandment of the Lord your God, which he commanded you; for now the Lord would have established your kingdom over Israel for ever. But now your kingdom shall not continue; the Lord has sought out a man after his own heart; and the Lord has appointed him to be prince over his people, because you have not kept what the Lord commanded you.

1 SAMUEL 13:13-14

God the Father punished Saul, not by deposing him immediately but by not allowing his son to succeed him. Even though Saul continued to reign as king, his kingdom had ended in terms of dynastic succession.

The events recounted in 1 Samuel 15 underscore how serious the Father was about his leaders keeping the commandments. Because the Amalekites were intent upon exterminating the Hebrews, God commanded Saul to completely obliterate this pagan people. So the king went to war against them and emerged victorious. But Saul and his army did not do as God had commanded. They utterly destroyed all that was despised and worthless but spared Agag, the Amalekite king, and kept the best of the sheep and the oxen and the fatlings of the lambs.

The word of the Lord came to Samuel: "I repent that I have made Saul king; for he has turned back from following me, and has not performed my commandments" (1 Sm 15:10).

The angry priest rose early in the morning to meet Saul, only to discover that the errant king had stopped at Carmel and set up a monument to himself and then continued on to Gilgal. Having to chase down Saul did nothing to improve Samuel's disposition. When they finally crossed paths, the king greeted him cheerily: "Blessed be you to the Lord; I have performed the commandment of the Lord" (v. 13).

Note the scathing irony of Samuel's response: "What then is this bleating of the sheep in my ears, and the lowing of the oxen which I hear?" (v. 14)

The self-righteous king replied, "Oh, that? The people spared the best of the sheep and the oxen to sacrifice to the Lord your God, and the rest we have utterly destroyed" (see v. 15).

Saul still seemed to miss the point. He had a real knack for tacking conditions onto God's commands, such as "if I feel like it," or "if it seems reasonable given the circumstances," or "to the extent I deem possible," or "but I shouldn't take this too literally or to inhumane extremes." (How often do we hear a command from God and subtly shift into low gear with a similar litany of excuses?)

Samuel probed a little deeper:

"Though you are little in your own eyes, are you not the head of the tribes of Israel? The Lord anointed you king over Israel. And the Lord sent you on a mission, and said, 'Go, utterly destroy the sinners ...' Why then did you not obey the voice of the Lord? Why did you swoop on the spoil, and do what was evil in the sight of the Lord?"

1 SAMUEL 15:17-19

But Saul still didn't get it. He maintained his innocence.

"I have obeyed the voice of the Lord," he insisted. "I have gone on the mission on which the Lord sent me, I have brought Agag the king of Amalek, and I have utterly destroyed the Amalekites. But the people took of the spoil, sheep and oxen, the best of the things devoted to destruction, to sacrifice to the Lord your God in Gilgal" (vv. 20-21).

In other words, "I thought I performed a difficult assignment quite well—with the slight exception of these few animals which the *people* spared to sacrifice. What more could you want, for crying out loud? Besides, it's their fault." Notice the shift of blame once again.

Samuel then uttered one of the most magnificent statements in the Old Testament: "Has the Lord as great delight in burnt offerings and sacrifices, as in obeying the voice of the Lord?" (v. 22).

As we've seen in previous chapters, God didn't require Israel to offer animal sacrifices until after the golden calf. Clearly, to obey is better than to sacrifice.

At last Saul got the point. "I have sinned," he said, "for I have transgressed the commandment of the Lord and your words, because I feared the people and obeyed their voice. Now therefore, I pray, pardon my sin, and return with me, that I may worship the Lord" (vv. 24-25).

Forced to admit his folly, this reluctant penitent wanted simply to sweep it under the cosmic rug and get back to business—at least until the next circumstantial tremor reopened this major fault line in his moral landscape.

Saul's casual contrition ran into a solid brick wall. Samuel replied, "I will not return with you; for you have rejected the word of the Lord, and the Lord has rejected you from being king over Israel" (v. 26).

As the priest-prophet turned to walk away, Saul grabbed the hem of his robe so that it tore. Samuel said to him, "The Lord has torn the kingdom of Israel from you this day, and given it to a neighbor of yours, who is better than you" (v. 28).

The people had asked for a king, "to be like the nations," and they got one. As a result, Israel learned a valuable lesson: Be careful what you ask for; you just might get it.

A New King in the Making

As soon as Saul lost the monarchy, God moved to raise up a new leader for his people. He knew that they would be lost without someone after his own heart. So God sent Samuel to Jesse the Bethlehemite, saying, "I have provided for myself a king among his sons" (1 Sm 16:1).

One by one, seven sons were rejected by the Lord for the

throne. The youngest, David, was out tending the sheep. "Arise, anoint him," the Lord said to Samuel, "for this is he" (v. 12).

David had to overcome tremendous obstacles before he could wear the crown, not the least of which was a Philistine giant who had been making sport of the Israelite soldiers and blaspheming God. Anyone who cheers for the underdog enjoys this favorite story about a fearless shepherd boy who toppled a giant with one well-aimed stone from his trusty sling (see 1 Sm 17).

Why wasn't David out tending sheep where he belonged? Having been tormented by an evil spirit, Saul had summoned the boy because of his reported skill on the lyre. David's music soothed and refreshed the king. And so the one who was losing his kingdom grew to love this new king-in-the-making, and soon made David his armor bearer (1 Sam 16:14-22).

In a further stroke of divine irony, a unique friendship blossomed between David and Jonathan, Saul's son, who was the crown prince and heir apparent. Thus the man who stood to lose everything if his father's dynasty ended became the best friend of the man who stood to gain everything if he established a new kingdom.

In a remarkable display of selflessness, Jonathan chose to be an obedient servant of God rather than fight to retain his royal rights and political power. After he became convinced of his father's murderous intentions toward David, Jonathan swore a covenant of family friendship with David that would yield fruit for generations to come (see 1 Sm 20).

The two ratified this covenant by meeting in a secluded field and pledging their loyalty. Jonathan exchanged his raiment as crown prince for his friend's garments befitting a minister in the royal court. By this symbolic gesture, Jonathan selflessly relinquished what he knew God didn't intend for him to inherit. The legitimacy of God's chosen king was now legally validated.

When Saul realized that his dynasty was beginning to fall apart, this man of once regal bearing was driven mad by evil spirits that haunted him day and night. The last several chapters of First Samuel recount the furious king's repeated attempts to find David and kill him. If his dementia weren't so sad, Saul's frantic chase could seem almost comical.

In one especially humorous story, the king took three thousand chosen men to search for this one man who so threatened his kingship (see 1 Sm 24). David and his men happened to be sitting in the innermost parts of the very cave that Saul entered to relieve himself. David could have easily surprised his demented persecutor and taken his life. But rejecting his comrades' advice to do so, the fugitive leader stealthily arose and cut off a piece of the king's robe instead.

After Saul rejoined his search party, David emerged from the cave and held up the remnant to prove his honorable intentions. "Saul, today the Lord delivered you into my hands, but I won't lay a hand on the Lord's anointed" (see 1 Sm 24:10). The chastened monarch called an end to the hunt—until the next fit of madness renewed his frenzy.

David's meekness came from his unconditional trust in his Father to provide; it also reflected a reverent regard for the divine authority invested in the king's office, in spite of the scoundrel who occupied it. There's much here for us to ponder and apply.

Saul finally met a shameful end (see 1 Sm 31). After the Philistines overtook him and his three sons, only Saul escaped. Badly wounded by a Philistine arrow, he committed suicide rather than be thrust through by "the uncircumcised." Enemy soldiers found his body the next morning, cut off his head and fastened his remains to the wall of Bethshan. Thus King Saul and all three of his sons fell in battle on the same day.

When David heard the news, he mourned and wept and fasted for Saul, Jonathan and the nation of Israel. The heartfelt words of David's lament are most revealing and instructive:

How are the mighty fallen!
Tell it not in Gath,
publish it not in the streets of Ashkelon;
lest the daughters of the Philistines rejoice,
lest the daughters of the uncircumcised exult....
Saul and Jonathan, beloved and lovely!
In life and in death they were not divided;
they were swifter than eagles,
they were stronger than lions.
Ye daughters of Israel, weep over Saul,
who clothed you daintily in scarlet,
who put ornaments of gold upon your apparel.

2 SAMUEL 2:19-24

What magnanimity is echoed in these lines, which David sang over the loss of Saul, his archrival but also his father-in-law and king.

For godly men, personal fortunes matter little when the welfare of God's family is at stake. David understood how Israel needed to rally around the living God, and the king whom he had chosen and anointed, even when that man, who was much less than a saint, had fallen into disgrace. This is a very important—but difficult—thing to do, in every age, including our own.

ELEVEN

"Thou Art the Man!":
From Kingdom to Exile

Gd often achieves his most awesome victories in the humblest ways: a childless old man leaves home without even knowing where he's going; a threatened baby in a basket is set afloat on a river; a shepherd boy armed with only a sling and five smooth stones faces a giant. In the last case, who in their wildest imagination could have foreseen the shepherd boy being crowned king of Israel and thus paving the way for the carpenter who would be the King of kings?

The Gates of Jerusalem Shall Not Prevail

A long civil war ensued between the house of Saul and the house of David while the other tribes tried to determine their own choices to replace the fallen leader. The Israelites from the north weren't too keen on this southern king from Judah. Finally all the tribes of Israel came to David at Hebron and proclaimed, "Behold, we are your bone and flesh" (2 Sm 5:1)—a covenant oath that essentially said, "We are all family, and we will follow you as a father."

So David made a covenant with the people, and the elders anointed him king. At the age of thirty, this seasoned leader, who was once a shepherd boy, became king over all twelve tribes of Israel. He reigned for forty years (v. 4).

In consolidating his kingdom, David decided to take over

Jerusalem, a city strategically located a little farther to the north. But that was easier said than done. One of the strongest fortresses in Canaan, Jerusalem was virtually impregnable. The Jebusites who defended it actually taunted David from the city walls: "You'll never come in here. Even the blind and the lame could ward you off" (see v. 6).

Nevertheless, David succeeded in capturing the stronghold of Zion and called it the city of David. The details are sketchy, but his warriors evidently gained access through some forgotten underground water shaft, perhaps with the help of insiders. King David went on to defeat the Philistines and secure relative peace with their enemies roundabout.

Scripture never bothers to explain why David decided to make Jerusalem his capital. The political and military advantages of the city are sufficient explanation in themselves; but the king may have sensed that there was some sacred purpose for which this place had been chosen by God.

It was here that Abram paid tithes to Melchizedek, priest-king of Salem, who blessed Abram and fed him with bread and wine (see Gn 14). It was also here that Abraham offered Isaac, and then heard God's oath to bless all the nations (see Gn 22). Moses had commanded a central sanctuary to be built here after Israel's conquest of the Promised Land and its surrounding enemies. So David had good historical grounds for thinking that Jerusalem might be the best place (Dt 12:10-14).

After all, God didn't specify the location; he simply had Moses say, "Go to the place where I will choose my name to dwell" (see Dt 12:5). It is quite plausible, then, that family traditions such as these influenced King David to consolidate his kingdom in Jerusalem, then begin to work on building a central sanctuary.

With that as a backdrop, Scripture goes on to describe an especially significant episode in terms of the covenant family of God. Having established his throne at Jerusalem, David gathered the best warriors of Israel, about thirty thousand in all, and set out to accomplish one task: to bring back the ark of the covenant from Baale-judah, where it had been kept since the days when the Philistines had returned it to the Israelites.

After a mishap and delay of a few months, David succeeded. Interestingly enough, in several ways his behavior at this point was as much like that of a priest as it was like that of a king. First, instead of royal garb, David donned an ephod, a sheer linen garment typically worn by the Levites to keep them cool during their priestly service in front of a blazing altar. Wearing this garment, the king danced before the Lord with all his might all the way to Jerusalem (see 2 Sm 6:5). The Hebrew term for dancing refers to liturgical dance; like a priest-king, David was whirling with joy around the ark of the covenant.

Besides wearing the priestly garb, King David also performed the priestly sacrifice before the ark along with the Levites (see 2 Sm 6:12-13). And when they reached Jerusalem, they set the ark of the Lord "inside the tent which David had pitched for it; and David offered burnt offerings and peace offerings before the Lord" (2 Sm 6:17). According to the Mosaic law, Levitical priests were to perform these sacred tasks. King David then "blessed the people in the name of the Lord," which is another task assigned by the law to priests (v. 18; see Nm 6:22-27). Finally, David distributed to each Israelite "a cake of bread, a portion of meat, and a cake of raisins" (v. 19). Several scholars prefer to render the Hebrew word for "meat" as "wine."[1] In other words, David came to Jeru-Salem dressed as a priest-king, blessed the people and gave them bread and wine. Shades of Melchizedek.

Why was David acting like a priest as well as a king? Having captured Jerusalem, the city of Abraham's priest-king, David had taken a giant step forward in realizing God's Abrahamic covenant plan: restoring his reign and rule over the entire human family through his chosen people. After all, God had initially wanted the people of Israel to be royal priests—not kings at the edge of a sword but kings who would rule through priestly service and teaching. David symbolized that intended role of the nation.[2]

Time for a Temple

David said to Nathan the prophet, "I dwell in this beautiful house of cedar while the ark of God dwells in a tent" (see 2 Sm 7:2). The king wanted permission to do what in the ancient Near East was a very royal-priestly thing: to build a temple.

Nathan at first consented. "Go, do all that is in your heart; for the Lord is with you" (v. 3). Then the word of the Lord came to the prophet that night and said, "Not so fast."

God sent the prophet back to David with another message, words that unlocked a whole new covenant. "Go and tell my servant David, 'Thus says the Lord: Would you build a house for me to dwell in? I have not dwelt in a house since the day I brought up the people of Israel from Egypt to this day, but I have been moving about in a tent for my dwelling'" (see vv. 5-6).

Translation: "Hey, you don't need to do me any favors. I'm God." The message continued:

In all places where I have moved with all the people of Israel, did I speak a word with any of the judges of Israel, whom I commanded to shepherd my people Israel, saying, "Why have you not built me a house of cedar?" Now therefore thus you shall say to my servant David, "Thus says the Lord of hosts, I took you from the pasture, from following the sheep, that you should be prince over my people Israel; and I have been with you wherever you went, and have cut off all your enemies from before you; and I will make for you a great name."

2 SAMUEL 7:7-9a

Shades of Abraham. After scattering the Babel-builders who tried to make a name (*shem*) for themselves and so repudiate the family rule of Noah, God made a similar promise to Abraham in calling him to the Promised Land. "I will make your name (*shem*) great; so I will restore the unity of the human family."

But this restoration didn't happen as quickly as Abraham had hoped. Now God announced his plan to renew—and fulfill—this promise with David:

> I will make for you a great name [*shem*], like the name of the great ones of the earth. And I will appoint a place for my people Israel, and will plant them, that they may dwell in their own place, and be disturbed no more ... and I will give you rest from all your enemies. Moreover the Lord declares to you that the Lord will make you a house.
>
> 2 SAMUEL 7:9b-11

God was promising David a great name and rest from his enemies. But what did he mean by a "house"?

The Hebrew term *bayith* can have various meanings. A house can be a family, a building, a temple or even a dynasty, like the House of Windsor or the House of Hapsburg. Within the context of this passage, "house" actually carries the senses of all four at once.

Nathan must have been up half the night, for God's promises to David continued:

> When your days are fulfilled and you lie down with your fathers, I will raise up your offspring after you, who shall come forth from your body, and I will establish his kingdom. He shall build a house for my name, and I will establish the throne of his kingdom for ever. I will be his father, and he shall be my son.
>
> 2 SAMUEL 7:12-14

Solomon was this son of promise, whose name comes from the Hebrew word for peace, *Shalom.*

Solomon clearly prefigured Jesus Christ, the eternal Prince of Peace: Son of David, king of Israel, temple builder, teacher of wisdom. Our belief in Christ's kingdom is built upon this very cornerstone. Jesus Christ, the Son of David, is Lord of lords and King of kings. There's not a single square inch of creation that escapes his dominion. As children of the King, we are called to be his servants and soldiers, to extend his reign into every corner of the world.

David's Humility

Even though David longed to build a temple and rule as a priest-king, God denied him this privilege. He promised to grant it to the king's son instead. Wouldn't you think David would be disappointed?

Yet how do fathers who fail to accomplish some dream react when they see their sons achieve it instead? They typically feel even greater satisfaction, as demonstrated in David's reply to God, which begins in this way:

> Who am I, O Lord God, and what is my house, that thou hast brought me thus far? And yet this was a small thing in thy eyes, O Lord God; thou hast spoken also of thy servant's house for a great while to come, and hast shown me *future generations.*
>
> 2 SAMUEL 7:18-19, emphasis added

The father's glee over God's generosity to his son was unbounded.

As the Revised Standard Version states in the margin, the Hebrew phrase translated "future generations" (*wasoth torath ha'adam*) is more naturally rendered "this is the law for humanity."[3] The two key words are *Torath*, which is a form of "torah," the word for covenant-law, and *ha'adam*, which is the Hebrew word for humanity ("adam").

King David thus announced a greater covenant blessing than God had ever given before, a "torah" for all nations, not just Israel. In other words, what the *torah* of the Mosaic covenant was to Israel, namely, a charter of divine guidance and blessing, the *torah* of God's covenant with David—and his son—would be for the Gentiles! The "torah" came to the Gentiles initially through Solomon, in the form of God's "wisdom" (see 1 Kg 3-10), and was subsequently collected and associated with what we call the Wisdom Literature (Proverbs, Ecclesiasticus, Song of Solomon, Wisdom of Solomon).

I would paraphrase the first part of David's response this way: "O God, you have done all these glorious deeds and made this promise for my house. You've pledged yourself to do great things for my dynasty. Yet all of this is small in your eyes, since what you have really given me is the covenant law for all the nations, your entire human family. I can't believe my ears. Who am I, your lowly servant, that you would do this for me and my son?!"

The Father had accomplished these glorious deeds because David thought of himself as nothing but a servant. If you feel like small stuff, a nobody, take heart: That qualifies you to play a role in God's plan. God has always been and still is looking for people who see themselves as lowly, who are humble before the Lord and who fear the Creator more than their fellow creatures. Such are the ones the Father will use to strengthen his human family and thus build the kingdom of heaven for his own name's sake.

David exhibited these very traits in his encounter with Goliath. Everybody quaked before this giant. Yet a mere shepherd boy stepped up to meet the challenge. He didn't claim to be fearless. In fact, David said in effect, "Hey, I would be afraid, too. But listen to this guy. He's blaspheming the God of Israel! Nobody can do that and get away with it, no matter *how* big he is. God will do anything for anybody willing to knock him down to size. After all, the bigger they are, the harder they fall."

David's faith allowed him to recognize the deeper import of God's promise: that his dynasty would be a universal kingdom. In fact, this worldwide decree was the means by which God would establish the corporate destiny of the human family. Through the Davidic covenant, he would give a constitution for all humankind, an international family charter offered freely to the nations.

As covenant mediator, King David went to work. He gradually transformed the *national* family of Israel into an *imperial* family, a dynastic kingdom. The difference is subtle but crucial. *A nation maintains sole sovereignty, whereas a kingdom exercises sovereignty over other states and nations.*

The ultimate purpose of this imperial rule was to share with all nations the wisdom, the truth and the righteousness that God had so generously poured out upon Israel. From the beginning, his desire was to father a worldwide family. He singled out Abraham, Isaac, Jacob and Moses, not because he plays favorites but because he is a wise father who knows how to use his firstborn son to influence the younger siblings who have been deceived by demonic powers.

God allowed the Davidic kings to make vassals out of the surrounding nations for their own good. After all, it was better to serve as a slave in God's family than to be free outside of his household. And in this way, the Father was preparing all the Gentile nations to receive the full gift of divine sonship through Jesus Christ.

For a brief time, the surrounding nations accepted this charter, much as Israel had initially said yes to God's call to be a kingdom of priests. And then Israel and the nations repudiated God's call. But we must not be too quick to condemn them: Sacrificing the lower goods of this world, setting our hearts on treasures in heaven and carrying our crosses, have never been easy and never will be.

The Royal Psalms

King David left one tangible legacy for all humankind: a rich treasury of psalms. These vignettes of agony and ecstasy, hate and love, despair and victory, scorn and praise capture this man's unusually sensitive nature as well as his gift with words and music. The so-called royal psalms offer an insightful commentary as to the real meaning of the Davidic covenant.

Psalm 2 is one of the best known of these songs. David reflects on the nations and kings of the earth who conspire together against the Lord and his Messiah, refusing to be ruled by God through his representative king. But the Lord has been listening in on their communications all along ... laughing at their schemes: "I have set my king on Zion, my holy hill" (v. 6). God wasn't worried about the kings and princes of the earth banding together to overthrow his righteous law. They may have deceived themselves and deluded others, but the Father knew their wayward hearts and rebellious plans and would make it all come back on their own heads. Psalm 2 thus highlights a particular aspect of the Davidic covenant: a worldwide theocratic family under God's fatherly law. The rulers of the earth who refuse to serve and worship the one true God court disaster and ruin.

Psalm 72 captures another angle of this vision. The psalmist prays that the royal son would reign with righteousness and justice, and that all kings would serve him. This is provisionally realized in Solomon, but ultimately fulfilled in the true Son of David, Jesus Christ.

Psalm 89 tells us that God will make the Son of David "the

firstborn, the highest of the kings on earth" (v. 27). The word "highest" in Hebrew is *elyon*, a title usually reserved for God himself. Yet the line of David shall endure forever as the means by which God the Father will reunify and restore the family he has created.

The last psalm to consider is Psalm 110, which is the most frequently quoted in the New Testament. It begins, "The Lord says to my lord (literally, Yahweh says to my lord [Adonai]): 'Sit at my right hand until I make your enemies your footstool'" (v. 1). Following the ancient tradition that attributes this psalm to David, Jesus referred to this verse and asked, "If David thus calls him Lord, how is he his son?" (see Mt 22:45). Like the other psalms we've cited, this points to the partial fulfillment of the Davidic covenant in Solomon and its perfect fulfillment in Christ.

The fourth verse is also significant: "The Lord has sworn, he will not change his mind; 'You are a priest for ever after the order of Melchizedek'" (Ps 110:4). Two things may be highlighted: first, this verse refers to God's covenant *oath* regarding David's son; and second, it reveals how God will bring blessings to Israel and all the nations, through Jesus Christ, our royal high priest (see Heb 5-7).

David's Undoing

For all his prowess and faith and poetic talent, King David exhibited a weakness for women that proved to be his downfall. You're probably familiar with the story (see 2 Sm 11). As Israel's commander in chief, David should have been out in battle. Yet the king was taking it easy at the palace. He was walking on the roof one day, late afternoon, when he saw a woman bathing on a nearby rooftop. And the woman was very beautiful.

Always a man of action, David sent and inquired about her. "Is not this Bathsheba, the daughter of Eliam, the wife of Uriah the Hittite?" (see v. 3). The king knew her because her husband was one of David's chief military advisers. So David asked for her, she came to him and he slept with her. Bathsheba returned home and soon found she was with child.

David started conniving at this point. "Send for Uriah. He's been at battle too long. I'm going to grant him some leave." When Uriah returned from the battlefield, the king told him to go home and relax and enjoy his beautiful wife.

Uriah refused. "How can I? God's people are out there in battle along with the ark of the covenant. I can't rest. I can't go in and sleep with Bathsheba."

David even tried getting this dutiful soldier drunk in hopes his resolve would weaken, but Uriah remained at the palace rather than go home and take pleasure with his wife. Desperate to cover his tracks, the king then implemented Plan B. He gave Uriah a sealed letter for Joab, the commanding general. It said in effect: "Joab, when you besiege the city, put Uriah up in the front lines, and then when the fighting gets hot and heavy, draw back and leave him up there by himself" (see v. 15).

David was sinking deeper and deeper with each step: first adultery, then murder. As intended, Uriah was cut down in battle. After the customary period of mourning for her husband, Bathsheba became David's wife and bore him a son.

God the Father was so displeased that he sent Nathan to tell David a quaint parable about a rich man who owned flocks and herds and a poor man who had only one little ewe lamb that was like his own child (see 2 Sm 12). Now the rich man wanted to prepare dinner for a wayfarer, but didn't want to waste a lamb from his own flock. So he stole the poor man's sole possession.

David's anger burned so hotly against such a rogue that he uttered an oath: "As the Lord lives, the man who has done this deserves to die; and he shall restore the lamb fourfold, because he did this thing, and because he had no pity" (vv. 5-6).

Then Nathan announced, "David, thou art the man!" And he went on to lay a solemn curse upon the house of David:

> Now therefore the sword shall never depart from your house, because you have despised me, and have taken the wife of Uriah the Hittite to be your wife.... Behold, I will raise up evil against you out of your own house; and I will take your wives before your eyes and give them to your neighbor, and he shall lie with your wives in the sight of this sun.
>
> 2 SAMUEL 12:10-11

David repented and the Lord spared his life, but the child of his adulterous union with Bathsheba died. In the aftermath of this tragedy, the contrite king wrote Psalm 51, the most profound song of repentance in Scripture. Bathsheba conceived a second child destined to inherit the throne of Israel. His name was Solomon.

David's life became more and more miserable, according to the curse spoken by Nathan. His son Amnon fell in love with one of his half-sisters, Tamar, and carried out a plan to rape her. Absalom, Tamar's brother, soon found out what his half-brother had done but waited a few weeks to see what his father would do about it. When David took no action, Absalom killed Amnon and fled out of fear of his father.

Relationships in God's family continued downhill from there. Absalom later returned to Jerusalem but didn't even see his father for two more years. As David's oldest son, he felt the crown rightfully belonged to him. So Absalom gathered strength and support and in time led a revolt against his father. He succeeded in ousting David and taking over Jerusalem.

As a shocking exclamation point to proclaim his dominion, Absalom stole his father's concubines and then slept with the royal harem in public. (According to the rules of the culture, whoever got the harem got the kingdom.) Nevertheless, Absalom's death in the ensuing struggle for power brought the greatest sorrow to David's fatherly heart.

Solomon's Legacy: Spiritual Collapse

David's sorrow only faintly reflected the broken heart of God the Father. Because of his sin, the house of David had been splintered by envy, hatred and lust for power. How would the Father keep his promise to establish an everlasting kingdom through David's son? God's grand design of fashioning a human family under his lordship may have been challenged, but it wasn't destroyed.

Against the vigorous protests of his older half-brothers, Solomon assumed the throne as David's chosen heir (see 1 Kgs 1-2). One of his first royal decrees was to establish a throne at his right hand for Bathsheba, the queen mother. From this point on until the end of the Davidic monarchy, we never see the king of Israel ruling without the queen mother at his right hand.

The Heavenly Father presented the new king with a special coronation gift: "I will give you anything you ask. Do you want wealth? long life? power?"

Solomon answered, "No. I want wisdom."

God said, "You've just pleased me. Because you asked for wisdom, I'll give you all the wisdom you could want and everything else as well" (see 1 Kgs 3:11-14).

Solomon's astounding wisdom was soon broadcast throughout the world. Kings and queens traveled from Africa, Europe and every inhabited continent to behold this wondrous gift. And with that wisdom, King Solomon set to work building the temple, a mammoth undertaking in terms of design, labor and materials.

When the king at last dedicated the temple with a magnificent prayer, fire came down from heaven and consumed the sacrifice on the altar (see 2 Chr 7:1). Needless to say, all the people present found themselves on their faces worshiping God.

Having restored the glory of his father's kingdom, Solomon then proceeded to drag the Davidic covenant through the mud by systematically violating all three rules enumerated in the "law of the king" in Deuteronomy 17. He became a tyrant like all the other kings, squeezing the treasuries of his vassal colonies dry (see 1 Kgs 10:14). Solomon also commanded the people to bring up to Jerusalem not just their bodies and souls to hear God's law but tons of their gold.

It is noteworthy that Solomon exacted from the nations *six hundred sixty-six* talents per annum for the privilege of using his lands and seas. Curiously, this number is used in another place in the Bible—the "number of the beast" (see Rv 13:17), which is given to those wishing to buy and sell—along with a call for "wisdom" to understand its meaning. Solomon had become like a proto-beast by misusing his wisdom and power for his own selfish gain, contrary to the needs of his younger brother-nations.

Anyone demanding that much money had to command an intimidating arsenal of weapons. So the king of Israel began to multiply for himself horses and chariots, standing armies and weapons, all in contradiction to God's command.

Finally, Solomon topped off his enormous wealth and weapons with the amorous pursuit of women: seven hundred wives and three hundred concubines. "Now King Solomon loved many foreign women: the daughter of Pharaoh, and Moabite, Ammonite, Edomite, Sidonian, and Hittite women" (1 Kgs 11:1). The Father had strictly forbidden his people to intermarry with these other nations, lest their hearts be turned away to other gods. But Solomon wanted to be a king like all the others, with the pleasure of making political alliances through marriages.

Solomon's rapid fall from grace continued. He actually began to construct idolatrous altars so that he could worship the Canaanite deities Asherah and Baal as well as Yahweh. But the Father wouldn't tolerate it. He sent enemies from within and without so that Solomon grew old watching his kingdom slip away.

One of his adversaries was Jeroboam, an Ephraimite and an able servant of the king. The prophet Ahijah spoke the word of the Lord to Jeroboam: "I will take the kingdom out of his son's hand, and will give it to you, ten tribes. Yet to his son I will give one tribe, that David my servant may always have a lamp before me in Jerusalem, the city where I have chosen to put my name" (1 Kgs 11:35-36). Thus God the Father still pledged to keep his promise to his son David, in spite of the failures of Solomon.

Two Nations Under God

Rehoboam, Solomon's son, ascended the throne at a time of perilous instability. Jeroboam and all the assembly of Israel promised to serve the new king if he would lighten their heavy tax burden. Rehoboam asked for three days to think it over.

The elders who had ministered to his father agreed with the wisdom of such a move. Then the king consulted with his buddies—the younger counselors who stood to gain the most from taxation. They recommended raising taxes even higher.

Rehoboam evidently didn't inherit Solomon's wisdom, one important component of which is to choose your counselors carefully. The new king delivered his decision to increase taxes with this inflammatory message: "You thought my father taxed you? My little finger is thicker than his loins and thighs" (see 1 Kgs 12:10-11). Or, to put it bluntly, you ain't seen nothin' yet!

Civil war ensued. Under Jeroboam's leadership, ten tribes split away, never to be reunited. Only the tribe of Benjamin was left with David's house. The northern kingdom, which was called Israel, dwarfed the southern kingdom of Judah, where Rehoboam was still king. The short-lived golden age of a united Davidic kingdom, an earthly prototype of God's heavenly kingdom, was now over.[4]

The millennium prior to Christ proved to be a crucible of purification and refinement for God's family. After revolting politically, the ten renegade tribes rebelled spiritually. The idolatrous stage was set by King Jeroboam, who reigned in the tenth century B.C.

One of the first official acts of King Jeroboam was to erect two golden calves to be worshiped, one at Bethel and one at Dan. He also expelled all the Levites. In effect, he undid the Sinai covenant. What was he thinking?

As a member of the tribe of Ephraim, perhaps Jeroboam was aware of the hybrid origins of his tribal progenitor. While Ephraim's father was Joseph, the son of Israel, his mother was an Egyptian named Asenath (see Gn 46:20). Jeroboam was living in Egypt at the time he was called upon to serve as the new king of the ten northern tribes (see 1 Kgs 12:2). Maybe he just wanted to start up his kingdom by mixing the religions of Israel and Egypt. If so, it's a clear case of false ecumenism.

Prophets and Losses

In response to this brazen presumption, God sent prophets to warn the northern kingdom, blockbusters such as Elijah and Elisha, not to mention Hosea and Amos. But in 722 B.C., the northern tribes were completely overrun by Assyria, the worst terrorist nation of antiquity.

These prophetic warnings plus the subsequent devastation sent shock waves throughout the Davidic kingdom of Judah, or what was left of it. It also led to some much-needed reforms, especially through kings such as Hezekiah and Josiah. However, these reforms failed to stem the tide of divine judgment.

Hezekiah's son, Manasseh, not only rebelled against God's covenant but perfected evil in Judah and Jerusalem as never before. He even sacrificed his own children on the fiery altar of the pagan god Molech and ordered the death of thousands of Jewish children on altars outside of Jerusalem.

For that alone, Jerusalem's fate would have been sealed. A century later, the best efforts of good King Josiah weren't enough to undo the damage done by Manasseh. Babylonian oppression began around 600 B.C., but the blackest year by far was 586 B.C., when the Babylonian king, Nebuchadnezzar, burned Jerusalem and carried the Jews away into captivity for seventy years.

The temple was destroyed, the priesthood decimated and the sacrifices stopped. God's covenant family appeared to have been extinguished. However, prophets like Isaiah, Jeremiah and Ezekiel saw the Babylonian exile as God's appointed period for purging and penance. It came to a partial close when the Medo-Persians overran Babylon. Their ruler, Cyrus, allowed the Jews to return home to Jerusalem and rebuild the temple (see Is 44-45).

With the restoration of temple worship came a rebirth of sorts for God's covenant people. Still without a Davidic king, the returning exiles saw Ezra, the high priest, as their head. He renewed the covenant and forced the Jewish men to divorce their foreign wives. Ezra also republished the law and oversaw the completion of the temple. From that time on, with a few brief interruptions during the Hasmonaean dynasty, the Jews lived as a priestly theocracy devoid of political or royal sovereignty. This temple-centered religious commonwealth spawned a new religious outlook, now known as Judaism.

Lacking political sovereignty or military power, the Jews were tossed around like a hot potato, constantly vanquished or tyrannized by Gentile powers—from Babylon and Medo-Persia, to Greece and the Ptolemy and Seleucid dynasties, until finally Rome had its turn, conquering Jerusalem in 63 B.C.

Devoid of kings and prophets, for the most part, even the priestly line became riddled by corruption and weakness. Yet during this period of suffering and subjugation and martyrdom, the Jews experienced a profoundly deep conversion to the Lord. Arguably, this period represents the climax of the Old Testament, at least from a spiritual perspective. In the absence of prophets and kings, the Jews had nothing to lean on but the Lord.

It was a time of waiting and trusting in the Father to fulfill his covenant promises. The prolonged period of waiting yielded some precious spiritual fruit. Prayer was cultivated, worship was refined and allegiance to God's law flourished as never before. Moreover, for the first time in Israel's history, many Jews were awarded the crown of martyrdom by suffering and dying for their faith. The deuterocanonical books, 1 and 2 Maccabees, give a very poignant and moving example of a mother who had to watch the torture and execution of her seven sons, all the while urging them to hold fast to—and suffer for—the faith of their fathers (see 2 Mc 7).

The refinement and purification of the Jews came in the crucible of intense suffering, where they were transformed into a holy priesthood. They now saw themselves as living sacrifices, and the world as one immense altar.

TWELVE

"It Is Finished!":
The Son Fulfills the Father's Promises

St. Augustine pointed out that the New Covenant is concealed in the Old, while the Old is revealed in the New. We've seen glimpses of God's ultimate plan through his covenants with Adam, Noah, Abraham, Moses and David. Now we'll consider various ways in which these are explained and fulfilled by the New.

As the Messiah, Jesus Christ is priest, prophet and king. He is the new Adam. He is the seed of Abraham. He is the new Moses. He is the Son of David. He is the Son of God. He is the Lamb of God. Jesus had to be all these things and more in order to fulfill all of the promises made by his Father. And he did.

What Did Jesus Mean?

I have a vivid recollection of a Sunday morning service back in 1982, when Kimberly and I were worshiping at a local evangelical congregation. I was still a seminarian at the time, preparing for the ministry. It was around Easter, and our favorite minister was in the middle of a very exciting sermon on the meaning of Jesus' sacrificial death on the cross at Calvary.

Suddenly, something he said grabbed my attention, and really stuck with me. In the middle of his sermon, he raised what sounded at first like a simple question: "In John 19:30, when Jesus cried, 'It is finished,' what did he mean? To what does the '*it*' refer?"

Instantly, the standard evangelical answer came to mind: Jesus' words referred to the completion of our redemption, at that very moment. "It is finished" means that nothing more was needed; our salvation was complete.

This preacher also happened to be an exceptional Scripture scholar, as well as one of my favorite seminary professors; so I was taken aback when he proceeded to convincingly prove that Jesus, by saying "It is finished," could not have possibly meant that.

For one thing, he pointed out how the New Testament teaches that our redemption wasn't complete until Jesus had been "raised for our justification," just as Paul says (Rom 4:25). And then he went on to explain how often Christians take their own theological views and impose them upon the biblical text, instead of drawing their conclusions from the text itself, read in its proper context.

Then, to my dismay, he candidly admitted that he didn't have an adequate answer to his own question. He simply hadn't found one!

I don't remember hearing another word of his sermon. My mind began racing in search of an answer. After we got home, the books came out and I started searching. And I didn't stop for ten months.

An answer finally came, long after graduation, during my first year as a pastor, while I was studying Scripture in preparation for a sermon on the "Lord's Supper," as we Presbyterians called it.

I still recall that thrilling sense of discovery, after such a long period of careful research into the historical background of several key biblical texts. In particular, four distinctive stages of the inquiry provided me with what proved to be invaluable clues.

Clue #1: Old Covenant Background

The first stage of my discovery process came in studying the Old Testament background to Jesus' Last Supper. The occasion was the Jewish feast of Passover (see Mk 14:12-16). As we've seen, this memorial celebrated God's deliverance of Israel from Egypt. During that fateful night, every firstborn son in Egypt perished except those in Israelite families where a lamb, without blemish or broken bones (see Ex 12:5, 46), was slain and eaten as a sacrificial meal. Then Moses led Israel out of Egypt to Sinai, where they received the law and the covenant, which was sealed through sacrifice and communion.

At the time, I had been studying the biblical idea of covenant for many years. So I was familiar with the work of scholars like D.J. McCarthy, S.J., who demonstrates how ancient covenants formed bonds of sacred kinship, in this case, between Yahweh and Israel, making them one family. These covenant bonds are described in familial terms: father and son (see Ex 4:22; Dt 1:31; 8:5; 14:1) as well as husband and wife (see Jer 31:32; Ez 16:8; Hos 2:18-20). Likewise, liturgical feasts and rituals renewed—and reinforced— the family bonds of covenant communion between Yahweh and Israel.

This was an important part of the Jewish understanding of Passover in Jesus' day. It is noteworthy that the Gospels only record Jesus using the word "covenant" one time, though it was on the momentous occasion of his last Passover, when he instituted the Eucharist in the Upper Room: "He took a cup, and when he had given thanks (*eucharistesas*) he gave it to them, saying, 'Drink of it, all of you; for this is my blood of the covenant, which is poured out for many for the forgiveness of sins'" (Mt 26:27-28).

What an awesome moment: the firstborn Son and Lamb of God fulfilled the Old Covenant Passover in himself, as a holy sacrifice for our sins. And it served as the occasion when Jesus deliberately announced the establishment of the New Covenant.

As I continued my hunt, I discovered that the Passover link involved more than just the Eucharist. This is especially clear in John's Gospel, where the entire succession of events, which began with the Last Supper and ended with Jesus' crucifixion, reflects the various themes of the Jewish Passover.

For example, when Jesus stood before Pilate (see Jn 18:33-37), John notes this seemingly unrelated fact: "Now it was the day of preparation of the Passover; it was about the sixth hour." Surely John knew that the sixth hour was the time when the priests were to begin slaughtering the lambs for Passover.

Likewise, John brings out the connection between Jesus on the cross and the Passover lamb by calling attention to the fact that his bones remained unbroken, just as Moses had stipulated for the Passover lamb (see Ex 12:46): "that the scripture might be fulfilled, 'Not a bone of him shall be broken'" (Jn 19:33, 36). For Jesus, the Passover extended all the way from the Upper Room to Calvary.

Another connection between Jesus' Passion and the Passover is found in John 19:29: "A bowl of vinegar stood there; so they put a sponge full of the vinegar on hyssop and held it to his mouth." Only John noticed that hyssop was used, the branch prescribed in the Passover law for sprinkling the blood of the lamb (see Ex 12:22).

Finally, John also calls attention to the garment that Jesus wore when the soldiers stripped him: a seamless linen tunic (see Jn 19:23-24). The same word for "garment" (*chiton*) is used in the Old Testament to refer to the official tunic worn by the high priest when sacrificing (see Ex 28:4; Lv 16:4). This alerts us to the fact that Jesus, our Passover Lamb, is also our High Priest.

Clue #2: The First-Century Jewish Passover: Four Cups

The second set of clues came from my study of the ancient Jewish Passover liturgy. The structure of the seder meal, also known as the Passover Haggadah, appears to have been formalized before the first century. The Gospel accounts seem to assume its structure in narrating the various details of the Last Supper.[1] In particular, the Passover meal was divided into four parts, which correspond to the four different cups that were served:

First, the preliminary course consisted of a solemn blessing (*kiddush*) pronounced over the first cup of wine, which was followed by a dish of bitter herbs. (This was meant to remind the Jews of the bitterness of Egyptian bondage.)

Second, the Passover narrative (see Ex 12) was recited, after which the "Little Hallel" (Ps 113) was sung. This was immediately followed by the drinking of the second cup of wine.

Third, the main meal was then served, consisting of lamb and unleavened bread, which preceded the drinking of the third cup of wine, known as the "cup of blessing."

Finally, the climax of the Passover came with the singing of the "Great Hallel" (Ps 114-18) and the drinking of the fourth cup of wine, the "cup of consummation."

Many New Testament scholars see this pattern reflected in the Gospel narratives of the Last Supper. In particular, the cup that Jesus blessed and distributed is identified as the third cup of the Passover Haggadah. This is apparent from the singing of the "Great Hallel" which immediately follows: "And when they had sung a hymn" (Mk 14:26). Paul identifies this "cup of blessing" with the cup of the Eucharist (see 1 Cor 10:16).

The Problem

However, at this point a real problem arises. For instead of proceeding immediately to the climax of the Passover, by drinking the fourth cup, we read: "And when they had sung a hymn, they went out to the Mount of Olives" (Mk 14:26). While it may be difficult for us Gentile Christians unfamiliar with the Haggadah to see the serious disorder this sequence represents, it is not lost to Jewish readers and students of the Passover. For them, Jesus' skipping the fourth cup is almost the practical equivalent of a priest's omitting the words of consecration at Mass or forgetting Communion! In sum, the fundamental purpose of the liturgy was seemingly overlooked!

Not only is the omission glaring, it even appears to have been noticed—and highlighted—by Jesus himself, in the preceding verse: "Truly, I say to you, I shall not drink again of the fruit of the vine until that day when I drink it new in the kingdom of God" (Mk 14:25). It seems as if Jesus intended *not* to drink what he knew his disciples expected him to drink.[2] But why not?

Some scholars speculate that psychological factors may account for Jesus' apparent forgetfulness. We read about how Jesus "began to be greatly distressed and troubled. And he said to them, 'My soul is very sorrowful, even to death'" (Mk 14:33-34). Perhaps he was simply too upset to be bothered with following the Passover rubrics with liturgical precision.

While this view is plausible, other considerations render it less than likely. For one thing, if Jesus was so distracted and confused, why did he expressly declare his intention not to drink the fourth cup, before interrupting and suspending the unfinished meal? And why did he go ahead and lead his disciples in singing the "Great Hallel"? In other words, why would Jesus declare his intentions so plainly before acting in such a disorderly fashion? Furthermore, his other actions that night seem to indicate a man admittedly distressed but in full possession of himself.

So the question remains: Why did Jesus choose not to drink?

Clue #3: The Cup in Gethsemane

The third stage of my discovery process started when I focused on where Jesus went—and what he did—after leaving the Upper

Room. In particular, I took a closer look at Jesus' prayer in the Garden of Gethsemane: "Going a little farther he fell on his face and prayed, 'My Father, if it be possible, let this cup pass from me; nevertheless, not as I will, but as thou wilt'" (Mt 26:39). Three times Jesus prayed for his Father to take away "this cup."

A rather obvious question then occurred to me: What cup was Jesus talking about?

Some scholars identify "the cup" Jesus mentioned as "the cup of God's wrath" frequently mentioned by the Old Testament prophets (see Is 51:17; Jer 25:15). And there is probably some connection, to be sure. But the connection seems indirect, since there's nothing in the immediate context to suggest it.

Instead, a more basic connection is provided by the immediate context of the Passover, which Jesus had just been celebrating with his disciples, that is, before he'd unexpectedly interrupted it.

Also note how Jesus' resolution not to drink "the fruit of the vine" seemed to resurface when Jesus was heading up to Golgotha: "They offered him wine mingled with myrrh; but he did not take it" (Mk 15:23). While the narrative does not explain his refusal, it was probably not unrelated to Jesus' solemn pledge *not* to drink "the fruit of the vine" until his kingdom was manifested in glory.

The Final Clue: Irony in John

The fourth stage of the process was reached when I found in the Gospel of John a pivotal clue for my hunt. That clue was John's use of irony. Let me explain.

For John, the hour of Jesus' Passion, crucifixion and death is also the hour of his greatest glory; his abject humiliations constitute his exaltation; his apparent defeat at the hands of his enemies is seen as his supreme triumph; and his death is actually *the* event that brings life to the world (see Jn 3:14; 7:37-39; 8:28; 12:23-33; 13:31—I urge you, look up these verses!).

From John's perspective, Jesus' paschal suffering is actually the event whereupon he manifests and enters into his kingdom glory! This is John's vision of Christ's sufferings, a strikingly profound—yet ironic—vision.

The Four Clues Reviewed

Recapping, then, these were the highlights of my hunt: First, I saw how the four Gospels depicted the whole succession of events surrounding Jesus' death, from the Upper Room to Golgotha, as closely connected to the Jewish Passover, both chronologically and theologically. Second, I discovered how during the Last Supper Jesus strikingly interrupted—and left unfinished—the Passover liturgy by not drinking the fourth cup. Instead, he promised *not* to drink it until his royal glory was revealed sometime in the future. Third, I recognized the significance of Jesus' prayer for a certain "cup" to be taken from him.

Just what is this "cup"? And when would he drink it? Is it supposed to be viewed as one long protracted draught of suffering, beginning with his arrest and trial and concluding with his death upon the cross? Or does it refer only to his crucifixion?

On the other hand, it seems very possible, even likely, given the larger Passover setting, that Jesus saw "the cup" in connection with the skipped "fourth cup" of the Jewish Passover liturgy and his solemn cup-saying.[3]

Finally, I discovered John's use of irony and how it offers us solid grounds for linking the hour of Jesus' death with the hour of his kingdom glory.

Having assembled these clues, it was now time to return to my original question: What exactly did Jesus mean when he said, "It is finished"? So I went back to the text and reread it in context:

> A bowl full of vinegar stood there; so they put a sponge full of the vinegar on hyssop and held it to his mouth. When Jesus had received the vinegar he said, "It is finished"; and he bowed his head and gave up his spirit.
>
> JOHN 19:28-30

As I brought my findings to bear on the text, something suddenly hit me. I believed that at last I had an answer to my question.

The "IT" that was finished was the Passover that Jesus had begun—but interrupted—in the Upper Room! And its completion was marked by the sign of Jesus' drinking the sour wine, the fourth cup! Or to be more precise, what was finished was Jesus' fulfillment of the Passover of the Old Covenant, through his transformation of it into the New Covenant Passover.

Ironically, the hour of his crucifixion and death constituted no defeat; it was rather "the day and the hour" of Jesus' entrance into the glory of his kingdom, when he'd drink of the vine anew,[4] just as he had said. But it isn't his will to drink alone; for Jesus calls us, as his disciples, to partake not only of the "third cup," that is, the "cup of blessing" which we share in the Eucharist (see 1 Cor 10:16), but also of the "fourth cup" by dying for him (Mk 10:38-39).[5] Only then is the paschal mystery truly fulfilled in us.

Sharing My Findings

It wasn't long before I presented these discoveries to my students and parishioners. One evening I was besieged with questions from one particular seminary student taking my graduate course on the Gospel of John. A former Catholic, Bob seemed to get very animated when I explained the close connection between the Eucharist and the Passover, on the one hand, and Christ's crucifixion on the other.

He then posed a very loud and loaded question: "So, Professor Hahn, what *are* you saying, is the Eucharist a sacrifice or not?"

"To be frank, Bob, I haven't had the time to think through all of the implications. But it certainly seems to follow, doesn't it?"

Without even knowing it, Bob had started a train of thought going in my brain that I wasn't able (or willing) to stop. Before long, the entire seminar was drawn into the discussion. In fact, it went on for another hour and a half, long past the end of class.

I still recall the conclusions we reached that night: First, the Synoptic Gospels clearly depict Jesus instituting the Eucharist within the context of the Jewish Passover. Second, the Jewish Passover was the covenant sacrifice that Jesus meant to fulfill by his own self-offering. Third, that Passover sacrifice should not be separated from Jesus' sacrificial death on the cross; Jesus didn't finish the Passover until Calvary, where he fulfilled it. Fourth, the Eucharist is also inseparably united to Jesus' death; for Calvary began with the Eucharist, while the Eucharist ended with Calvary. In fact, they are one and the same sacrifice!

Bob stopped me on the way out of the seminar room that night. "Do you realize, Professor Hahn, that what you shared tonight fits perfectly with what I was taught in the *Baltimore Catechism?*"

I replied softly, "Bob, this may sound a little stupid, but what's the *Baltimore Catechism?*" I had never heard of it before.

He then explained how it was the basic guide for catechizing Catholics in America since the last century. It had never occurred to him, since leaving the Catholic Church years before, that its teachings on the Eucharist could be explained from Scripture.

It also had never occurred to me. After all, I'd long prided myself on my firm anti-Catholic convictions, along with my efforts to help Catholics find the truth of Jesus and leave their Church for the true gospel, as I understood it. Besides, I'd never even attended a single Mass.

My last words were from the heart: "Bob, all I can say is that I'm only following Scripture." Then I promised that I'd look into the *Baltimore Catechism*. And I did. Sure enough, he was right.

Further Confirmation From Scripture: John 6

Further study of the matter led me to additional revisions. For one thing, I sought confirmation and clarification elsewhere in Scripture for my conclusion regarding the inseparable union between Jesus' Passover sacrifice in the Eucharist and on Calvary.

Deeper research into John's Gospel shed considerable light on the matter, especially in Jesus' discourse on the Bread of Life in chapter six. The occasion for the discourse is explicitly stated: "Now the Passover, the feast of the Jews, was at hand" (6:4). John shows how Jesus miraculously provided bread for five thousand after "he had given thanks (*eucharistesas*)," evoking eucharistic imagery. Jesus then identified himself as the "true bread from heaven" (v. 32) and the "bread of life" (v. 35), drawing a parallel with Moses, through whom God supernaturally fed manna to the Israelites while forming a covenant with them after the first Passover (Ex 16:4ff.). John thus prepared his readers to recognize how Jesus would form the New Covenant by means of his own eucharistic sacrifice as High Priest and paschal victim. Even clearer testimony came in Jesus' amazing declaration:

> Truly, truly, I say to you, unless you eat the flesh of the Son of man and drink his blood, you have no life in you; he who eats my flesh and drinks my blood has eternal life, and I will raise him up at the last day. For my flesh is food indeed, and my

blood is drink indeed. He who eats my flesh and drinks my
blood abides in me, and I in him.

JOHN 6:53-56

Jesus used the strongest possible language to convey the truth
of his real presence in the Eucharist, as our Paschal Lamb, even in
the face of unbelief and scandal (see Jn 6:60-69).

Jesus' words horrified devout Jews for good reason: Leviticus
strictly prohibited the drinking of blood. Those who did so would
be cut off from their family. Did Jesus backpedal when he heard
their objections and say, "I'm just speaking figuratively?"

No. He said, in effect: "You've got it right. If you drink my
blood, you'll be cut off from all your kinsmen in the old Israel, and
cut off from the entire natural family of the old Adam as well.
Only then can I unite you to myself, in my flesh and blood, and
make you a part of the supernatural family of the New Adam, the
new Israel of God (see Gal 6:16). This is what I came to do, to
form God's New Covenant family in my own eucharistic flesh and
blood."

Clearly, Jesus wasn't just speaking figuratively or merely using a
metaphor. If that's all he was doing, it would have been very
easy—and absolutely essential—for him to have clarified his point.
And if he had done so, his Jewish listeners would've easily understood; in which case, there'd have been no cause for offense.

Actually, Jesus' audience back then had a much better excuse
for not believing than we do, because he hadn't died yet, much
less instituted the Eucharist. We can't get off so easily, for Jesus'
fulfillment of the Passover is now plainly manifest. He is the firstborn Son who was slain, the Lamb without blemish or broken
bones, the one who is slaughtered, whose blood is sprinkled—and
whose body must therefore be eaten.

The key to unlocking Jesus' hard saying is found in the original
Passover, on that fateful night in Egypt when Israel was about to

be set free. The rules were simple enough. You had to kill the lamb, sprinkle its blood and then eat it.

But suppose one of the Hebrew slaves in Egypt just couldn't stomach lamb. Let's say he killed the lamb and sprinkled the blood and then threw away the lamb chops in favor of steak, or baked some lamb-shaped cookies and ate them instead. What would've happened? That Hebrew would have awakened the next morning to find his oldest son or brother dead. Obeying two out of three instructions wasn't enough. They couldn't just *kill* the lamb; they had to *eat* it.

After all, death was only one aspect of the divine command to sacrifice. But God's ultimate purpose was to restore communion with Israel. And this is what was vividly represented and actualized by eating the Passover lamb. So God instructed every Israelite family as to what they must do. And they *had* to eat the lamb.

Thus, it is clear that Jesus' sacrificial death, begun in the Upper Room and finished on Golgotha, wasn't the full end of *his* Passover sacrifice either. Since the main purpose is to restore communion, we too have to eat the Lamb. This is why Jesus instituted the Eucharist.

Paul's Perspective

Paul shared a similar view of the matter, which he wrote to the Corinthians: "Christ, our paschal lamb, has been sacrificed" (1 Cor 5:7). Notice he doesn't conclude, "There is nothing more to be done." Instead he says in the very next verse, "Let us, therefore, celebrate the festival, not with the old leaven... but with the unleavened bread of sincerity and truth" (1 Cor 5:8). In other words, Paul understood that something more remains for us to do. We must feast upon Jesus, the Bread of Life and our Passover Lamb.

Paul confirmed this realistic outlook on the Eucharist later in the same epistle: "The cup of blessing which we bless, is it not a participation (or communion, *koinonia*) in the blood of Christ? The bread which we break, is it not a participation (*koinonia*) in the body of Christ?" (1 Cor 10:16). Such language reflects a solid belief in the real presence of Christ in the Eucharist. That's why Paul warned his fellow believers: "For anyone who eats and drinks without discerning the body eats and drinks judgment upon himself" (1 Cor 11:29).

The Letter to the Hebrews

I also found a similar outlook in the Epistle to the Hebrews. This came as a surprise, since I had always taught, as I had been trained, that Hebrews, more than any other New Testament book, contradicted the Catholic doctrine of the Eucharist as a sacrifice. The main theme of Hebrews is the priesthood of Jesus, particularly as it relates to his "once for all" sacrifice (see Heb 7:27; 9:12, 26; 10:10). This is succinctly stated:

> Now the point in what we are saying is this: we have such a high priest, one who is seated at the right hand of the throne of the Majesty in heaven, a minister in the sanctuary and the true tent which is set up not by man but by the Lord.
>
> HEBREWS 8:1-2

Unlike the Jewish priests in the Old Covenant, Jesus doesn't make daily offerings of distinct sacrificial victims (see Heb 7:27).

On the other hand, as our High Priest, Jesus must have something to offer as a sacrifice on our behalf: "For every high priest is appointed to offer gifts and sacrifices; hence it is necessary for this priest also to have something to offer" (Heb 8:3). Does this mean that Jesus' "once for all" sacrifice is exclusively past? On the contrary, it clearly implies that Jesus' sacrifice, precisely because of its "once for all" character, has become the one perfect offering that he continually presents in heaven. In other words, it's never-ending. That's why the Church calls it a "perpetual" sacrifice. As one of my teachers put it: "How can you repeat that which never ends?"

Jesus is no longer bleeding, suffering or dying (see Heb 9:25-26). Rather, he is enthroned in heaven with his resurrected body and with our glorified humanity, which he as our oldest brother, High Priest and King offers to the Father (see Heb 7:1-3). It is precisely in this manner that the Father beholds this perfect and perpetual offering in the living body of his Son.

If Jesus' offering has ceased, there would be no basis for his ongoing priesthood; but Jesus' priesthood is said to be permanent and to "continue forever" (see Heb 7:24). Moreover, there would be no reason for an earthly altar if Jesus' offering was ended. But the author of Hebrews teaches that we do: "We have an altar from which those who serve the tent have no right to eat" (Heb 13:10).

In sum, the "once for all" character of Jesus' sacrifice points to the perfection and perpetuity of his self-offering. It can be represented upon our altars in the Eucharist, by the power of the Holy Spirit, so that "through him [we] continually offer up a sacrifice of praise to God" (Heb 13:15).

Apocalyptic Perspective

Final confirmation came for me when I found a very illuminating feature of John's vision of Christ in the Book of Revelation. Upon hearing the angel announce the appearing of Jesus as "the Lion of the tribe of Judah," John looks and beholds "a Lamb standing, as though it had been slain" (Rv 5:5-6). In other words, he who is our celebrant priest and reigning king in the liturgical worship of the heavenly assembly also appears continually as the Passover Lamb of the New Covenant. He appears as the Lamb since his sacrificial offering continues. And it will abide with us until he restores and perfects communion with all of his children in the Eucharist. It will continue for God's family forever into eternity, for John depicts our everlasting blessedness as "the marriage supper of the Lamb" (Rv 19:9; 21:2-10; 22:17). But that's the last chapter.

Postscript: What Is the New Covenant Gospel?

At the close of deep discussions, like this one, I often ask my students to summarize what we've covered, and in the simplest terms possible. Wouldn't that be a nice thing to try right about now? So let me attempt to sum up the Gospel of the New Covenant, starting at the beginning and going to the end, in ten basic steps.

First, we start with the good news of creation: God is more than the wise Creator, he is also our loving Father. That's why he made us "in his own image," to live as his children, by his grace. "He is not far from any of us, and he gives us the power to live, to move, and to be who we are. 'We are his children.'"[6]

Second, God established a covenant with us from the beginning. A covenant is a sacred family bond in which persons give themselves to one another in loving communion. God calls us into a covenant relationship to share friendship with him and each other, as his family. To keep his covenant, we must trust and obey our Father in everything, just as we love each other as his sons and daughters. "Have we not all one father? Has not one God created us? Why then are we faithless to one another, profaning the covenant of our fathers?" (Mal 2:10, CEV).

Third, all of us have broken God's covenant. That's what sin is about. More than broken laws, sin results in broken lives, broken homes and broken hearts. We see it all around us: in society, at work and at home. We're selfish, dishonest, mean and miserable. "They are proud, conceited and boastful, always thinking up new ways to do evil.... They know God has said that anyone who acts this way deserves to die. But they keep on doing evil things, and they even encourage others to do them" (Rom 1:29-32, CEV). That's why the Father punishes sin with death, because sin kills the life of God within us and others.

Fourth, we desperately need God's mercy and grace. We'd like to think there's a simpler solution—more education, laws, technology or money. But that's almost like prescribing aspirin for AIDS! Sin's infection is too deep and deadly. But we shouldn't despair or get depressed. Our Father knows what we need better than we do. "Once we were also ruled by the selfish desires of our bodies and minds. We had made God angry, and we were going to be punished. But God was merciful! We were dead because of our sins, but God loved us so much that he made us alive with Christ" (Eph 2:3-4).

Fifth, the solution to our sin came when God became man in Jesus Christ. Jesus took on our weak and mortally wounded nature, not only to heal and perfect us, but to elevate us to share in his own life of divine sonship, to make us one with his Father. "Jesus and the people he makes holy all belong to the same Family. That is why he's not ashamed to call them his brothers and sisters" (Heb 2:11). Jesus did what no one else could do: he took out sin at its source. "We are people of flesh and blood. That is why Jesus became one of us. He died to destroy the devil, who has the power over death. But he also dies to rescue all of us who live each day in fear of dying" (Heb 2:14-15). Through his suffering and death, we are healed and brought home. This gives us the greatest confidence and hope. "See what love the Father has given us, that we should be called children of God; and so we are" (1 Jn 3:1, CEV).

Sixth, Jesus seals the New Covenant with us through his self-offering. This sacrifice began in the Upper Room, at the Passover meal, when he said to his disciples: "'Take, eat; this is my body'.... And he took a cup, and ... he gave it to them, saying, 'Drink of it, all of you; for this is my blood of the covenant, which is poured out for many for the forgiveness of sins'" (Mt 26:26-28, CEV). Christ sacrificed himself for us, first by instituting the Eucharist, and then by dying for us on Calvary. It is all of one piece.

Seventh, Jesus was raised from the dead by the power of the Holy Spirit. And the Holy Spirit is his gift to us. "Now that we are his children, God has sent the Spirit of his Son into our hearts. And his Spirit tells us that God is our Father" (Gal 4:6). God promises to give the Spirit to all who ask: "As bad as you are, you still know how to give good gifts to your children. But your heavenly Father is even more ready to give the Holy Spirit to anyone who asks" (Lk 11:13).

Eighth, the Holy Spirit comes to us through the sacraments in a powerful way; for Jesus instituted them, and now administers them to us, beginning with baptism. "Now the name of our Lord Jesus Christ and the power of God's Spirit have washed you and made you holy and acceptable to God" (1 Cor 6:11). The greatest of the seven sacraments is the Eucharist. It is the sacrifice of the New Covenant and the family meal that nourishes us with Jesus' own body and blood, just as he promised: "I am the bread of life.... My flesh is the true food, and my blood is the true drink. If you eat my flesh and drink my blood, you are one with me and I am one with you" (Jn 6:48, 55-56). Now he calls us to share this living Bread at the Father's table. "Listen! I am standing and knocking at your door. If you hear my voice and open the door, I will come in and we will eat together" (Rv 3:20).

Ninth, the Catholic Church is God's worldwide family that the Father sent the Son to establish by the Spirit. "Just as I am one with you and you one with me, I also want them to be one with us" (Jn 17:21). So we love the Church as our Mother, revere it as Christ's bride and obey its teachings, all because we trust that Jesus will be true to his word: "On this rock I will build my Church, and death itself will not have any power over it" (Mt 16:18). But Jesus doesn't stop there; he also gives us his mother, Mary, to be our own spiritual mother. "When Jesus saw his mother and the disciple whom he loved standing there, Jesus said to his mother, 'Woman, there is your son.' Then he said to the disciple, 'There is your mother'" (Jn 19:26-27; see Rv 12:1-2, 5, 17). Mary's grace all comes from Jesus. That's what makes her so powerful in God's family. No one ever honored his mother like Jesus; he now wants us to imitate him.

Tenth, as God's children, we are earthly pilgrims heading home to heaven. This makes heaven our true homeland, and death a true homecoming! "We are citizens of heaven and are eagerly awaiting for our Savior to come ... and make these poor bodies of ours like his own glorious body" (Phil 3:20-21). And the angels and saints who have gone before us are our older brothers and sisters. "You have now come to Mount Zion and to the heavenly Jerusalem. This is the city of the living God where thousands and thousands of angels have come to celebrate. Here you will find all of God's dearest children.... And you will find God himself" (Heb 12:22-23).

THIRTEEN

Here Comes the Bride:
The Son Rises Over the New Jerusalem

When people say "Church," what generally comes to mind? Structure, institution, hierarchy, rules, buildings, St. Peter's Basilica, the Pope. All this is true, but there's more to it.

In the Book of Revelation, John describes a vision of the Church as the New Jerusalem and the Bride of Christ, beautiful and pure. Yet this vision of the Church does not always fit with the experience many people have: scandal, hypocrisy, bland liturgies, false teaching.

In this last chapter we'll consider how Christ views the Church by examining various biblical images (bride, city, body, temple). This should help us to see ourselves—through the eyes of faith—as Christ sees us, even if we're not all yet canonizable saints.

The purpose of the New Covenant was not to abolish the earthly manifestations of the Old but to fulfill and expand them to their uttermost. Christ does this by establishing the New Jerusalem—one *worldwide* family of God, the Catholic Church. As the Father's final and definitive Word, Jesus did it all. But he's still doing it, even now—through us, his Church—to fulfill his Father's promises.

Apocalyptic Liturgy in the Heavenly Temple

After Jesus appeared to John (see Rv 1) and dictated the seven letters to the seven churches (see Rv 2-3), he invited John to "come up hither" (Rv 4:1). The Spirit whisked John into heaven and showed him a wondrous vision, blazing and colorful and noisy and crowded: the heavenly liturgy in the New Jerusalem. "It is in this eternal liturgy that the Spirit and the Church enable us to participate whenever we celebrate the mystery of salvation in the sacraments" (#1139).

In the Mass we hear the same call as John did. When the priest says, "Lift up your hearts (*sursum corda*)," Christ is inviting us—through the priest—to raise our vision and join with all the elect angels and saints in the heavenly worship, as it was revealed to St. John.[1]

Here and throughout the Book of Revelation John bombards the reader with the sights and sounds of his vision—sights and sounds we find meaningless, even bizarre, until we realize that the same sights and sounds would have been found in the Jerusalem temple.

John and his first-century readers would have realized immediately that the heavenly temple that John sees resembles the Jerusalem temple because, according to Scripture, the design of the earthly temple followed that of the heavenly (see Wis 9:8; 1 Chr 28:19). More importantly, the vision would have brought to mind not just the temple itself but everything it represented; for the temple and its trappings pointed to higher realities.

"The Temple ... is a microcosm of which the world itself is the macrocosm."[2] As we've seen, the Jerusalem temple represented the world in miniature. Conversely, the faithful see the world as a macrotemple. The temple was "the world in essence ... the theology of creation rendered in architecture."[3] This is also true of the new creation. As we'll see, John's visions all take place within the heavenly temple, which corresponds to "a new heaven and a new earth" (Rv 21:1).

Cosmic Worship: The Liturgy of Creation (Rv 4)

At the beginning of Revelation 4, the Spirit catches John into heaven and shows him the heavenly temple. He sees the throne and the One seated on the throne. Round the throne and supporting it are the four living creatures, the cherubim, just as there were four cherubim in the Holy of Holies, which was the throne room of the temple; two cherubim formed the mercy seat of the ark, while the other two overshadowed the ark (see Ex 37:7; 1 Kgs 6:23; Ps 80:1). From the throne issue thunder and flashes of lightning, as they did from the cloud of God's presence on Mount Sinai. Before the throne is a sea of glass, crystal clear, like the pavement seen on Mount Sinai (see Ex 24:9-10). These elements were also in Solomon's temple: the bronze sea and the Shekinah glory cloud (see 1 Kgs 7:23; 8:10-11).

John sees the cherubim as winged creatures, symbolizing the power behind the physical creation: the lion signifies power and authority; the ox, strength; the man, intelligence and wisdom; the eagle, motion and speed. Their heads indicate that they hold within themselves all living creatures and every part of the universe.

The twenty-four elders minister in the sanctuary, serving a royal priestly role: they are crowned, seated on thrones and dressed in the white garment of the priest (see Rv 4:4-10). The Greek word for elders is *presbyteroi*, whence the English word "priest."

A rainbow encircles the heavenly throne (see Rv 4:3). Since the time of Noah, the rainbow was the sign of God's covenant with creation. Just as God covenanted himself with man through Noah to renew physical creation, so has Christ renewed all of creation, physical and spiritual, and covenanted it to himself.

Revelation 4 thus describes the liturgy of creation, so called primarily because the participants in the heavenly worship glorify God as Maker, that is, the one who "didst create all things" (v. 11). Liturgy is worship of God by his creatures—a worship that is corporate, public, physical, orderly and glorious. All the earth is God's temple; everything in it joins to worship the Creator, praising God in the liturgy of the cosmic temple.

That all creation finds a place in the liturgy of the cosmic temple is evident in various sacred symbols. Recall how the act of divine creation described in Genesis 1 established the liturgical rhythm of the Old Covenant. God created the world in six days and rested on the seventh. This set the rhythm, a sabbatical "time signature" to creation. God stamped this liturgical rhythm into both space and time: "God said, 'Let there be lights in the firmament of the heavens ... and let them be for signs and for seasons and for days and years'" (Gn 1:14). "Signs and seasons" is a phrase used frequently throughout the Old Testament in connection to Israel's sacred calendar. "Seasons" are more than just spring, summer, winter and fall; they refer to the festivals of covenant renewal.

In the Old Covenant the sacred calendar was closely linked to the seasonal cycles of nature. At Pentecost the Jews celebrated the first fruits of the wheat harvest in the late spring. It was also known as the "Feast of Weeks," because it came seven weeks after Passover. (Significantly, the Hebrew word for "weeks" is *sheva'ot*, which can also be translated as "sevens" or "oaths.") The Feast of Tabernacles celebrated the fruit harvest in the fall. Because the cycle of the moon determined the months, the moon also determined when certain feast days fell.

Not just the act of Creation but the very being of creation worships God. Psalm 148 calls all levels of creation to praise the Lord: the heavens, the angelic hosts, the lights of the firmament, the earth, the sea, the mountains, the trees, the creatures, the elements.

On Earth As It Is in Heaven

An innumerable host of angels performs countless tasks in the ordering of creation. The angels are the instrumentalists; the things of creation are their instruments. Their service is the hymn of "Holy, Holy, Holy" before the throne of God, a command performance for the King and Creator and Author of the score.

At his creation man participated in the symphony. Original sin introduced discord. Man, the meeting place of physical and spiritual, represents the focal point of the universe. His sin not only declared war between body and spirit in himself but in all creation. The union of divinity with humanity in the person of Jesus Christ reunited physical and spiritual not just in man but in all creation. The drama of human salvation introduced the redemption of the entire world. To use the musical metaphor, the Incarnation reharmonized the symphony of creation.

We aren't accustomed to contemplating the symbolic meaning and divine mystery present within the world. Since the Enlightenment, many people have viewed God as a clock maker, winding up the universe and letting it run its course. (One might almost say that our scientific worldview is closer to ancient Baal worship, which held impersonal forces of nature as supreme powers in this world.)

Rather, the world was created to be a sacrament. In other words, everything on earth was made to point to heavenly realities. Science has stripped reality down to a barren rationalism. In so doing it has blurred reality; faith corrects our vision so that we can see the splendor and mystery—and romance—that is reality.

Throughout the world God has placed signs that symbolize invisible realities, signs that point to him. Tragically, his people are not familiar with those signs. So we end up missing the richness of the liturgy, which is meant to reflect the worship of the heavenly Jerusalem.

With My Body I Thee Worship:
The Liturgy of Redemption

God united divinity and humanity in the person of Christ not to free us from our bodies but to redeem them and all creation. God made us with souls and bodies. God wants us to worship him with our whole being—body and soul. Bowing and kneeling, robes, thrones and crowns, white, scarlet and purple, incense, candles and bells aren't just nice extras. They belong in our worship.

> The worship of God, surely, should be the place where men, angels, and devils may see human flesh once more set free into all that it was created to be. To restrict that worship to sitting on pews and listening to words spoken is to narrow things down in a manner strange to the gospel. We are creatures who are made to bow, not just spiritually (angels can do that) but with knee-bones and neck muscles. We are creatures who cry out to surge in great procession, 'ad altare Dei,' not just in our hearts (disembodied spirits can do that) but with our feet, singing great hymns with our tongues, our nostrils full of the smoke of incense.[4]

From the prostrations and worship and singing of the elders and the four living creatures, John directs his attention to the One on the throne, who holds in his hand a scroll with seven seals. No one is worthy to open the scroll but the Lion of the tribe of Judah, who is Jesus (see Rv 5:1-5; Gn 49:9).

John looks around. Instead of a lion, he sees Christ as a Lamb looking as though he has been slain. Why would Jesus, in his resurrection glory, resemble a slain lamb? To demonstrate that he remains in a perpetual state of sacrificial victimhood. Like the twenty-four elders he is both Priest and King; but he is also the sacrificial victim, perpetually offered for our salvation.

As both Priest and Victim, Christ offers the one perfect gift of self (see Heb 8:1-3). Unlike the sacrificial animals offered by the Levite priests, Christ no longer suffers, bleeds or dies. Yet he truly offers himself—both in heaven and upon our altars in the Mass—in order to sanctify us and deepen our communion with him.

John hears the living creatures and the elders proclaim the liturgical phrase "Worthy are thou" (see Rv 5:9-10) which first appeared in chapter four. The repetition reflects continuity between chapters four and five, but it also points to differences. In Revelation 4, the liturgy of creation, the living creatures and the elders worship and glorify God who created them (see v. 11). In Revelation 5, the liturgy of redemption, they worship and glorify the Lamb whose blood redeemed them (see v. 9). Other parts of Revelation 4 reappear: the throne and the One on the throne, the living creatures and the elders, incense, singing, prostrations. This is a unified liturgy with two distinct parts: one celebrates God for making us, while the other celebrates Christ for saving us.

The Lamb's sacrifice made him worthy to take the scroll. It made him worthy to be Priest and King. His sacrifice transformed the old order into the new to fulfill the covenant of Creation, and thus the living creatures and the elders sing a new song, the song of the New Covenant, the song that will always be new, even millions of years after its first performance.

The Lamb's sacrifice fashioned for God a kingdom of priests to reign on earth. As royal priests, we offer ourselves, in union with our High Priest and Lamb, as he offers himself to the Father on our behalf. We do this in the eucharistic liturgy, where we gather as royal priests and join with the living creatures and the elders in singing, "holy, holy, holy" and "Worthy art thou." Our participation in the Eucharist gives us the power to plod along and to overcome. History is controlled from the throne of the Lamb; but through the Church's liturgical worship, all of us can share in Christ's reign.

Worship As Warfare

In our liturgical worship, we approach Christ, the Lion who reigns, the Lamb who was slain. But we don't see him as Lion or Lamb. All we see is a wafer. Revelation 4 and 5 help us see that when we participate in the eucharistic liturgy, we participate in the heavenly liturgy; the "wafer" is really the Lamb who was slain. The song of praise of the heavenly congregation is woven into the fabric of Catholic liturgy. The Mass ushers us into the presence of the Father and of the Lamb, and into worship with the four living creatures, the elders, the saints and the myriads of angels. Although we cannot see them, we share the dignity and privilege of worshiping with them.

Our earthly worship environment should help us see what we can't see. It should strive to imitate its heavenly counterpart, which we glimpse through Revelation. Too often our liturgical art, music and architecture bow to utility and economy, when they should bow to the transcendent. John's vision inspires us to rethink the ways we design our churches. The visible should be a vehicle for the invisible, giving our senses a taste of the glorious mystery in which we partake, filling our beings with reverence and awe, lifting our minds and hearts to heaven.

In Revelation we discover our vital role as royal priests, as we affect the course of history and the destiny of nations through our worship. God's sovereignty extends to the whole world, but he exercises his rule—and executes his saving plan—in conjunction with the Church at prayer. We are part of a grand battle plan.

The following chapters of Revelation demonstrate how the prayers, chants and songs of liturgical worship determine covenant history. The liturgy does not end with Revelation 5 but continues through the rest of the book, forming the background for the other events of the vision and occasionally returning to the forefront. Liturgy is the setting for everything else.

Every subsequent vision of Revelation reveals the political, military and economic fallout of the heavenly liturgy and our participation in it—the influence of liturgy on covenant history. God rains down his judgment, he avenges our suffering, he protects and delivers us in direct response to the liturgy.

Christ's Bride and Body

In the opening verses of John's final vision, the Church is described in two ways: as the holy city, new Jerusalem; and as the beautiful Bride of Christ. We will consider both of these images, beginning with the Church as Christ's Bride.

> Then I saw a new heaven and a new earth; for the first heaven and the first earth had passed away, and the sea was no more. And I saw the holy city, new Jerusalem, coming down out of heaven from God, prepared as a bride adorned for her husband.
>
> REVELATION 21:1-2

The Holy City is the Bride of the Lamb (see Rv 21:9-10), loved by him, redeemed by his blood and cleansed and sanctified by him that he might present her to himself (see Eph 5:25-27). The heart of the universe, the goal of history, is love, romance and marriage. And new life.

Paul says that the Church is the body of Christ (see Eph 1:22-23; Col 1:24). "Now you are the body of Christ and individually members of it" (1 Cor 12:27). As members of the Church, we are members of Christ's body. Through participation in the Eucharist "we who are many are one body, for we all partake of the one bread" (1 Cor 10:17).

In Ephesians Paul explains how the Church is the bride of Christ. "Husbands should love their wives as their own bodies....

For no man ever hates his own flesh, but nourishes and cherishes it, as Christ does the church, because we are members of his body. 'For this reason a man shall leave his father and mother and be joined to his wife, and the two shall become one.' This is a great mystery, and I mean in reference to Christ and the church" (Eph 5:28-32).

In both passages Paul points back to Genesis 2. When God first made man, he formed the marital covenant. He caused Eve to come forth from Adam's side. When he saw her, Adam proclaimed her "bone of my bones and flesh of my flesh" (Gn 2:23).

At the beginning of time God drew an image of what things would be like at the end. Paul describes the picture painted in this primordial moment, when Adam and Eve became natural, physical, earthly signs of a supernatural, spiritual, heavenly reality: Jesus Christ and his Church. The Church is Christ's Body just as Eve was Adam's.

Paul discovered this by studying Genesis; John got it straight from Christ in a mystical vision.

This ties together in an exciting way our vision of the Church as Christ's Body and the Church as Christ's Bride. Too often we think of these as disconnected metaphors. Paul shows us otherwise.

The Church as the New Eve

From Adam's side came forth one who was both body and bride: Eve, formed from his body, was bone of his bone, flesh of his flesh. Joined to him in marriage, she became one body with him, his body, as he became her body. Similarly, from the side of Christ pierced by a lance came the Church. "The origin and growth of the Church are symbolized by the blood and water which flowed from the open side of the crucified Jesus."[5] Joined in nuptials to him, she who received life from his side became also his body. Just as Eve came from Adam and was united with him as one body, so the Church comes from Christ and is united to him as one body, his Body. The Church is Christ's Body, and as such is his Bride. The Church is Christ's Bride, and as such is his Body.

This is a remarkable vision—Adam and Eve, Christ and the Church—but how does it happen here and now?

Nuptial Signs of the New Covenant

When two become one in marriage, the bridegroom gives the bride his flesh and blood; the bride receives him, his flesh and blood. (The Greek word *haima*, usually translated "blood," can refer to other bodily fluids, including the man's "seed." See Jn 1:13.) When he gives and she receives, they bring new life into the world. When does Christ, the Bridegroom, unite himself with his Bride? When does he give his flesh and blood in order to bring new life? In the Eucharist. The Eucharist is the sacrament of the consummation of the marriage between Christ and his Church. In the Eucharist he renews the New Covenant, which is his marriage covenant with her. It is much more than a banquet. It is a wedding feast. We the Bride receive our Bridegroom's Body in the Eucharist.

The marital imagery of Christ's love for his Church becomes a powerful symbol for the sacrament of marriage. Or is marriage a powerful symbol of Christ's love for his Church—for each of us?

We may need to execute a sort of Copernican revolution in our understanding of love. Just as God's Fatherhood is the perfect reality that human fatherhood portrayed, though imperfectly, so the marriage of Christ and the Church is the perfect reality portrayed by human marriage. Our vision for marital love and sexual intimacy should reflect this reality.

This challenges believers, especially married ones, to make marriage and family life a sign of Christ's intimate union with his bride. This makes sex more than "four bare legs in a bed," as C.S. Lewis said. Every marital act becomes a sign and a renewal of the New Covenant, a reaffirmation of the intense love Jesus has for each of us. Every child becomes a reflection of the new life Christ has poured into his people. Fidelity to the marriage covenant images Christ's enduring fidelity to his Church.

Western society has made an idol out of sex. Sex dominates our entertainment, it sells our cars, it controls the way we think of ourselves. Our society is driven by sex; it lives for sex. Our longing for sexual intimacy is among our deepest desires and strongest passions. God has placed in us these natural desires, which reflect supernatural desires fulfilled only in him.

For example, we hunger for food. We eat food, we are filled. This images a spiritual longing within us, satisfied only when God fills us with himself. We long for beauty. We discover it in the things around us; but only when God's beauty ravishes us do we find peace. We desire intimacy, sexual union. We find it in other persons. But that desire points to a deeper desire, which only union with God can meet; and union with God proves to be deep intimacy, unimaginable ecstasy, infinite fulfillment of the desire to love and be loved, to give and receive totally, to become one with the other.

This is a truth that only the mystic can really understand; but then, mystics are lovers. And God wants us all to be lovers.

The New Covenant Fulfills the Old

In the Old Testament God took Israel as his bride. When she played the harlot, the Lord cast her off: "I will deal with you as you have done, who have despised the oath in breaking the covenant" (Ez 16:59; see also Hos 1-3). But he did not abandon her forever. He promised to remember his covenant and establish with her an everlasting covenant (see Hos 2:14-20; also Is 54; Ez 16:60).

Revelation 21:3-7, thick with Old Testament references, proclaims the fulfillment of God's promises to his people. On the cross, when his sacrifice was completed, Jesus announced, "It is finished" (Jn 19:30). Now that he has died and is risen, now that the vestiges of the Old Covenant have been swept away and the New Covenant is in place, Jesus can shout with his Father, "It is done!"

God promised his people that he would "dwell" (Hebrew *shakan*, literally "tabernacle") with them. Intimate presence was the sign of the covenant. And he did dwell with them, through his presence in the Shekinah glory cloud over and around the ark of the covenant. But when the ark disappeared and Babylon vanquished the country, God renewed his promise for a future and more glorious fulfillment: "I will make a covenant of peace with them; it shall be an everlasting covenant with them; and I will ... set my sanctuary in the midst of them for evermore. My dwelling place shall be with them; and I will be their God, and they shall be my people" (Ez 37:26-27)—the classic covenant formula. He promised to overcome death and change sorrow to joy (see Is 25:6-9; 65:17-18). He promised divine sonship: "I will be his father, and he shall be my son" (2 Sm 7:14).

It is all done in Christ. "The Word became flesh and dwelt among us" (Jn 1:14); literally, he pitched his tent among us. He is Emmanuel, God with us (see Is 7:14). Through him we are God's people, and in him we are sons of God. We are all made new: "If any one is in Christ, he is a new creation; the old has passed away, behold, the new has come" (2 Cor 5:17).

What God did in the Old Testament through Israel, God is continuing in the New Testament Church today. He is fathering his family, restoring the human race to his household.

The New Jerusalem: The Church on Earth

When in Revelation 21:9-21 John describes the dimensions and adornments of the New Jerusalem, he describes the heaven enjoyed by the saints at the end of time, the ultimate fulfillment of the New Covenant. We will enter into the fullness of the New Covenant, but only in eternity. We will enter fully into the new creation and the New Jerusalem when we enter heaven in our resurrected, glorified bodies. But John's vision can't be interpreted exclusively as a future reality. The kingdom of God, which can never be fully realized on earth, does find partial (but real) fulfillment in us on this side of heaven. We experience the fulfillment of the New Covenant now.

How? In the Church. The Church is the New Jerusalem. When we become members of the Church, we become citizens of the heavenly Jerusalem. Through the liturgy, through the sacraments, in the prayers and works of the people of God, we participate in heavenly life.

We don't experience this heavenly life with our earthly senses, but it is real. More real than the physical world. When the world ends, the Church will continue triumphant in heaven, and we will see and experience God's life fully, completely, ecstatically and eternally.

Time Intersects Eternity

"And he who sat upon the throne said, 'Behold, I make all things new'" (Rv 21:5). If these verses referred only to the end of time, then Christ would have said, "I have made all things new"; but the verb is in the present tense. "Therefore, if any one is in Christ, he is a new creation; the old has passed away, behold, the new has come" (2 Cor 5:17). Christ now makes all things new.

The complete renewal of the universe awaits the end of time; but renewal occurs even now—eternity breaking into time.

The Bride of the Lamb, the Holy City, is temporal. It exists here and now; but we discern the eternal realities of the New Covenant only through the eyes of faith. When we see temporal realities in the Spirit, we see eternity. Revelation describes things in temporal and eternal terms to teach us to live by faith, looking forward to sights to come. We do not have to choose between the eternal and the temporal. The temporal is shot through with the eternal, just as the eternal is signified and prefigured by the temporal. Revelation 21 reflects a marvelous dualism, both temporal and spatial. The New Jerusalem is now, but it is to come. The New Jerusalem is on earth below, but it is also in heaven above.

The Old, the New and the Eternal

God's plan unfolds in three stages: the Old Covenant is promise; the New Covenant is fulfillment; eternity is consummation. The time period between A.D. 30 and 70 represents a momentous turning point in God's covenant plan as it unfolds in history. All Old Covenant signs had to give way to New Covenant realities. Likewise, at the end of time, the New Covenant signs (the sacraments)—which actually do what they signify—will give way to the tangible realities of eternity.

While the fulfillment is spiritual and invisible, its reality cannot be underestimated. The New Jerusalem is now. This is not another piece in the puzzle of covenant-historical interpretation. This is the puzzle; this is the picture. This is the climax of the Old and New Testaments.

The True Holy of Holies

John says there is no temple in the city, and he says that there is a temple in the city—and he states both things in the same sentence (see Rv 21:22). First, why does he say there is no temple? John prepares us by measuring the city. It's a cube, the same shape as the Holy of Holies of the Old Covenant temple. And the word he uses for temple, *naos*, refers specifically to the inner sanctuary, as opposed to *hieron*, which indicates the entire temple structure. God dwelt in this inner shrine; and his people did not have direct access to him there. Now the veil has been rent, the Holy of Holies has been laid bare, the divisions of the Old Covenant temple have been destroyed. Now the entire city is the dwelling place of the Lord. Instead of shrouding himself in a dark cloud, God bathes the city and its citizens in his glorious light. All its citizens enjoy face-to-face fellowship with God.

There is no temple, no closed-off inner shrine; but there is a temple: the Lord and the Lamb (see Rv 21:22). John emphasizes that the temple of the New Jerusalem is not a temple such as God's people have known. It is not an impersonal building that erects barriers to separate the people from their God. The temple is the Savior, whom the old temple signified. The temple is the Lamb, the Paschal Victim, the eucharistic sacrifice, the new Adam from whence comes the Church, his Mystical Body and Bride, the New Jerusalem.

Saints as Living Sacraments

It may seem that the Church John envisions is a far cry from the Church that we have experienced. We see scandal and hypocrisy, bland liturgies, false teaching, broken families, sin and sinners everywhere. Down the street a new "nondenominational" fellowship may be serving up the Bible hot and spicy; its members are more rigorously observing God's law and more devoutly praying to him. Millions of Catholics have joined so-called Bible-believing churches because in them they see greater fervor. What do we do?

"We walk by faith, not by sight" (2 Cor 5:7). By faith we understand that the Church's essential identity is heavenly. We can't judge her by our earthly experience. She is only fully herself in heaven.

A Crisis of Saints

Here on earth the Church is a field full of both wheat and weeds, as Jesus himself taught in the parables of the kingdom of heaven (see Mt 13:24-30, 36-43). But she is really and truly the heavenly kingdom even here on earth. "The Church [is] ... at once holy and always in need of purification" (#827). She embraces saints and sinners. Sometimes we see only the sinners.

Through Scripture we must train ourselves to attain a sacramental vision of the Church. Don't ever let the mixed bag that is the Church on earth cause you to leave her or stay out of her. When you allow scandal to make you leave the Church or stay out of the Church, you are not only depriving yourself of the spiritual food of the sacraments, you are spurning Christ's Bride.

St. Cyprian once said, "You cannot have God as your Father without the Church as your Mother." Perhaps John would paraphrase this, "If you will not have the Bride, then you cut yourself off from the Bridegroom."

Sinners are in the Church, but they do not embody the Church. For them the Church is a hospital for healing—so they can be made into saints. The sacraments, the liturgy and especially the saints embody the Church's true essence. The saints embody John's vision of what the Church is and what her members are supposed to be.

The crisis of the Church is not reducible to the lack of good cat-echists, liturgies, theologians and so forth. It's a crisis of saints. But it's a crisis that our Father can be trusted to handle, especially if we allow him to keep his promises to us. "I am sure that he who began a good work in you will bring it to completion at the day of Jesus Christ" (Phil 1:6). So with Pope John Paul II, I urge you, "Make yourselves saints, and do so quickly!"

NOTES

ONE
Kinship by Covenant

1. The fatherly pedagogy that is revealed in the different stages of the divine economy of salvation history is summarized by St. Augustine: "The education of the human race, represented by the people of God, has advanced, like that of an individual, through certain epochs, or, as it were, ages, so that it might gradually rise from earthly to heavenly things, and from the visible to the invisible. This object was kept so clearly in view, that, even in the period when temporal rewards were promised, the one God was presented as the object of worship, that men might not acknowledge any other than the true Creator and Lord of the spirit, even in connection with the earthly blessings of this transitory life.... It was best, therefore, that the soul of man, which was still weakly desiring earthly things, should be accustomed to seek from God alone even these petty temporal boons, and the earthly necessities of this transitory life, which are contemptible in comparison with eternal blessings, in order that the desire even of these things might not draw it aside from the worship of Him, to whom we come by despising and forsaking such things" (*City of God*, Book X, 14).

2. Pope John Paul II, *Dives in Misericordia*: "The cross of Christ stands beside the path ... of that wonderful self-communication of God to man, which also includes the call to man to share in the divine life by giving himself ... and like an adopted son to become a sharer in the truth and love which is in God and proceeds from God" (v. 7).

3. St. Thomas Aquinas, *Summa Theologica* I, Q1. a.10: "The author of Sacred Scripture is God, in whose power it is to accom-

modate not only words for expressing things (which even man is able to do) but also the things themselves." He notes: "Now as words formed by man are signs of his intellectual knowledge; so are creatures formed by God signs of His Wisdom" (III, Q12. a.3).

4. For a fuller treatment of the familial aspects of covenants and oaths, and how they relate to the divine plan of salvation history, see S.W. Hahn, "Kinship by Covenant: A Biblical Theological Study of Covenant Types and Texts in the Old and New Testaments" (Ann Arbor, Mich.: University Microfilms, 1995).

5. *Against Heresies,* Bk. I, ch. X, no. 3. See Wisdom 12:21.

6. See D. Michaélidès, *Sacramentum Chez Tertullien* (Paris: Études Augustineiennes, 1970), who shows how Tertullian introduced the Latin term "sacramentum" into the Western tradition not only as a translation of the Greek term, "mysterion," but also with reference to the divine promises in salvation history that were backed by a covenant oath. See J.D. Laurance, *'Priest' as Type of Christ* (New York: Peter Lang, 1984), 60–64. Also for a profound and insightful treatment of the sacrament of baptism done in terms of covenantal oath-swearing, see M.G. Kline, *By Oath Consigned* (Grand Rapids, Mich.: Eerdmans, 1968).

7. This explanation of covenant in terms of sacred kinship reflects a broad consensus among scholars from among the various traditions. For a **Catholic** perspective, see D.J. McCarthy, S.J., *Old Testament Covenant: A Survey of Current Opinions* (Richmond: John Knox Press, 1972) 33: "There is no doubt that covenants, even treaties, were thought of as establishing a quasi-familial unity. In the technical vocabulary of these documents a superior partner was called 'father,' his inferior 'son,' and equal partners were

'brothers.'" Also see Paul Kalluveettil, *Declaration and Covenant* (Rome: Pontifical Biblical Institute, 1982), 212: "The idea, 'I am yours, you are mine' underlies every covenant declaration. This implies a quasi-familial bond which makes sons and brothers. The act of accepting the other as one's own reflects the basic idea of covenant: an attempt to extend the bond of blood beyond the kinship sphere." From a **Protestant** perspective, see F.M. Cross, "Kinship and Covenant in Ancient Israel" (Cambridge, Mass.: Harvard Biblical Colloquium, 1991), 10: "The language of covenant, kinship-in-law, is taken from the language of kinship-in-flesh." And: "The failure to recognize the rootage of the institution of covenant and covenant obligations in the structures of kinship societies has led to confusion and even gross distortion in the scholarly discussion of the term *berit*, 'covenant,' and in the description of early Israelite religion" (p. 14). See D. Smith, "Kinship and Covenant in Hosea," *Horizons of Biblical Theology* 16 (1994), 42: "Both the language of biblical covenant and treaty language developed in a social environment in which kinship was the primary model for understanding all human interaction. It was natural ... that international treaties, national (league) covenants, and individual covenants used kinship language to describe their content." From a **Jewish** perspective, see D.J. Elazar, *Covenant and Polity in Biblical Israel* (London: Transaction, 1995), 38: "Covenant links *consent* and *kinship*." Also see J.D. Levenson, *The Death and Resurrection of the Beloved Son* (New Haven, Conn.: Yale University, 1993), 40: "To us, these covenantal uses of familial language seem to be straightforward metaphors, but that is only because our culture makes a sharp distinction between biological and other types of relationship and attributes greater reality to the former.... Ancient Israel, following a different convention, could comfortably see a father and a son or two brothers in people who were known to have no blood relationship." See C. Baker, *Covenant and Liberation* (New York: Peter Lang, 1991), 38: "We might take as our working definition of covenant … a solemn and externally manifested commitment which strengthens kinship and family concern between both parties."

8. See N. Glueck, *HESED in the Bible* (Cincinnati, Ohio: Hebrew Union College Press, 1967), who defines "*hesed* as the mutual relationship of rights and duties between the members of a family or tribe" (p. 38). Elsewhere he notes: "Between the members of an alliance, just as between blood relatives, *hesed* was the only possible mode of conduct" (p. 46). He states: "The *hesed* which Israel showed Yahweh was the *hesed* that members of a family were obliged to show toward one another" (p. 60). And: "*Hesed* was the content of every *berith* [covenant] as well as every covenantal relationship" (p. 70).

9. Cited in J.L. McNulty in "The Bridge," *The Bridge* I (1955), 12.

10. *Redemptor Hominis* (Boston: Daughters of St. Paul, 1979), 17. Also see his encyclical *Dives in Misericordia*: "This covenant, as old as man—it goes back to the very mystery of creation—and afterwards many times renewed." (v. 7).

11. Pope John Paul II, *Puebla* (Boston: DSP, 1979), 86. Notably, the next line reads: "This subject of the family is not, therefore, extraneous to the subject of the Holy Spirit."

TWO
Creation Covenant and Cosmic Temple

1. The pentateuchal narrative itself often refers to Moses as writing its contents (see Ex 17:14; 24:4-7; 34:27; Nm 33:2; Dt 31:9-26). This is also affirmed elsewhere in Scripture, both in the Old

Testament (see Jos 1:7-8; 8:31-34; 23:6; Neh 8:1-14; Dn
9:11-13; Sir 24:23) and the New (see Mt 19:7-8; Mk 7:10;
10:3-5; 12:19-26; Jn 1:17; 5:45-47; 7:19; 8:5; Acts 3:22; Rom
10:5). Our respectful adherence to the traditional view of the
Mosaic authorship of the Pentateuch doesn't rule out the possibility that earlier sources were used or later editing was done. Indeed,
both are likely, but not necessarily in the way that modern critics
have often assumed; see P.J. Wiseman, *Ancient Records and the
Structure of Genesis: A Case for Literary Unity* (New York: Nelson,
1985). The Catholic Church's official affirmation of the "substan-
tive Mosaic authenticity and integrity of the Pentateuch" was pro-
mulgated by the Pontifical Biblical Commission (June 27, 1906);
see *Rome and the Study of Scripture* (St. Meinrad, Ind.: Abbey,
1964), 118–19. For a clear exposition and balanced defense, see
Archbishop Smith, *Mosaic Authorship of the Pentateuch* (London:
Sands, 1913). A more technical treatment of the critical arguments
is found in Augustin Cardinal Bea, *De Pentateucho* (Rome:
Biblicum, 1933). Also, many non-Catholic scholars, both
Protestant (R.K. Harrison, O.T. Allis, G.A. MacRae) and Jewish
(B. Jacob, U. Cassuto), accept and defend Mosaic authorship. The
Catholic Magisterium exemplifies prudent flexibility in the way it
maintains the traditional view of Mosaic authorship, which is
reflected in more recent statements, such as the famous 1948 letter
from Fr. Voste, Secretary of the Pontifical Biblical Commission, to
Cardinal Suhard of Paris (see *Rome and the Study of Scripture*,
150–53). Founded in the last century by Pope Leo XIII, the
Pontifical Biblical Commission was originally made up of cardinals,
to serve as an organ of the Magisterium. Then in 1971 it was
"demoted" to a mere advisory body of exegetes under the
Congregation for the Doctrine of the Faith. Decrees issued by the
Commission prior to 1971 were issued as authoritative norms and
binding guidelines for Catholic exegetes, though not strictly or
necessarily infallible *per se*. For a strong affirmation of the original

Commission's authority, see Pope St. Pius X, "Praestantia Sacrae Scripturae" (*Rome and the Study of Scripture*, 40–42).

As to what we mean by "greater explanatory power," see J. Ratzinger, *Behold the Pierced One* (San Francisco: Ignatius, 1986), 44–46: "From a purely scientific point of view, the legitimacy of an interpretation depends on its power to explain things. In other words, the less it needs to interfere with the sources, the more it respects the corpus as given and is able to show it to be intelligible from within, by its own logic, the more apposite such an interpretation. Conversely, the more it interferes with the sources, the more it feels obliged to excise and throw doubt on things found there, the more alien to the subject it is. To that extent, its explanatory power is also its ability to maintain the inner unity of the corpus in question. It involves the ability to unify, to achieve a synthesis, which is the reverse of superficial harmonization. Indeed, only faith's hermeneutic is sufficient to measure up to these criteria."

2. For a patristic example of a literal reading, see St. Augustine, *The Literal Meaning of Genesis*, 2 vols. (New York: Paulist, 1982). The reason why "literal" advocates are called "fundamentalists" is that, in the twentieth century, most of them are. Plus, the tendency to interpret Scripture in an overly literal manner *is* a fundamentalist trait, and that's what many "literal" advocates do. However, there are too many other (more basic) defining traits of fundamentalism to justify classifying every "literal" advocate as a fundamentalist. Some of these other features include apocalyptic millennarianism, Zionism, separatism and the wholesale rejection of other allegedly unredeemable items like historical criticism, sacramentalism, the patristic tradition of spiritual/allegorical exegesis, etc.

By way of historical background, fundamentalism started early in the twentieth century as a reactionary movement among conservative Protestants who were opposed to the liberal takeover of mainline denominations. It gets its name from a list of core beliefs which were enumerated and expounded by conservative Protestant writers in a multivolume series published under the title *The Fundamentals* (edited by R.A. Torey; Los Angeles: Bible Institute, 1917). "True believers" were able to identify each other by their adherence to five "fundamentals": biblical inerrancy, Jesus' divinity, virgin birth, atoning death and bodily resurrection and future advent. Noteworthy is a comment from the Biblical Commission's recent document *The Interpretation of the Bible in the Church*: "Fundamentalism is right to insist on the divine inspiration of the Bible, the inerrancy of the Word of God and other biblical truths included in its five fundamental points. But its way of presenting these truths is rooted in an ideology which is not biblical." (Boston, DSP, 1993), 73.

3. For a useful analysis of the similarities between Genesis and ancient Near Eastern Creation myths (e.g., Enuma Elish, Atrahasis Epic), and the much greater dissimilarities, see D.T. Tsumura, "Genesis and Ancient Near Eastern Stories of Creation and Flood: An Introduction," in R.S. Hess and D.T. Tsumura, eds. *"I Studied Inscriptions From Before the Flood": Ancient Near Eastern, Literary and Linguistic Approaches to Genesis 1-11* (Winona Lake, Ind.: Eisenbrauns, 1994), 27–57.

4. The *Catechism of the Catholic Church* speaks of "the history of the fall narrated in Genesis" (#388), and asserts that "the account of the fall in Genesis 3 uses figurative language, but affirms a primeval event, a deed that took place at the beginning of the history of man," which was "committed by our first parents" (#390). For authoritative guidance on the much harder question of what narrative elements of Genesis 1–3 should be regarded as historical, one should consult the Biblical Commission's *responsum*, "On the Historical Character of the First Three Chapters of Genesis" (June

30, 1909), which lists nine "narrated facts" whose "literal and historical meaning" should not be "called in question": (1) the creation of all things... by God at the beginning of time; (2) the special creation of man; (3) the formation of the first woman from man; (4) the unity of the human race; (5) the original happiness of our first parents in a state of justice, integrity and immortality; (6) the divine command laid upon man to prove his obedience; (7) the transgression of that divine command at the instigation of the devil under the form of a serpent; (8) the fall of our first parents from their primitive state of innocence; (9) the promise of a future redeemer. See *Rome and the Study of Scripture*, 123.

5. See *The Catechism of the Catholic Church*, #1951–60.

6. *Summa Theologica* I–II, q. 91, art. 4–5. While these notions of nature and grace may seem abstract and elusive, with a little bit of effort they should start to stick. They're also useful for building bridges between biblical exegesis and dogmatic theology, something badly needed these days. These notions also dovetail with classical Catholic principles of how grace relates to nature: (1) The orders of nature and grace are distinguished in order to be united, not separated; (2) grace doesn't abolish—but builds upon—nature: by healing it, perfecting it and elevating it. Christians in every generation need to grasp these notions; for in this area, errors can be very harmful and confusing, especially these days, when they assume rather subtle forms (e.g., "Man isn't religious by nature, only by grace"; "Law is a secular and public matter, while religion and morality are merely spiritual and private").

7. Joseph Ratzinger, *A New Song for the Lord* (New York: Crossroad, 1996), 69: "[I]t is fundamental that the Sabbath is part of the story of creation. One could actually say that the metaphor of the seven-day week was selected for the creation account

because of the Sabbath. By culminating in the sign of the covenant, the Sabbath, the creation account clearly shows that creation and covenant belong together, from the start, that the Creator and the Redeemer can only be one and the same God. It shows that the world is not a neutral receptacle where human beings then accidentally become involved, but that right from the start creation came to be so that there would be a place for the covenant. But it also shows that the covenant can exist only if it conforms to the yardstick of creation." Also see R. de Vaux, *Ancient Israel* (New York: McGraw-Hill, 1961), 2:481: "Creation is the first action in the history of salvation; once it was over, God stopped work, and he was then able to make a covenant with his creature.... The 'sign' of the covenant made at the dawn of creation is the observance of the sabbath by man (cf. Ez 20:12, 20)."

8. The view of the Creation Sabbath as God's covenant oath seems to have been commonplace in ancient Judaism, especially around the time of Christ. For instance, we read in Jubilees 36:7, "I will make you swear by that great oath—because there is not an oath which is greater... [than] the glorious and honored... and mighty Name which created heaven and earth and everything together—that you will fear and worship him." We also read in 1 Enoch 69:15-27: "He then revealed … the power of this oath, for it is power and strength itself.... By that oath, the sea was created.... By that oath the depths are made firm.... By the same oath the sun and the moon complete their courses.... This oath has become dominant over them." This is also echoed later in *Sifre Deut.* 330: "When the Holy One, blessed be He, created, He did not create except by an oath." See R. Murray, *The Cosmic Covenant* (London: Sheed and Ward, 1992), 2–13.

9. See Joshua Berman, *The Temple: Its Symbolism and Meaning Then and Now* (Northvale, N.J.: Jason Aronson, 1995), 10–14.

10. Abraham Joshua Heschel, *The Sabbath* (New York: Farrar, Straus and Young, 1951), 29: "The Sabbath itself is a sanctuary which we build, a sanctuary in time." See A. Green, "Sabbath as Temple: Some Thoughts on Space and Time in Judaism," in R. Jospe and S.Z. Fishman, eds., *Go and Study* (Washington, D.C.: B'nai B'rith-Hillel Foundations, 1980), 287–305; J.D. Levenson, "The Temple and the World," *Journal of Religion* 64 (1984): 275–98.

11. See Jubilees 8:19: "Noah knew that the garden of Eden was the holy of holies and the dwelling of the Lord." Also see G.J. Wenham, "Sanctuary Symbolism in the Garden of Eden Story," *Proceedings of the Ninth World Congress of Jewish Studies* (Jerusalem: World Union of Jewish Studies, 1986), 19–25.

THREE
Splitting the Adam

1. *Table Talk*, May 1, 1830; cited by K. Burke, "On the First Three Chapters of Genesis," in R. May, ed., *Symbolism in Religion and Literature* (New York: George Braziller, 1960), 119.

2. The *Catechism* states: "As long as he remained in the divine intimacy, man would not have to suffer or die" (#376). If Adam was tested with the prospect of suffering and death, as we'll argue below, it does *not* follow that—by giving consent to the loss of all things, for the love of God—Adam would have experienced suffering and death, at least as we know it (viz., disintegration, corruption). On the contrary, it would have produced the purest passion and ecstatic joy that the human soul can know, coming as it were from the fire of divine love within the heart, as witnessed in the

deaths of many martyrs. For a remarkable treatment of this much neglected datum of the Church's living tradition, see Louis Chardon, *The Cross of Jesus,* 2 vols. (St. Louis: Herder, 1957).

3. Later in Scripture the apostle Paul reflects on this text when he says: "[Man] is the image and glory of God; but woman is the glory of man" (1 Cor 11:7). Many readers assume that Paul meant that woman doesn't bear God's image as much as man. In fact, Paul is making the opposite point, that is, to paraphrase: "If man, as God's image-bearer, is the climax of creation, then woman, with all her beauty, is the most glorious expression of God's image in man."

4. The narrative also doesn't mention how much, if any, time elapsed between their betrothal and the confrontation with the serpent-tempter in the next chapter. For the reader, therefore, this confrontation occurred on the same day, at least in terms of narrative time, since no passage of days is indicated.

5. Cited by J. Higgins, "Anastasius Sinaita and the Superiority of Woman," *Journal of Biblical Literature* 97 (1978), 254; this quote is taken from her translation of a disputed fragment from Irenaeus.

6. God's curse on the serpent (crawling on its belly, eating dust, and having its head crushed; see Gn 3:14-15) shouldn't be taken to mean that the serpent couldn't have been anything more than a harmless snake. In the first place, the curse resulted when the serpent plunged the family of God into the spiritual ruin of original sin and death. It does not seem fitting if the punishment entailed nothing more than what's reflected in the lowliness of the snake's natural habitat at present. Such a punishment would hardly be a curse of any consequence; indeed, it would almost appear trivial compared to the enormity of the crime which the serpent perpe-

trated. While God's curse may be connected to the snake's lowly condition after the Fall, at least in some provisional sense, nonetheless that curse is probably meant for a fulfillment of much greater magnitude, that is, when God delivers the ultimate deathblow to "the great dragon, that ancient serpent," by means of the woman and her "seed" (see Rv 12:9). Indeed, only such a punishment would fit the serpent's crime and represent an absolute humiliation to Satan. Moreover, it would constitute the kind of decisive victory that God alone would be able to accomplish. See Psalm 74:14, where "the serpent" is said to be divinely dispatched in a similar manner: "Thou didst crush the heads of Leviathan."

7. See the *Apocalypse of Abraham* 23:1-12: "My eyes ran to the side of the garden of Eden, and I saw a man very great in height.... entwined with a woman who was also equal to the man in aspect and size. And behind the tree was standing (something) like a *dragon* in form.... [It was] Azazel himself." Azazel was a common name for Satan in Jewish writings from the intertestamental period. Pope John Paul II, *Jesus Son and Savior* (Boston: Pauline Books, 1996), 28–29: "Especially to be noted is the Book of Revelation ... according to which 'the great dragon was thrown down ... that ancient serpent [this is an explicit reference to Genesis 3], who is called the Devil and Satan.'"

8. See E. Van Wolde, *Words Become Worlds: Semantic Studies of Genesis 1-11* (Leiden: E.J. Brill, 1994), 17: "[T]his pericope [is] characterized by a considerable togetherness ... which appears from the fact that in all the verses of this episode the verbs and pronominal suffixes are in the plural, all in all twelve times in seven verses."

9. M. Kolarcik, *The Ambiguity of Death in the Book of Wisdom 1-6* (Rome: Pontifical Biblical Institute Press, 1991), shows how death has the same ambiguous double meaning in the trial of the

righteous by the unrighteous in Wisdom 1-6. The righteous man they kill is the one who truly lives and whom God rewards with glory, while in the act of killing him, the killers truly die themselves (Wis 2-3).

10. *Catechism of the Catholic Church,* #398.

11. Everett Fox points out that the serpent's opening line, in the Hebrew, is really an incomplete phrase, known as "aposeopoesis," which "leaves it to the reader to complete the speaker's thought which in the Bible is usually an oath or a threat (see also, for instance, 14:23, 21:23, 26:29, 31:50)" (*The Five Books of Moses* [New York: Schocken Books, 1995], 21).

12. See Fr. John Hugo, *Your Ways Are Not My Ways* (Pittsburgh: EWS, 1986), 135: "*Even before the Fall,* Adam and Eve were tested by mortification, for they were required to give up 'the fruit…' which stands for all earthly goods, in order to die by giving up their own wills." Also see St. Leo the Great (A. Field, trans.), *The Binding of the Strong Man* (Ann Arbor: Word of Life, 1976), 25: "If the first man had obeyed God and preserved the dignity with which he had been endowed, this spiritual part of his make-up would have lifted up the material part with itself to heavenly glory. But he listened to the deceiver and was taken in by his suggestions. He thought he could forestall the hour and win the honor that was in store without having to undergo *probation*" [emphasis added].

13. See C.M. Pate, *The Glory of Adam and the Afflictions of the Righteous* (Lewiston, N.Y.: Mellen, 1993); M. Fishbane, *The Kiss of God: Spiritual and Mystical Death in Judaism* (Seattle: University of Washington Press, 1994), 126: "Heavenly love is activated by human death. Self-sacrifice thus stands at the heart of Being—a sacrament of love."

14. For an excellent presentation of the evidence showing how Genesis 3:15 is fulfilled by Jesus and Mary, as the New Adam and New Eve, see D.J. Unger, *The First Gospel: Genesis 3:15* (St. Bonaventure, N.Y.: Franciscan Institute, 1954).

15. This outlook is reflected in the remarkable statement at the end of a first-century Christian document, the Didache: "Then the creation ... will come to the fire of testing, and many will fall away and be lost, but those who endure their faith will be saved by the curse itself" (Didache 16:5).

16. In explaining original sin, this text was "perhaps more often quoted by the Fathers than any other," according to Neil Forsyth, *The Old Enemy: Satan and the Combat Myth* (Princeton, N.J.: University Press, 1987), 300. See *Catechism of the Catholic Church*, #407.

FOUR
Shape Up or Ship Out

1. Notice how sin is symbolized as a beast of prey. This predatory image closely parallels the *modus operandi* and guise of Satan as a deadly serpent in the previous chapter. It may also point to the symbolic significance surrounding the origins of animal sacrifice.

2. On envy as a pervasive (but seldom recognized or acknowledged) social force in Western society, see H. Schoeck, *Envy: A Theory of Social Behavior* (New York: Hartcourt, Brace & World, 1966). Also see Max Scheler, *Ressentiment* (New York: Free Press, 1961); J.H. Berke, *The Tyranny of Malice: Exploring the Dark Side of Character and Culture* (New York: Summit, 1988).

3. On the "mark" of Cain as a covenant oath sign, see M.G. Kline, "Oracular Origins of the State," in G.A. Tuttle, ed., *Biblical and Near Eastern Studies* (Grand Rapids, Mich.: Eerdmans, 1978), 132–41. The "mark" may be seen as an oath-sign of Cain's new bond of allegiance with Satan, the murderous serpent (see the "mark of the beast" in Rv 13); thus it would warn others to steer clear.

4. See P.S. Alexander, "The Targummim and Early Exegesis of 'Sons of God' in Genesis 6," *Journal of Jewish Studies* 23 (1972): 60–71.

5. The language of covenant "renewal," which is explicitly used in Genesis 9, certainly implies an already existing covenant, namely, the creation covenant (see Jer 33:20; Is 54:9); see W.J. Dumbrell, *Covenant and Creation* (New York: Thomas Nelson, 1984), 11–46; and idem, "The Covenant with Noah," *Reformed Theological Review* 38 (1979): 1–8. There are several optional views of the covenantal significance of the bow as the sign of (1) God's oath (Gunkel); (2) peace from God hanging up his war-bow (Batto); (3) the restored domed firmament of heaven (Turner); (4) God's allowance for hunting and meat eating (Coote and Ord).

6. See F.W. Bassett, "Noah's Nakedness and the Curse on Canaan: A Case of Incest," *Vetus Testamentum* 21 (1971): 232–37; D. Steinmetz, "Vineyard, Farm, and Garden: The Drunkenness of Noah in the Context of Primeval History," *Journal of Biblical Literature* 113 (1994): 199–200; R.W.E. Forrest, "Paradise Lost Again," *Journal for the Study of the Old Testament* 62 (1994): 3–18. The other two major interpretive options (homosexual rape and castration) utterly fail to explain why Noah cursed Canaan rather than Ham.

7. This view is taken in Targum Onkelos, Philo, Maimonides, Rashi, Ibn Ezra and various midrashim (Joma 10a; Gen. R. 36).

8. See J.H. Charlesworth, ed., *The Old Testament Pseudepigrapha*, vol. 2 (Garden City, N.Y.: Doubleday, 1985), 35–142.

9. See M. Fishbane, *Text and Texture* (New York: Schoken, 1979), 38; and D. Smith, "What Hope After Babel?" *Horizons in Biblical Theology* 18 (1996): 169–91.

10. It is interesting to note, in this connection, how Shem has been frequently identified with the mysterious figure of Melchizedek, the priest-king of Salem, who blessed Abram and offered him bread and wine, after receiving his tithes (Gn 14:18). This common interpretive outlook is reflected in many ancient Jewish sources (targumic, midrashic, rabbinic), and not without textual reasons. See M. McNamara, *Palestinian Judaism and the New Testament* (Wilmington, DE: Michael Glazier, 1983), 208: "An analysis of the dates and life-spans of the post-diluvian patriarchs in Genesis 11 indicates that Shem lived into, and well beyond, the time of Abraham. What is more natural than to identify the mysterious Melchizedek of Abraham's day with him, as for instance is done in the Palestinian Targum (all texts)." Also see J. Fitzmyer, who notes: "The haggadah identified Melchizedek with Shem, the eldest son of Noah, because from Adam to Levi the cult was supposed to have been cared for by the firstborn" ("Now This Melchizedek... [Heb 7:10]," *Catholic Biblical Quarterly* 25 [1963], 312, n. 32; citing Spicq, *Hebreux* II, 205). Also see Robert Hayward, "Shem, Melchizedek, and Concern with Christianity in the Pentateuchal Targumim," in Kevin J. Cathcart and M. Maher, eds., *Targumic and Cognate Studies* (Sheffield, UK: Sheffield Academic Press, 1996), 67–80.

Identifying Melchizedek with Shem also serves to explain where Melchizedek got the blessing that he gave to Abram, since Shem was the last one to have received a blessing in this Genesis narrative (see Gn 9:26). Perhaps not surprisingly, this Shem-as-Melchizedek view also came to be shared by many ancient Christian interpreters like Ephrem and Jerome (both saints and doctors of the Church). It later became a commonplace in the Medieval period, as it appears in Alcuin, Sedulius, Scot, Aimon d'Auxerre, and Peter Lombard; it ever shows up in the marginal annotations of the *Glossa Ordinaria (PL* 198:1094–95), not to mention Martin Luther's commentary on Genesis.

It should be noted that the text of Hebrews 7:3 ("He is without father or mother or genealogy, and has neither beginning of days nor end of life") does not contradict the identification of Shem with Melchizedek. The author of Hebrews is often misinterpreted as though he were simply arguing from the silence of Scripture as to the origins of Melchizedek. Quite apart from fallacious reasoning, that line of argument fails to account for the fact that Jesus had a genealogy (see Mt 1 and Lk 3), which the author already knew well to be Judahite (see Heb 7:14). Instead Hebrews 7:3 must be interpreted in view of the technical requirements that candidates needed before they could qualify for the Levitical priesthood: they had to prove their pure Levitical pedigree by producing a paternal and maternal genealogy, which also confirmed their age of eligibility (from 30 to 50); see Ex 32:29; Nm 3:45; 4:3; 8:24-25; Ezr 2:61-63; Neh 7:63-65). But this arrangement only came into being after the firstborn sons of Israel had forfeited their priesthood with the golden calf episode at Sinai (Ex 32; Nm 1-8). The pre-Levitical priesthood that was passed from fathers to firstborn sons was thus cancelled, at least until God the Father sent his firstborn son to restore it (see Hebrews 1:6). This seems to be what Heb 7:12 is referring to: "For when there is a change in the priesthood, there is necessarily a change in the law" (Heb 7:12).

For the author of Hebrews, then, Shem-Melchizedek was an earthly prototype of Jesus, God's firstborn son (Heb. 1:6), whose royal high priesthood is administered in the heavenly Jerusalem (see Heb 12:22-24), where he offers himself in the form of heavelnly bread and wine, the New Covenant Eucharist (see Heb 8-10). For additional background and argumentation, see Hahn, "Kinship by Covenant," pp.. 153–65; 171–81; 568–92.

FIVE
How Do You Spell Belief?

1. From a Christian perspective, Melchizedek is a type of Christ. As the royal priest of the earthly Jerusalem, Melchizedek blessed Abram and his family by giving them bread and wine; so Jesus is enthroned as our royal High Priest in the heavenly Jerusalem, where he blesses Abraham's spiritual family by offering to them heavenly bread and wine in the Eucharist. For the symbolic aspects of this story within the Genesis narrative, see D. Steinmetz, *From Father to Son: Kinship, Conflict and Continuity in Genesis* (Louisville, Ky.: Westminster, 1991), 147: "The story of Abraham's battle with the kings is crucially linked to the forging of God's covenant with Abraham immediately following. We read the terms of the covenant and come to see that the future of Abraham's descendants will have the shape of Abraham's own past. And, looking back at the battle with the kings, we realize that, at the precise moment that Abraham had enacted the primeval blessing, he had enacted the destiny of the future nation of Israel." In short, Israel's conquest of the Promised Land, along with their subsequent divine blessing, was foreshadowed by Abram's experience in Genesis 14. This indicates how the Israelites were meant practically to meditate on the law, which certainly includes Genesis, by contemplating their divine mission in history in light of the narrative of their forefather's life.

2. See H.C. Brichto, *The Names of God* (New York: Oxford University, 1998), who notes: "In Ch. 15 the territory promised to his descendants was to extend from 'the river of Egypt to the Great River, Euphrates.' In neither direction ... did historic Israel ever attain—perhaps even aspire to—such distant borders. But YHWH never limited his promise to a single branch, nor even to two or three branches, of Abram's line." It may be useful to distinguish the larger scope of the land promised to *Abram's* "seed" in Genesis 15:18, which includes the land of Arabia as Ishmael's, from the narrower scope of the divine promise of Canaan to *Abraham's* "seed" in Genesis 17, which was only meant for Israel.

3. T. Thompson, "The Origin Tradition of Ancient Israel" (*Journal for the Study of the Old Testament*, 1987), 89: "The fulfillment of Abraham's childlessness in 16:15 ... is only an *apparent* fulfillment.... Ishmael's birth in Genesis 16 becomes the opening episode of a story of the *displace-ment* of Ishmael." He adds: "It is with Isaac and Isaac alone that God establishes his covenant (Gn 17:19, 21)."

4. See Levenson, *Death and Resurrection of the Beloved Son*, 121: "The idea that Moriah was always another designation of the Temple Mount in Jerusalem is as rare among critical scholars as it is ubiquitous in Jewish tradition.... The same cult-site almost certainly lies behind the use of the name 'Salem' in Genesis 14:18, a name that otherwise occurs only in Psalm 76:2, where it parallels 'Zion.' The midrashic notion that Jerusalem received the second half of its name in Genesis 14 and the first in Genesis 22, though still unscientific, is thus less far-fetched than at first seems the case." For this midrashic notion, see Genesis Rabbah, 56.10A: "Abraham called it 'will choose.' Shem called it Shalem based on 'AND MALKIZEDEK KING OF SHALEM' (Gn 14:18). Said the Holy One, if I call it *yir'eh* (will choose) as Abraham called it, then

Shem, the just one, will be upset; if on the other hand, I call it Shalem as Shem called it, Abraham, also a just man, will be upset; then let me combine their names, Yerushalem: Yir'eh-Shalem" (*Midrash Rabbah*, eds., Freemen and Simon [London: Soncino, 1951]). Also see L. Ginzberg, *Legends of the Jews* (Philadelphia: Jewish Pubns, 1956), 1:285ff; and M. McNamara, *Palestinian Judaism and the New Testament* (Wilmington, Del.: Michael Glazier, 1983), 159–204.

SEVEN
"Let My People Go!"

1. In this text (Ex 8:25-27), we find a valuable clue to solve a modern-day puzzle (Why did God command animal sacrifice?), one that seems to have been much less puzzling to the early Church fathers and ancient rabbis. In ancient Jewish interpretive traditions, it was clearly understood that God commanded Israel to sacrifice to him the animals that were worshiped in the Egyptian cult as gods: Hathor under the form of a cow, and Aries under the form of sheep. It is stated matter-of-factly by Josephus (*Apion* I:26) and emphasized by Philo: "The most horrible form of idolatry is the worship of irrational beings ... animals, as done by the Egyptians.... They have even deified the fiercest and most savage of wild animals" (cited in P. Borgen, "Man's Sovereignty Over Animals and Nature According to Philo of Alexandria," in T. Fornberg and D. Hellholm, eds., *Text and Context* [Boston: Scandanavian University Press, 1995], 380). Borgen continues: "Philo gives here his own version of the kind of criticism and ridicule of Egyptian animal worship which was quite widespread among non-Egyptians in the Graeco-Roman world" (381). This is also a typical interpretation echoed in the Midrashim (Lev. Rab. 22s), along with the medieval rabbis (Rashi, Maimonides,

Nachmanides), and found in some modern Jewish scholars (Weinfeld, Cassuto). This interpretation also represents a virtual consensus among the early Church fathers (*Didascalia Apostolorum*, Athanasius, Justin Martyr, Irenaeus, Origen, Eusebius, Gregory of Nyssa, Basil, Gregory Nazianzus, John Chrysostom, Ephrem, Aphrahat, Augustine, Jerome), through the medieval period (Anselm, Hugh of St. Victor, Thomas Aquinas). For a thorough summary treatment of all of these rabbinic, patristic and medieval figures, replete with sources and citations, see the remarkable book by S.D. Benin, *The Footprints of God: Divine Accommodation in Jewish & Christian Thought* (Albany: SUNY Press, 1993). Also see Hahn, "Kinship by Covenant," 42-50. Very few modern scholars even seem to be aware of this view; see B. Childs, *Exodus* (Philadelphia: Westminster, 1974), 157; J. Davis, *Moses and the Gods of Egypt* (Grand Rapids, Mich.: Baker, 1986), 116-17. However, it has been recently treated by Egyptologist, J.D. Hoffmeier: "It has long been maintained that ... a specific degrading of Egyptian deities is evident in the plague narratives. Ex 12:12 and Nm 33:4 point out that plagues and exodus were God's executing judgment on 'the gods of Egypt.' Furthermore, Jethro ... said, 'Now I know that the Lord is greater than all gods' (Ex 18:11a; RSV). Some have tried to see an Egyptian deity behind each plague... e.g., Nile and the god Hapi; frogs and the goddess Heket; the cows and bulls struck by the murrain as representing Hathor and Apis respectively; the Sun being obscured and the god Re." ("Egypt, Plagues in," *Anchor Bible Dictionary*, vol. 2 [New York: Doubleday, 1992], 376). Interestingly, many of the interpreters listed also understand the prohibition by Moses of "unclean" animals in terms of the animals that were sacrificed—but never worshiped—by the Egyptians (e.g., pigs). See V.L. Trumer, *The Mirror of Egypt in the Old Testament* (London: Marshall, Morgan & Scott, 1932), 100.

For an insightful presentation of this interpretive tradition, explained in terms of "the principle of normative inversion" (i.e., Moses required what the Egyptians prohibited, prohibited what they commanded, and then sacrificed what they venerated), see the new book by the renowned Egyptologist from the University of Heidelberg, J. Assmann, *Moses the Egyptian* (Cambridge, Mass.: Harvard University Press, 1997). He shows how the Mosaic reversal of Egypt's idolatrous practices was recognized not only by ancient Jewish and Christian interpreters, but also in the descriptive accounts of Mosaic religion written up by Egyptian historians like Manetho (third century B.C.), and later by the Roman historians: Tacitus, Strabo, and Hecataeus.

EIGHT
Israel's Calf-Hearted Response

1. On the link between the royal priesthood and firstborn sons, see H.C. Brichto, "Kin, Cult, Land and Afterlife: A Biblical Complex," *Hebrew Union College Annual* 44 (1979): 46: "There is ample evidence that the role of priest in the Israelite family had at one time been filled by the firstborn." This is echoed in the rabbinic sources (Rashi, Maimonides), and patristic and medieval writings (Jerome, Nicholas of Lyra, Thomas Aquinas). See G. van Groningen, *Messianic Revelation in the Old Testament* (Grand Rapids, Mich.: Baker, 1990), 221: "In the firstborn the dual capacity of king and priest is implicitly present." For additional sources, see Hahn, "Kinship by Covenant," 214–26.

2. See R. de Vaux, *The Early History of Israel* (Philadelphia: Westminster, 1978), 446–47: "The blood of ... a sacrificial animal created a bond, strengthened an oath or sealed a pledge between men. A primitive tradition, then, is preserved in Ex 24:3-8." M.W. Smith comments on "The Covenant Oath: This was the actual

pledge made by the vassal to the lord. It involved the killing of an animal ... each party touching blood. This affirmed the idea they were one blood and had a shared life. It also indicated the type of punishment fitting for one who broke this oath and betrayed his covenant lord" (*What the Bible Says About Covenant* [Joplin, Mo.: College Press, 1981], 14).

3. D.J. McCarthy, *Treaty and Covenant,* 1st ed. (Rome: Pontifical Biblical Institute, 1963), 171–72: "Besides the sacrifice and blood rite there is the tradition of the covenant meal.... The rites mentioned ... have in common the idea of creating kinship between the parties. The covenant meal means admission into the family circle of another." Also see R. Sklba, "The Redeemer of Israel," *Catholic Biblical Quarterly* 34 (1972): 11: "Yahweh had accepted them as His own relatives and kinsfolk. The election is sacramentalized in the meal of Ex 24:11."

4. See W. Harrelson, *Interpreting the Old Testament* (New York: Holt, Rinehart and Winston, 1964), 92: "Yahweh has set aside for Israel the portion belonging to the first-born son, and thus Israel is to exercise the privileges *and the responsibilities* of the first-born of all God's sons—the other nations and peoples of the world.... Israel is to be a kingdom of priests.... The most probable interpretation is this: Israel is to be the priest nation for the nations ... exercising the responsibility of priestly instruction and intercession in behalf of all peoples before Yahweh.... The passage thus carries out the thought of the Yahwistic summons to Abraham in Genesis 12:3." Also see Hahn, "Kinship by Covenant," 220–24.

5. L. Smolar and M. Aberbach, "The Golden Calf Episode in Post-Biblical Judaism," *Hebrew Union College Annual* 39 (1968), refer to the golden calf incident as "the nearest Jewish equivalent to the concept of original sin" (105).

6. See Benin, *Footprints of God*, 24–41; and Hahn, "Kinship by Covenant," 232–53.

7. Maimonides, *Guide for the Perplexed*, 3:46 (New York: Pardes, 1946), 359. See Benin, *Footprints of God*, 76–112.

NINE
Beloved Backsliders

1. G. von Rad, *Deuteronomy* (Philadelphia: Westminster, 1966), 14, suggests that we "understand Deuteronomy along the lines of an interpretation on the Law for the laity." See S.D. McBride ("Polity of the Covenant People: The Book of Deuteronomy," *Interpretation*, 1987, 41:229), who shows how Josephus saw Deuteronomy as a "divinely authorized and comprehensive 'polity' or national 'constitution.'"

2. Midrash Tanhuma, Nitzavim 3, on Deuteronomy 29:1: "Three times did the Holy One Blessed be He cut a covenant as they went out of Egypt. Once as they stood before Sinai, once in Horeb, and once here. Why did the Holy One Blessed be He cut a covenant with them here? He did so because the covenant that He made with them at Sinai had been nullified by saying, 'These are your gods ...' Therefore, he returned and made another covenant with them in Horeb and set before them a curse for those who would go back on His words" (cited in D. Elazar, *Covenant and Polity in Biblical Israel*, 370). See T.V. Farris, *Mighty to Save: A Study in Old Testament Soteriology* (Nashville: Broadman, 1993), 103: "The covenant at Mount Sinai must also be distinguished from the transaction that is described in the Book of Deuteronomy. That confusion should cloud the distinction between these two

covenants is strange in light of the explicit statement of the text.... Two visible surface features indicate the difference: (1) the covenants were negotiated at different places, and (2) they were instituted at different times. The two locales are clearly marked by the contrast between Moab and Horeb.... Accordingly, miles and years of desert wandering separated the two incidents as they are described in the Books of Exodus and Deuteronomy." The recent disaster at Beth-peor is mentioned in D euteronomy 3:29; 4:3-4.

3. On the distinctive elements of the Deuteronomic covenant, see Hahn, "Kinship by Covenant," 108–19.

4. St. John Chrysostom, *Discourses Against Judaizing Christians* (Washington, D.C.: Catholic University of America Press, 1979), 90: "After they kept the festival in honor of the evil demons, God yielded and permitted sacrifices. What he all but said was this: 'You are all eager and avid for sacrifices. If sacrifice you must, then sacrifice to me.' But even if he permitted animal sacrifices, this permission was not to last forever; in the wisdom of his ways, he took the sacrifices away from them again. Let me use the example of the physician again.... After he has given in to the patient's craving he gets a drinking cup from his home and gives instructions to the sick man to satisfy his thirst from this cup and no other. When he has gotten his patient to agree, he leaves secret orders with the servants to smash the cup to bits; in this he proposes, without arousing the patient's suspicion, to lead him secretly away from the craving on which he has set his heart. This is what God did, too. He let the Jews offer sacrifice but permitted this to be done in Jerusalem and nowhere else in the world. After they had offered sacrifices for a short time, God destroyed the city. Why? The physician saw to it that the cup was broken. By seeing to it that their city was destroyed, God led the Jews away from the practice of sacrifice, though it was against their will."

5. St. Augustine, *The Spirit and Letter*, 34.

TEN

"Choose This Day Whom You Will Serve!"

1. D.T. Olson, *Deuteronomy and the Death of Moses* (Minneapolis: Fortress, 1994), 135: "Moses commands the Levites who carried the ark of the covenant to 'take this book of the law and put it beside the ark of the covenant' (31:26). In the present context of the passage, one must identify this book of the *torah* as the book of Deuteronomy itself." Also: "Moses commands the Levites to place the written book of the *torah* (Deuteronomy) 'beside' the ark of the covenant. While the book of the *torah* is *beside* the ark, the stone tablets containing the Ten Commandments ... are *inside* the ark (10:5). The Decalogue's placement inside the ark suggests its primal and authoritative character. Therefore, in relation to the Ten Commandments ... the rest of Deuteronomy is visualized as extended and secondary commentary or exposition of the primal Decalogue" (15-16). See M. Weinfeld, *Deuteronomy 1-11* (New York: Doubleday, 1991), 1: "Although the words *mshnh htwrh hz't* in Deut 17:18 may mean 'a copy of this Torah,' it is true that Deuteronomy constitutes a second covenant besides the Sinaitic one (cf. 28:69/29:1) and thus may have been rightly considered to be secondary."

2. R.P. Carroll, *From Chaos to Covenant* (New York: Crossroad, 1981), 217: "Indeed, according to the deuteronomistic history, that covenant was broken with a regularity which almost beggars the imagination." Thus, he concludes: "If ever an institution was created which was a complete failure from the beginning, it must be the deuteronomistic covenant!"

3. See Berman, *The Temple*, 66–67: "What is the import of the fact that God granted David safety from all the enemies around him? This is of immense significance in light of the conditions for erecting the temple set down in Deuteronomy, chapter 12, and the state of affairs prevailing in the Jewish state during the previous four centuries. The language of Deuteronomy 12:10 is clear. Offerings will be brought to the place God selects to establish His name when... '*He grants you safety from all your enemies around you.*'... The fact that God had granted David 'safety from all the enemies around him' is particularly salient for a discussion of the conditions necessary to build a temple, in light of the history of the Israelites during the period of the Judges. The Book of Judges is a chronicle of a three-century period in which Israel entered a recurring cycle of disobeying God's commandments and of servitude and subjugation by foreign powers, separated by intermittent periods of redemption. When David defeated the Philistines (2 Samuel 5)—the perennial foe of the Israelites during the period of the Judges and the reign of Saul—it marked the fulfillment of the prerequisite of Deuteronomy 12:10 for the first time in three centuries. For the first time, Israel would not be the subject of scoff and derision among its neighbors.... Under these circumstances, thought David, the time could be ripe for building a house for the establishment of God's name—His reputation as universal sovereign."

ELEVEN
"Thou Art the Man!"

1. W.R. Arnold, *Ephod and Ark* (Cambridge, Mass.: Harvard University Press, 1917), 65–66; C.F. Keil and F. Delitzsch, *Biblical Commentary on the Books of Samuel* (Grand Rapids, Mich.: Eerdmans, 1973), 337.

2. W.J. Dumbrell, "The Davidic Covenant," *Reformed Theological Review* 39 (1980), 46: "In the light of this fuller covenantal exposition of 2 Sam. 7, more may be said about the role of Davidic kingship which it introduces.... In its contemplation of a priestly kingship (see Ps 110:4) what appears to be being entertained is that in the person of the king, the covenant demand contemplated for all Israel in Exodus 19:3b-6, has been embodied.... Davidic kingship is thus to reflect in the person of the occupant of the throne of Israel and as representative of the nation as a whole, the values which the Sinai covenant had required of the nation."

3. See R. Gordon, *1-2 Samuel* (Sheffield: JSOT Press, 1984); W.C. Kaiser, "The Blessing of David: The Charter for Humanity," in J. Skilton, ed., *The Law and the Prophets* (Nutley, N.J.: Presbyterian and Reformed Publishing, 1974), 298–318; W.J. Beecher, *The Prophets and the Promise* (Grand Rapids, Mich.: Baker, 1977). For a good treatment of the theologically significant difference between the (Mosaic) Sinai Torah and the (Davidic) Zion Torah, see H. Gese, *Essays on Biblical Theology* (Minneapolis: Augsburg, 1981), 79–85; and P. Stuhlmacher, *Reconciliation, Law, Righteousness: Essays in Biblical Theology* (Philadelphia: Fortress, 1986), 110–133.

4. See N. Frye, *The Great Code: The Bible and Literature* (London: Routledge & Kegan Paul, 1982), 83: "The most important single historical fact about the Old Testament is that the people who produced it were never lucky at the game of empire."

TWELVE
"It Is Finished!"

1. While many deny that the Last Supper was a Passover meal, all the synoptic Gospels explicitly assert that it was (see Mt 26:17-19; Mk 14:12-16; Lk 22:7-15). The *Catechism of the Catholic Church* affirms it: "By celebrating the Last Supper with His Apostles in the course of the Passover meal, Jesus gave the Jewish Passover its definitive meaning" (#1340). Also see J. Jeremias, *The Eucharistic Words of Jesus,* 3d ed. (London: SCM, 1965).

2. W.L. Lane, *The Gospel According to Mark* (Grand Rapids, Mich.: Eerdmans, 1974), 508: "The cup which Jesus abstained from was the fourth, which ordinarily concluded the Passover fellowship.... Jesus had used the third cup, associated with the promised work of redemption, to refer to his atoning death.... The cup which he refused was the cup of consummation." Jesus' refusal of the fourth cup is clearly seen by D. Daube, *The New Testament and Rabbinic Judaism* (Peabody, Mass.: Hendricksen, 1995), 331: "The implication is that they go out directly after the 'hymn' without drinking the fourth cup."

3. See R. Brown, *The Death of the Messiah: From Gethsemane to the Grave* (New York: Doubleday, 1994), 2:1007: "In 18:11 Jesus said that he wanted to drink the cup the Father had given him; when Jesus drinks the offered wine, he has finished this commitment made at the beginning of the P[assion] N[arrative]."

4. G. Feeley-Harnik, *The Lord's Table: Eucharist and Passover in Early Christianity* (Philadelphia: University of Pennsylvania, 1981), observes: "He resists the cup from his 'Father' in the garden of Gethsemane, but he will drink it if it is his Father's will.... He refuses the wine mixed with sedative myrrh (Mark 15:23)...

which the Roman soldiers offer him immediately before the crucifixion. When he finally cries out in agony, 'My God, my God, why
hast thou forsaken me?' (Matthew, Mark; according to John he
says 'I thirst'), they offer him vinegar.... He drinks the fourth cup
and dies the accursed death.... The wine does it. The blood of the
lamb that saved the firstborn Israelites when they painted it on the
lintels and doorposts of their houses with hyssop is the wine of
wrath that kills the firstborn Israelite when it is handed up to him
on hyssop (John 19:29)" (145).

5. "On the basis of the cup-sayings of Jesus the cup becomes a
symbol of martyrdom in early Church writings. The dying
Polycarp prays [in The Martyrdom of Polycarp, 14:2]: 'I bless thee
in that thou hast deemed me worthy ... that I might take a portion among the martyrs in *the cup* of thy Christ'" (L. Goppelt,
"πινω" in G. Kittel and G. Friedrich, eds., *Theological Dictionary
of the New Testament*, Vol. 6 [Grand Rapids, Mich.: Eerdmans,
1968], 6:153). It is important to note, by way of practical
reminder, that the "fourth cup" is not strictly in our future; just as
it doesn't require martyrdom as much as a daily dying to self (or
what is sometimes referred to as martyrdom—on the installment
plan).

6. Acts 17:27-28. (All Scripture texts in this final section are taken
from the Contemporary English Version.)

THIRTEEN
Here Comes the Bride

1. The early Church fathers' understanding of the Eucharist as our
participation in the heavenly liturgy is echoed in many documents
of the Magisterium. For example, The Constitution on the Sacred

Liturgy (*Sacrosanctum Concilium* 8): "In the earthly liturgy we share in a foretaste of that heavenly liturgy which is celebrated in the Holy City of Jerusalem toward which we journey as pilgrims, where Christ is sitting at the right hand of God, Minister of the sanctuary and of the true tabernacle. With all the warriors of the heavenly army we sing a hymn of glory to the Lord; venerating the memory of the saints, we hope for some part and fellowship with them." (see #1090). Likewise, the *Catechism of the Catholic Church:* "The book of Revelation of St. John, read in the Church's liturgy, first reveals to us, 'A throne stood in heaven, with one seated on the throne': 'the Lord God.' It then shows the Lamb, 'standing as though it had been slain': Christ crucified and risen, the one high priest of the true sanctuary, the same one 'who offers and is offered, who gives and is given'" (#1137).

2. J.D. Levenson, *Sinai and Zion* (New York: Winston, 1985), 139.

3. Levenson, 139.

4. T. Howard, *Evangelical Is Not Enough* (San Francisco: Ignatius Press, 1984), 37.

5. Lumen Gentium, n. 3; see Jn 19:34.